Commodore John Rodgers

New Perspectives on Maritime History and Nautical Archaeology

UNIVERSITY PRESS OF FLORIDA

Florida A&M University, Tallahassee
Florida Atlantic University, Boca Raton
Florida Gulf Coast University, Ft. Myers
Florida International University, Miami
Florida State University, Tallahassee
University of Central Florida, Orlando
University of Florida, Gainesville
University of North Florida, Jacksonville
University of South Florida, Tampa
University of West Florida, Pensacola

NEW PERSPECTIVES ON MARITIME HISTORY AND NAUTICAL ARCHAEOLOGY
James C. Bradford and Gene A. Smith, Series Editors

Maritime Heritage of the Cayman Islands, by Roger C. Smith
(1999; first paperback edition, 2000)

The Three German Navies: Dissolution, Transition, and New Beginnings, 1945–1960,
by Douglas C. Peifer (2002)

The Rescue of the Gale Runner: *Death, Heroism, and the U.S. Coast Guard*,
by Dennis L. Noble (2002)

*Brown Water Warfare: The U.S. Navy in Riverine Warfare and the Emergence of
a Tactical Doctrine, 1775–1970*, by R. Blake Dunnavent (2003)

*Sea Power in the Medieval Mediterranean: The Catalan-Aragonese Fleet in the War
of the Sicilian Vespers*, by Lawrence V. Mott (2003)

An Admiral for America: Sir Peter Warren, Vice-Admiral of the Red, 1703–1752,
by Julian Gwyn (2004)

Maritime History as World History, edited by Daniel Finamore (2004)

Counterpoint to Trafalgar: The Anglo-Russian Invasion of Naples, 1805–1806,
by William Henry Flayhart III (first paperback edition, 2004)

X Marks the Spot: The Archaeology of Piracy, edited by Russell K. Skowronek
and Charles R. Ewen (2006)

Life and Death on the Greenland Patrol, 1942, by Thaddeus D. Novak,
edited by P. J. Capelotti (2006)

*Industrializing American Shipbuilding: The Transformation of Ship Design
and Construction, 1820–1920*, by William H. Thiesen (2006)

Admiral Lord Keith and the Naval War against Napoleon, by Kevin D. McCranie (2006)

Commodore John Rodgers: Paragon of the Early American Navy, by John H. Schroeder (2006)

Commodore John Rodgers

Paragon of the Early American Navy

JOHN H. SCHROEDER

Foreword by James C. Bradford and Gene A. Smith, Series Editors

University Press of Florida
Gainesville · Tallahassee · Tampa · Boca Raton
Pensacola · Orlando · Miami · Jacksonville · Ft. Myers

11 10 09 08 07 06   6 5 4 3 2 1

LIBRARY OF CONGRESS CATALOGING-IN-PUBLICATION DATA:
Schroeder, John H., 1943–
Commodore John Rodgers: paragon of the early American navy /
John H. Schroeder; foreword by James C. Bradford and Gene A. Smith.
p. cm. (New perspectives on maritime history and nautical archeology)
Includes bibliographical references and index.
ISBN 0-8130-2963-5 (alk. paper)
1. Rodgers, John, 1773–1838. 2. United States Navy—Biography.
3. United States—History—War of 1812—Naval operations, American.
4. United States—History—Tripolitan War, 1801–1805—Naval operations,
American. 5. United States—History, Naval—To 1900. I. Title. II. Series.
E353.1.R7S37 2006
973.5'245092—dc22
[B]   2005058239

The University Press of Florida is the scholarly publishing agency for the State
University System of Florida, comprising Florida A&M University, Florida Atlantic
University, Florida Gulf Coast University, Florida International University, Florida
State University, University of Central Florida, University of Florida, University of
North Florida, University of South Florida, and University of West Florida.

University Press of Florida
15 Northwest 15th Street
Gainesville, FL 32611-2079
http://www.upf.com

To my wife, Sandra, again

Contents

Illustrations

Chronology

John Rodgers (1773–1838)

1773	Born in Harford County, Maryland
1786	Enters Merchant Marine
1798–99	First lieutenant on the *Constellation* in the Quasi-War with France
1799–1801	Captain of the *Maryland* during the Quasi-War
1802	Meets Minerva Denison
1802–3	Captain in the Mediterranean during the Barbary War
1804–6	Captain and commander-in-chief in the Mediterranean during the Barbary War
1806	Marries Minerva Denison
1807–11	Commander of the New York squadron and naval station
1811	The *Little Belt* affair
1812–13	Captain of the *President* on four cruises during the War of 1812
1814	Commander of the Delaware Naval Flotilla
1814	Leads naval forces in the defense of Baltimore
1815–24	President of the Board of Navy Commissioners
1825–1827	Commander-in-chief of the Mediterranean squadron
1827–37	President of the Board of Navy Commissioners
1832	Contracts cholera
1838	Dies in Philadelphia

Foreword

Water is unquestionably the most important natural feature on earth. By volume, the world's oceans compose 99 percent of the planet's living space; in fact, the surface of the Pacific Ocean alone is larger than that of the total surface of all land bodies. Water is as vital to life as air. Indeed, to test whether other planets or the moon can sustain life, NASA looks for signs of water. The story of human development is inextricably linked to the oceans, lakes, and rivers that dominate the earth's surface. The University Press of Florida series "New Perspectives on Maritime History and Nautical Archaeology" is devoted to exploring the significance of the earth's water while providing lively and important books that cover the spectrum of maritime history and nautical archaeology broadly defined. The series includes works that focus on the role of canals, rivers, lakes, seas, and oceans in history; on the economic, military, and political use of those waters; and on the people, communities, and industries that support maritime endeavors. Limited by neither geography nor time, volumes in the series contribute to the overall understanding of maritime history and can be read with profit by both general readers and specialists. This biography of John Rodgers provides insight into several of these topics.

John Rodgers does not reside in the pantheon of American naval heroes. His name is not as famous as John Paul Jones, Stephen Decatur, David Farragut, or George Dewey, yet, as John Schroeder amply demonstrates in this biography, Rodgers deserves to be better appreciated. In many ways he was a typical officer of the early navy. He went to sea as a teenager and became a merchant captain trading between North America, the West Indies, and Europe. After entering the U.S. Navy in 1798, Rodgers saw service in all the early wars of the young republic. During the Quasi-War with France, he became a captain and commanded a ship in the Caribbean; during the Tripolitan War, the ship he commanded captured one enemy ship and destroyed another; and during the War of 1812, he led a squadron across the Atlantic in pursuit of a British convoy. After the war, Rodgers was assigned to the new Board of Navy Commissioners—a body he eventually headed—that administered the navy during much of the antebellum era.

Despite this record of service, Rodgers is often remembered less for his own naval career and more for being, with his brother George Washington Rodgers, a progenitor of the "Rodgers Family," one of the great naval families of American history. It included John's son John Rodgers (1812–82) and his grandson William Ledyard Rodgers (1860–1944). Another of John's sons, Army Colonel Robert Smith Rodgers, married a daughter of Commodore Matthew C. Perry, and their children included Rear Admiral Frederick Rodgers (1842–1917) and Rear Admiral John Augustus Rodgers (1848–1933). The latter's son, Commander John Rodgers (1881–1926), was a pioneer naval aviator. The brother of "our" John Rodgers, the subject of this biography, was George Washington Rodgers (1787–1832). He and his wife, Anna Marie Perry, a sister of Commodore Oliver H. Perry and Matthew C. Perry, had three sons, including Commander George W. Rodgers (1822–63), who died while his ship was attacking Charleston during the Civil War, and Rear Admiral C.R.P. Rodgers (1819–92), whose two sons, Raymond Perry Rodgers (1849–1925) and Thomas Slidell Rodgers (1858–1931), both became rear admirals in the early twentieth century. Together these officers represent the Rodgers family legacy for the navy, but, more important, they reflect the influence of Rodgers as a role model for officers during his career, a particularly long one that spanned nearly four decades at a time prior to the establishment of the U.S. Naval Academy, when officers learned their craft at sea under the tutelage of their seniors rather than in the classroom and on the drill field ashore in Annapolis.

John Schroeder, a biographer of Matthew C. Perry and author of a book on the Mexican War and on the role of the U.S. Navy in shaping the American maritime empire of the mid-nineteenth century, is the perfect person to put the life of John Rodgers in context. Schroeder demonstrates that Rodgers was intensely patriotic, hungered after fame and glory, possessed a pronounced sense of personal honor, and fairly exuded the qualities of a natural-born leader. His career lacked the brilliant highlights of those more famous, but Rodgers operated at the top of the American sailing navy for longer than any other officer save perhaps Admiral David Dixon Porter (1813–91). Though disliked by many fellow officers, Rodgers avoided involvement in the internecine quarreling that led to several nasty feuds and duels among naval officers of the era. He also refused to participate in the graft and corruption so common in the spoils system of the decades he served on the Board of Navy Commissioners. Schroeder's is a balanced account of Rodgers's long career that finds much to admire as well as much to criticize. In addition to its intrinsic interest, this life of Rodgers provides valuable insights into the early history of United States and the development of its infant navy.

James C. Bradford, Texas A&M University
Gene A. Smith, Texas Christian University, Series Editors

Preface

Commodore John Rodgers was the preeminent and most influential naval officer of his generation. His historically eventful career was long, varied, and fascinating. From 1798 to 1837, Rodgers fought with distinction in three wars, led a major naval diplomatic mission to the Mediterranean, and shaped the peacetime navy for two decades after the War of 1812. Like Thomas Truxtun, his mentor, and Edward Preble, Rodgers worked tirelessly and effectively to establish and maintain the highest standards of naval efficiency, discipline, and conduct. For four decades as a commander, warrior, diplomat, administrator, and exemplary officer, he won respect for and shaped the early American navy.[1] Senator Thomas Hart Benton, longtime senator from Missouri and no lenient judge of character, would later recall that Rodgers "was to me the complete impersonation of my idea of the perfect naval commander: person, mind, and manners."[2]

Rodgers began his naval career on the *Constellation*, where, under the command of Captain Thomas Truxtun, he led a boarding party in the hard-fought and bloody capture of the French frigate *L'Insurgente* and then, under harrowing conditions, brought the prize safely into port two days later. During two cruises in the Barbary War between 1802 and 1806, Rodgers commanded single warships and then the Mediterranean squadron in combat operations. His military leadership and diplomatic skills helped to preserve peace with Morocco in 1804, to end the war with Tripoli in June 1806, and to intimidate recalcitrant Tunisian officials into peace terms several weeks later.

Commodore Rodgers played a significant part in the events leading to the war with England and in the subsequent War of 1812. It was Rodgers who commanded and gave the order for the *President* to fire on HMS *Little Belt* in May 1811. This controversial engagement between the American frigate and the overmatched British sloop of war won the approbation of President James Madison but provoked both praise and criticism for Rodgers himself.

During the war, Rodgers commanded the *President* on four different cruises in the Atlantic during 1812 and 1813. On each mission, he disrupted British commerce and exasperated British naval commanders by consistently eluding the British navy. Although he captured few prizes and only one small British warship, Rodgers's ability to evade the vastly superior British navy preserved his own warship, which was itself a vital part of the tiny American navy.

In the immediate aftermath of the capture and sacking of Washington, D.C., in August 1814, Rodgers played a critical role in the defense of Baltimore. When panic in Baltimore followed the fall of Washington, Rodgers's presence, reputation, and expertise as commander of U.S. naval forces there was vital in restoring public morale and preparing the city's defenses for the coming assault. When the battle began, different units of Rodgers's men fought successfully on both land and sea to repel the British and defend the city.

In the two decades after 1815 as president of the Board of Navy Commissioners, Rodgers was instrumental in shaping the nation's peacetime navy. Although it is largely forgotten today, the Board of Navy Commissioners dominated the administration of the Navy Department from 1815 to 1842 because most of the naval secretaries were second-rate figures with little naval experience or knowledge. At a time when many politicians were suspicious of and even hostile to the American navy, Rodgers's professional stature and visible presence in Washington, D.C., helped to protect the navy's reputation. As president of the board, Rodgers brought his long experience as a flag officer, his technical expertise, and his energy as an administrator to bear on the task of institutionalizing the exemplary standard of conduct and performance that had been set by the first generation of American naval officers.

Rodgers's two long terms as president of the board were interrupted in the mid-1820s when President John Quincy Adams asked him to lead a major naval and diplomatic mission to the Mediterranean. In addition to raising the morale and restoring the discipline of the Mediterranean squadron, Rodgers achieved both the naval and the diplomatic objectives the administration had defined. His well-disciplined squadron impressed European, Greek, and Turkish observers wherever it sailed. He also won the respect of both Greek and Turkish protagonists in the Greek Revolution while preserving American neutrality in the conflict. In addition, by impressing high-level Turkish officials he smoothed the way for the first formal treaty between the United States and the Ottoman Empire, which was signed several years later.

Rodgers's ambition, patriotism, and determination constituted an integral part of his character. As a young man, he chose a naval career because he believed it would bring him fame, glory, and fortune. According to the prevailing values of his time, the pursuit of immortal fame through sacrifice and service to country was viewed as an exalted and admirable motive. Rodgers was a fervent patriot who loved his country and devoted forty years of his life to the navy. Like other leading officers of the "old navy," Rodgers set high professional standards for himself and for those who served under him because he believed that, once established, these standards would be emulated by future generations of American naval officers.

Rodgers was also an intense and passionate man. With his great physical strength and energy, Rodgers exhibited an indomitable will, sharp temper, and forceful (some said overbearing) manner. Although he never exhibited it professionally, Rodgers could be a sensitive and romantic person. After he first met young Minerva Denison in 1802, the twenty-nine-year-old Rodgers acted, on occasion, more like a smitten schoolboy than a tough navy captain. Minerva was the great love of Rodgers's life, and the two engaged in a candid and passionate correspondence over their frequent physical separations. Their letters have enriched this biography by revealing a side of Rodgers that his male naval peers never witnessed or even suspected existed. John Rodgers, then, remains an important and compelling historical figure for whom a modern biography is long overdue.

In preparing this book, I have benefited from the assistance of a number of individuals and institutions. I want to acknowledge the personal support of University of Wisconsin System president-emeritus Katharine Lyall as well as the financial support of the University of Wisconsin-Milwaukee and the UWM Foundation. I am grateful for the considerable assistance that I received from the Golda Meir Library at UWM, particularly the director's office, the interlibrary loan office, and the professional staff of the American Geographic Society housed in the library. Librarians and archivists at various repositories provided invaluable assistance, including those at the Manuscript Division of the Library of Congress, the National Archives, the Historical Society of Pennsylvania, the New York Historical Society, the Wisconsin Historical Society, and the William L. Clements Library of the University of Michigan. The Tourism and Visitor Center at Havre de Grace, Maryland, assisted me in getting oriented physically to the town where John Rodgers spend his childhood.

The completion of this book was facilitated by the special efforts of several individuals. I appreciate the encouragement to undertake this project that I received from James Bradford and Paul Wilderson. At the University Press of Florida, the manuscript benefitted from the professional expertise of director Meredith Morris-Babb and her staff and was enhanced by the meticulous copyediting of Susan Brady. On a visit to Havre de Grace, Ellsworth Shank invited me into his home and shared his knowledge of local history and legend with me. In Ann Arbor, Michigan, our good friends Jeanne and Jim Snyder rolled out the red carpet and entertained Sandra and me when I worked at the Clements Library. In the office of the history department at UWM, Anita Cathey explained some of the mysteries of my word-processing program. On several occasions, Louise Whitaker took a considerable amount of time and went above and beyond her own duties to print or make an additional copy of the manuscript when I was unable to do so. Christopher McKee generously shared his detailed knowledge of early American naval history by reading my original proposal and making helpful suggestions that enhanced the manuscript. Spencer Tucker read the final manuscript with care and both provided constructive suggestions as well as alerted me to various errors in the text. As he had with my previous books, Reginald Horsman shared his extensive command of early American history as he read and provided innumerable constructive criticisms of the manuscript. As always, my wife, Sandra, furnished invaluable assistance. She carefully read, reread, and improved the manuscript by posing numerous queries, correcting grammatical mistakes, and improving its stylistic quality. In addition to being a skilled editor, she remains my best and most abiding critic.

Maryland Merchant Captain and Navy Lieutenant, 1773–1799

The most gratifying sight any eyes ever beheld was seventy French pirates (you know I have just cause to call them such) wallowing in their gore, twenty nine of whom were killed and forty one wounded.

Lieutenant John Rodgers of the American boarding party,
on the capture of the French frigate *L'Insurgente*, 1799

John Rodgers founded a distinguished American naval family that served the United States with distinction from the eighteenth until well into the twentieth century. There was, however, little evidence in his family background or in his childhood to presage a naval destiny for him. The Rodgers family traced its genealogical roots to Scotland, where the name was familiar and the clan numerous. John Rodgers, the father of John Rodgers, was born in Scotland about 1726. He migrated to the middle colonies in 1755 and in 1760 married Elizabeth Reynolds of Delaware. Her father was a Presbyterian minister, and the family was prominent in Delaware. In the 1760s, the couple moved south, across the Susquehanna River, and settled near the village of Lower Susquehanna Ferry in Maryland. Originally in Baltimore County, the village became part of Harford County when it was formed in 1774. Although the small, poor village was in a remote part of the colony, it was located near the mouth of the Susquehanna on Chesapeake Bay and on the main post road between Philadelphia and Baltimore. The couple first lived on a farm, but later Rodgers moved to town and opened a tavern in 1774. A popular stopping place for travelers, the tavern was known as one of the best inns in the region.[1]

Rodgers was not active in local politics, but he strongly supported the American patriot cause. In 1775, he served as a solicitor and signer of a pro-revolutionary petition of the local Association of Freemen. After hostilities erupted in Massachusetts in the spring of 1775, Rodgers raised and took command of a local militia company, one of several in Harford County. Designated a captain, he served under Colonel Francis Holland and Major John B. Hall until 1778, when he received an official commission from the governor and council of Maryland. On several occasions during the war, Rodgers was reported to have given "signal proofs of great personal gallantry and patriotism."[2]

Rodgers prospered during the revolutionary conflict. He acquired a sawmill, a mill race, and a dam and built a grist mill with a partner. He purchased another farm in Harford County and, in 1780, a tavern across the Susquehanna in Cecil County. For a time, he also operated a ferry on the river. It was at the farm in Harford County that son John Rodgers was born in 1773, the fourth of eight children—four boys and four girls. His mother, Elizabeth, was a resourceful woman "of an uncommonly vigorous and masculine character." With her husband absent during the Revolutionary War, a foraging party of British soldiers entered her farm and approached the house. As they neared, she armed several "of her Negroes with some muskets which had been accidentally left at the home, and fired upon" the intruders. Although no one was hit, the British retreated "and left her without further molestation."[3]

In 1784, the name of Lower Susquehanna Ferry was changed to the more appealing name of Havre de Grace, allegedly because when General Lafayette traveled through town on one occasion, he remarked that the village bore a striking resemblance to the French town of the same name. The physical reality of the town did not live up to the elegance of its new name. Indeed, one traveler who stayed at Rodgers's tavern praised it as a "very good House" but described the small, quiet village of several hundred residents as "a wild, bleak place."[4] Despite its location near the mouth of the Susquehanna and the head of Chesapeake Bay, Havre de Grace was neither a bustling commercial center nor the local hub of a prosperous agricultural county. The town handled only local commerce and grew slowly. Philadelphia was seventy-five miles to the northeast. Baltimore, which stood thirty-five miles to the southwest, controlled most of the commerce of the upper Chesapeake. Harford County was farm country, but most farms "were small and semi-subsistence because the soil was not particularly rich. Harford County was also a slave county. According to the 1790 census, the total population of 14,979 people included 3,417 (or 23 percent) slaves and 775 (or 5 percent) free blacks. At the same time, only 30 percent of the white families owned any slaves, and only 13 percent owned more than five slaves. Among the slave owners was the Rodgers family, which owned several slaves. Harford County and Havre de Grace, then, remained an undeveloped, underpopulated, and somewhat backward frontier during the 1770s and 1780s.[5]

Young John Rodgers apparently enjoyed a typical rural childhood. He received a rudimentary education at home and in a neighborhood school. Spending most of his extracurricular time engaged in outdoor activities, young John was an active, hardy, and vibrant child known early on for his physical strength and courage. He was also remembered as a ringleader of other boys in their various feats of daring and strength. Apparently keen to hunt and fish, he was known to break the "thin ice and swim after the wild ducks which he had shot from the shores of the Susquehanna."[6]

With two significant exceptions, the childhood of John Rodgers was like those of many other American boys growing up in small, remote villages in the 1780s. First, the Chesapeake Bay and the Susquehanna River lay near his doorstep. Playing, hunting, and fishing along their shores, he developed a passion for the sea as he watched schooner-rigged ships come and go. Second, his father's tavern on the main post road between Baltimore and Philadelphia provided a window on a more dynamic world beyond Harford County. The reputable inn attracted a steady stream of visitors, some of them well known or even famous. George Washington, General Lafayette, and numerous military officers were said to have stayed there. With them came news and stories from Baltimore, Philadelphia, and beyond. As a young boy, he no doubt heard at second and third hand some exciting (and embellished) tales of revolutionary glory and descriptions of distant and romantic places in the colonies and across the sea. This information had to be an elixir that stimulated the imagination of this energetic and curious youngster and instilled dreams of adventure and glory. As he grew older, he inevitably came to learn that opportunity and excitement lay elsewhere.

Young Rodgers also "came to fancy the life of a sailor" as a result of books he read on nautical subjects. By the time Rodgers was thirteen, he had decided to go to sea. He apparently told neither his schoolmates nor family. He left home and walked alone to Baltimore, thirty-five miles away. Hearing of his son's plans, Rodgers's father pursued him on horseback and intercepted him as he approached Baltimore. The father attempted to persuade his son to return home, but young John remained adamant. Finally Colonel Rodgers relented, went into Baltimore with his son, and helped him find a spot as an apprentice for a five-year term with Captain Benjamin Folger. An experienced and highly respected sea captain, Folger had served the patriot cause on several privateers during the Revolution. After the war, Folger became a merchant captain. In 1786, Folger commanded the *Maryland*, which he co-owned with Samuel and John Smith of Baltimore. In the next several years, Rodgers made a number of voyages to Europe on the *Maryland* and other merchant ships with Folger, who proved to be an excellent mentor.

In comparison to his boyhood home, Baltimore was a vibrant base for Rodgers. It offered abundant opportunities to young men who wanted a place on a merchant ship. With a population of almost thirteen thousand by the late 1780s, Baltimore was quickly becoming an important urban and commercial center. Wheat provided a solid economic foundation as the town's economy was geared to process, store, and ship the grain to markets in the United States, the Caribbean, and Europe. At this time, Baltimore ranked behind only Boston, New York, and Philadelphia in its domestic and foreign shipping traffic.[7]

As it grew in both economic and political importance, Baltimore also offered opportunities for an ambitious young man to development friendships and personal contacts with the city's elite. Of particular importance to Rodgers was his association with the Smith family. John Smith and his son General Samuel Smith headed one of Baltimore's most successful and influential merchant families. Samuel was also heavily involved in local politics. Although initially a Federalist, Samuel switched to the Jeffersonian Republicans in 1796 and thereafter became an influential force in the Republican Party. Samuel Smith's brother, Robert, a lawyer, also became actively involved in local and national politics during the Jefferson administration. After Samuel turned the position down, Robert served as secretary of the navy during Jefferson's two presidential terms. Although he was never close to Samuel, Rodgers became good friends with Robert Smith;, each man later named one of his own sons for the other. Although young John Rodgers could not know it at the time, Baltimore provided not only his chance for a career at sea but also the beginnings of a lasting personal association that would serve him well in his adult years.

John Rodgers took readily to the demands of life at sea. Beginning as an apprentice and becoming a mate by his eighteenth birthday, Rodgers matured physically and learned his chosen trade well. Under his experienced mentor, Captain Folger, Rodgers mastered the intricacies of seamanship, the details of successful command, and the various skills needed to succeed in his profession. Learning quickly and working diligently, Rodgers became a skilled sailor with a reputation for great physical strength and an intimidating personality. When they had parted in Baltimore, Rodgers's father made an "earnest request" that his son never use "ardent spirits," a vice common to sailors and one that Rodgers avoided. His resolve "never to touch ardent spirits" was strengthened during his apprenticeship when he witnessed an intoxicated captain endanger the safety of his vessel and the lives of his crew. Always a temperate man who drank wine and beer in moderation, Rodgers was proud that he kept his vow never to consume hard liquor.[8]

Rodgers quickly matured into a capable commander, becoming a "master," or commander of a merchant ship, by age nineteen. His first command in 1793 was the 300–ton *Jane* owned by the Smiths. As captain of the *Jane* from 1793 to 1797, he sailed and traded in Caribbean, English, and European ports on annual voyages. Although it usually took only two to three months to cross the Atlantic, merchant ships typically made only one voyage each year because of the time required to sell the cargo overseas and to purchase a new one for the return trip. Rodgers was proud that he never lost a ship at sea or grounded a vessel he commanded.

As a commander, Rodgers exuded confidence and authority. He was also a passionate man with a reputation for relentless determination and great courage. According to family legend, the only challenge ever to his command authority or hint of a mutiny occurred during these years and proved short-lived. On one of his early voyages to Europe, Rodgers's ship was blown off course into the "adverse winds and currents" of the North Sea. Three men froze to death in one night. With their provisions nearly exhausted and the remaining crew members in "sullen despair," they refused his order to go aloft in such terrible conditions and "secure the frozen rigging." Indignant, the powerful young captain stripped off his jacket and shirt and climbed aloft himself, shouting to his crew that he would demonstrate "what a man could do." After wavering between "fear and shame," the crew followed their commander. They secured the rigging and the ship managed to reach port safely.[9]

An American patriot whose pride was easily wounded, Rodgers could exhibit a hypersensitivity to insults against his country. In Liverpool, in May 1796, Rodgers and some American companions were dining when a loud campaign procession passed outside the inn. The supporters of candidate General Banastre Tarleton carried a banner that depicted the British veteran of the American Revolutionary War on a horse charging a band of fleeing Americans whose national flag was being trampled by his horse and discolored by blood from his battle wound. The banner infuriated Rodgers, who charged outside and reportedly "knocked down the astonished standard bearer and trampled across his banner." Rodgers then returned to the inn, armed himself with a saber and pistols, proceeded to the hustings, and confronted Tarleton. The American demanded an explanation. Tarleton explained that he was not responsible for the banner and apologized to Rodgers for the misunderstanding, thus ending the incident.[10]

On several other occasions in England and in Europe, Rodgers showed "great sensitiveness when he imagined his flag was not properly respected . . . [and] often hazarded his personal safety in attempting to vindicate its honor." In Hamburg, he got into a melee at a theater when he demanded that the orchestra play "Washington's March." In response, some English patrons insisted that "God Save the King" be played. On the ensuing evening, Rodgers with some American friends returned to the theater and again demanded "Washington's March." Again the British demanded "God Save the King." Confusion followed as Rodgers and his compatriots jumped onto the stage, warded off the British attempting to dislodge them, and threatened the orchestra musicians with violence should they refuse to play the request. Finally, the orchestra "struck up Washington's March," after which the Americans departed.[11]

By his early twenties, Rodgers had developed into a somewhat hot-headed and arrogant man whose physical courage sometimes outweighed his good judgment. Still, his physical presence, abundant pride, and personal bravado permitted Rodgers at a surprisingly young age to effectively command crews of tough veterans under demanding conditions at sea.

In 1793, the outbreak of war between France and Great Britain complicated the challenges of commanding an American merchant ship. As each side attempted to attack and cut off the overseas trade of the other, American commerce was inevitably caught in the middle of the war. The British attempted to suppress American merchant ships trading with France or the French West Indies while the French attempted to capture American vessels trading with England or its overseas colonies. On several occasions, Rodgers was stopped and inspected by first one belligerent and then by the other before being allowed to proceed.

The situation between the United States and France deteriorated sharply after the Washington administration negotiated the Jay Treaty with England in 1794. From France's perspective, the United States had turned its back on its old friend and ally to enter into a virtual, if undeclared, alliance with England. Once the Jay Treaty was finally approved in 1796, French interference with American shipping intensified. In early 1797, Rodgers switched ships and took command of the *Hope*, owned by the firm of Buchanan and Young of Baltimore. With the change of ships came bad luck. In February 1797, Rodgers was wounded when the *Hope*, bound for Falmouth with a cargo of tobacco, was captured by a French privateer and taken into L'Orient. On 6 March 1797, a French tribunal condemned the cargo because a document containing the details of the cargo lacked a certificate properly identifying the notaries who had signed it. In addition, the clearance and manifest did not carry an official seal, and only one of the three bills of lading contained the correct destination as Falmouth. Since these errors seemed minor technicalities, the owners appealed; however, the tribunal rejected the appeal and condemned the vessel and the cargo, together valued at $23,000. A resentful Rodgers quickly recovered from his injury and returned to the United States.[12]

After new president John Adams took office in 1797, relations with France continued to deteriorate. On 31 May 1797, the French refused to receive the new American minister, Charles Cotesworth Pinckney. Adams then appointed a three-person commission to negotiate a new treaty of amity and commerce, but the French government refused to receive the delegation officially unless the Americans provided a $240,000 bribe. When the American refused to make concessions, the chance for negotiations failed. Although President Adams still sought peace, he prepared to fight. Between March and July 1798, Congress passed twenty acts attempting to ready the nation for war. In addition to the well-known Alien and Sedition Acts, which attempted to curb dissent, Congress imposed new taxes, increased the size of the military, formally established the Navy Department, and created the Marine Corps. As tensions worsened, the two nations drifted into an undeclared naval war—now referred to as the Quasi-War—and many Americans expected a formal war to follow.

It was in this political environment that John Rodgers decided to join the American navy. The humiliation of losing the *Hope* was very fresh in his mind as Rodgers contemplated the welcome prospect of naval action against the French. His timing was good. In 1794, Congress had authorized the construction of six frigates, but none had yet been completed; nor had the officers and crews been recruited or trained even though the beginning of the Quasi-War had hastened naval recruitment. Because the navy had no training facility or apprentice program, it turned to a few veterans of the Revolutionary War and, more often, to experienced commanders and crewmen from the American merchant service. Ready to serve were a number of excellent young merchant captains. They were intense patriots and skilled sailors who welcomed adventure at sea and the glory that military action would bring. In addition to Rodgers, the group included experienced merchantmen like Thomas Tingley, Thomas Truxtun, Stephen Decatur Sr., Samuel and James Barron, Edward Preble, William Bainbridge, and David Porter.[13]

Rodgers's age, experience, and reputation worked to his advantage as he sought a commission. His personal and family connections enhanced his credibility. He had the support of the prominent Smith merchant family of Baltimore as well as that of the Maryland Pinkneys. William Pinkney, who was then on a diplomatic assignment in England, was a prominent Maryland attorney who had practiced law for a time in Harford County and there married John Rodgers's sister Ann Marie in 1790. In March 1798, Rodgers received an appointment as second lieutenant on the new frigate the *Constellation*. When the first lieutenant resigned, Rodgers was promoted to first lieutenant and executive officer of the ship. The *Constellation* had been built at the shipyard of David Stodder in Baltimore according to the plans of marine architect Joshua Humphreys. Known as an elegant ship of beautifully balanced proportions, the *Constellation* had a keel length of 161 feet, a beam of 40 feet, a speed of 10 to 12 knots, and a tonnage of 1265 tons; it carried a complement of 340 men. Although rated at thirty-six guns, the ship actually mounted forty-four.[14]

In June 1798, Benjamin Stoddert became the nation's first secretary of the navy. A member of a prosperous mercantile firm in Maryland, Stoddert, born in 1751, had fought in the Revolutionary War and had served as secretary of the Board of War, a position in which he dealt with the myriad war issues of men, material, and money. A loyal Federalist, Stoddert proved to be an excellent appointment whose tenure helped place the navy on sound footing. Energetic, sensible, and administratively capable, Stoddert understood that as his decisions set important precedents for the navy, his leadership would determine the new navy's success or failure. He expected his senior officers to embody exemplary standards of character and conduct to inspire and shape young officers. Accordingly, he placed a high priority on identifying and promoting outstanding officers and eliminating incompetents.[15]

The man who had supervised the construction of the *Constellation* and served as her first captain was Thomas Truxtun. Although he did not realize it at the time, Rodgers was fortunate to have such a talented and experienced man as his commander and his naval mentor. Truxtun was, in fact, well on his way to becoming a legend in the infant American navy. At age forty-three in 1798, Truxtun had had more than three decades of experience at sea. During the Revolution he had successfully commanded several privateers. After the war, he had commanded merchant ships to China and India. A stern, egotistical man, Truxtun insisted on rigorous discipline on the ships he commanded. As one of the first captains of the new navy, Truxtun understood that his conduct and leadership would set important precedents for the new service and must instill high standards for younger officers and his successors to emulate. This dedicated and gifted officer of great vision was not simply commanding one of the first American frigates; he was establishing a tradition of excellence for the navy.[16]

Truxtun also believed that naval service held promise for young officers to achieve honor and glory in the patriotic service of their nation. He advised one junior officer that to "become conspicuous," he needed "night and day" to think of his duty and be "laboriously industrious and active, in whatever appertains to your duty, and respects order and good discipline, and [do] not lose the Golden Moment . . . that chance and perhaps good fortune has thrown in your way." Accordingly, he dedicated much time to writing rules and regulations that addressed every aspect of his warship's operations. As an admirer of the British navy, he borrowed heavily from its rules, procedures, customs, and tactics. If the ultimate purpose and test of a warship was success in battle, her officers and crew must be organized, disciplined, and drilled to achieve that goal. Everyone needed not only to know his duty and be thoroughly trained in executing it but also to be so disciplined that, in the frightening uncertainty of battle, each man would do his duty or follow any order without hesitation. As he would later explain to a junior officer, Truxtun believed "that good discipline is considered by all who know anything . . . as the vital part of a ship of war."[17] In fact, Truxtun set a model for discipline that was followed by many other American naval officers for years to come.

Small in stature, Truxtun became known for his harsh and egotistical demeanor. More than thirty years later, one of the young midshipmen on the *Constellation*, Commodore David Porter, would vividly remember Truxtun as a "petty tyrant." Porter recalled Truxtun as a "proud and tyrannical though gallant naval commander," a "little tyrant who struts his few fathoms of scoured plank, dare not unbend, lest he should lose the appearance of respect from his inferiors which their fears inspire." Enjoying "no society, no smiles, no courtesies for or from any one," the captain had to shut "himself up from all around him" and stand "alone, without the friendship or sympathy of one on board; a solitary being in the midst of the ocean." Indeed, this "man of war" was a "petty kingdom . . . governed by a petty despot, exacting from his subjects, all the respect and homage, that are voluntarily and spontaneously bestowed on a higher order of legitimate sovereigns."[18]

Rodgers's appointment as first lieutenant on Truxtun's *Constellation* proved fortuitous. As difficult and tyrannical as he could be, Truxtun was still an excellent mentor for Rodgers. At age twenty-five, Rodgers was a veteran merchant captain without any military experience. On his merchant ships he had used a direct, hands-on style of command over small numbers of crewmen. Now, as the executive officer of the *Constellation*, Rodgers would direct the daily activities of more than three hundred officers and crewmen on a ship whose operations were much more complicated than any on which he had served. He also had to learn how to delegate some

responsibility to commissioned and warrant officers. While his previous experience had prepared him well, Rodgers still had much to learn in his new
assignment.

The *Constellation* was launched in Baltimore in September 1797, but various problems delayed her preparation for sea until the following spring. As
a result, Lieutenant Rodgers's first assignment was to recruit a full crew.
He opened a recruiting rendezvous in Baltimore at Cloney's Tavern in Fell's
Point. Here he offered able seamen at first fifteen, and later seventeen, dollars per month while ordinary seamen received ten dollars per month for
a one-year enlistment term. He could also offer a two-month pay advance
to those men who could produce security against disappearing before they
actually boarded the ship. Truxtun's orders allowed Rodgers one dollar per
man for the rendezvous expenses of "fire, candle, liquor, house rent, etc."
in addition to a reasonable amount for "music to indulge and humour the
Johns in a farewell frolic." In five weeks, Rodgers enlisted about one hundred men. Although many experienced sailors were available in the thriving
port town of Baltimore, they had more attractive options than a demanding,
closely supervised, and low-paying term on a warship. So to fill out the crew,
Truxtun opened additional rendezvous at Norfolk and at Alexandria. As the
recruiting continued, Truxtun worked assiduously to supply and fit out his
new ship as well as to organize and train his officers and men. He prepared
a quarter bill and a list of standing orders, which he posted alongside the
Articles of War to supplement them. The quarter bill outlined the specific
duties of each crewman as the ship prepared for battle. The detailed and
specific standing orders required careful study by the officers who were in
charge of executing and enforcing them. Every commissioned and warrant
officer also received a written statement detailing his own specific duties and
responsibilities.[19]

In a detailed letter to his first lieutenant, Truxtun outlined his require-
ments. Most important, he expected unquestioning obedience from all officers and men on board to ensure that all orders were executed "without
hesitation or demur." He instructed his commissioned officers to be "Civil
and polite to everyone" because "Civility does not interfere with discipline."
He also warned them against excessive and arbitrary punishment as well as
"improper familiarity with petty Officers" because it undermined their authority. At the same time, he expected petty officers and crewmen to observe
appropriate etiquette. When delivering a message to a commissioned officer,
for example, they were to "Speak holding their hats in hand." Although he
did not demand total abstinence, Truxtun warned his officers against the
frequent and "detestable vice drunkenness." "I do not mean that a Convivial

fellow is a drunkard, who may become Chearful [*sic*] in Company, the distinction is too great . . . to draw any line on that Subject."[20]

Finally on 26 June 1798, the *Constellation* sailed on her shakedown cruise. The Navy Department had instructed Truxtun to sail from Cape Henry to the "Southern Limits" of the United States in order to protect the American coast and vessels of the United States against French privateers or warships. Specifically, Truxtun was to seize and "bring into any Port of the United States" any French vessels that shall have "committed, or which shall be found hovering on the Coasts of the United States, for the purpose of committing Depredations" on any U.S. vessel. His orders also authorized him to "retake" any American vessel captured by the French.[21]

Shortly after the *Constellation* sailed, trouble brewed among the ranks of the newly formed crew. Truxtun became aware of some grumbling and discontent. The issue was his water rations, which limited each man to only four and one-half pints per day to be served at four different times. As the *Constellation* was heading south into a hot climate, the captain feared that some men would become bloated or contract dysentery if they drank excessive amounts of water. Some of the crew, however, thought the water ration unduly capricious. As they labored under a hot sun, why shouldn't they be allowed to drink as much water as they needed whenever they became thirsty?

A particular irritant, the water ration compounded the general tension of an inexperienced crew still being molded to Truxtun's rigorous discipline and training regimen. When he overheard some men complaining audibly in small groups, Truxtun reacted quickly. On 2 July, he assembled the entire crew, had the Articles of War read, and read a statement of his own. Noting that "several mutinous assemblies" had occurred "with a view to excite, cause and effect a Mutiny," he issued a "public warning" to the crew. In the event that he ever heard "a Murmur in the Ship, or any Expressions, that have a Tendency to disorganize, or cause Disorder, or Discontent," he would "comply strictly" with the Articles of War and put the offenders to death. "You have the Law before you . . . you know the Consequences, if, in the future, you transgress I must and will do my duty."[22] Truxtun then had a marine seized and flogged "at the Gang Way . . . for Insolence to the Sergeant of the Marines and endeavoring to arrest a Pistol out of his hands." This public punishment ended any threat of mutiny and restored discipline. On 22 July, Truxtun increased the water ration to five pints per day and then on 10 August ended it altogether.[23]

Truxtun's decisive reaction made good sense in the general disciplinary climate of the day. Recent events in the British navy had alerted naval commanders to the potential for mutiny. In 1797, large naval mutinies had occurred in the British navy, not on a single ship but within two fleets. In response to harsh conditions, thousands of British sailors protested and then mutinied in the Channel Fleet at Spithead. The idea of a general mutiny then spread to the fleet near the mouth of the Thames River. These uprisings were suppressed, but they involved thousands of men on more than one hundred British naval vessels. More recently, the crew of the British frigate *Hermione* had mutinied in the West Indies. Her captain, Hugh Pigot, was a brutal commander known for his harsh and capricious discipline. After one incident, the crew murdered the captain and most of his officers, seized control of the ship, and then surrendered it to the Spanish, who were then at war with England. While some of the crew also surrendered to the Spanish, others scattered. One culprit was John Watson, who made his way to Norfolk, changed his name to Hugh Williams, and signed on as a seaman with the *Constellation* shortly before she sailed in June 1798.[24]

Several weeks after dealing with what he perceived to be a threat of mutiny on his ship, Truxtun received a warning letter via pilot boat from Secretary of Navy Stoddert. The secretary himself had received an anonymous letter from a crewman on the *Constellation*. Stoddert informed Truxtun that the letter spoke of a "spirit of Mutiny" onboard and urged that it "be suppressed by every prudent Means." Truxtun again acted quickly. He assembled the crew and read the names and descriptions of the *Hermione* mutineers in an effort to determine whether any of them was onboard. Shortly thereafter, he identified seaman Williams, immediately placed him in irons, and eventually delivered him to the British consul at Norfolk in late August.[25]

After a two-month shakedown cruise, the *Constellation* returned to Norfolk and then headed for Cuba, where she and the twenty-gun *Baltimore* were to convoy American merchant vessels and to combat French privateers. This second cruise provided little excitement or action, but it did furnish ample opportunity for regular drills and gunnery practice. Truxtun worked constantly to prepare his ship and her officers and crew for the ultimate test of combat. Initially, Second Lieutenant William Cowper and Marine Lieutenant James Triplett were inattentive to detail and sloppy in executing their duties. After speaking to him several times, Truxtun reprimanded Cowper in writing for not having "a Sail trimmed or a Brace hawled properly," for permitting "various ropes" to be towed in the water, for talking with common seamen, and for permitting petty officers to "box on Deck."[26]

In contrast, First Lieutenant Rodgers worked well with his captain and gained Truxtun's respect as the two slowly molded the men of the *Constellation* into fighting trim. Rodgers admired and adapted Truxtun's system of firm discipline. He understood its purpose, absorbed its principles, and enthusiastically executed its rules. His style of discipline would be one of Truxtun's legacies that Rodgers brought to warships that he later commanded. At the same time, Rodgers's conduct and character so impressed Truxtun that he recommended to the Navy Department that his first lieutenant be promoted to captain. When his recommendation was not accepted by December, Truxtun continued to press for the promotion.[27]

In late 1798, Secretary Stoddert revised his instructions to his senior commanders. Based on the reports of Truxtun and other commanders, Stoddert realized that French privateers rarely approached the American coastline and posed little threat to American coastal trade. On 8 December, Stoddert now authorized American warships to move into the West Indies in search of French ships. In December, the secretary divided the American fleet into four small squadrons. Truxtun was to command one and to cruise between St. Kitts and Puerto Rico with the brig *Richmond* and four smaller ships.[28]

Once he reached St. Kitts, Truxtun began to arrange convoys for homeward-bound American merchant ships and cruised the area. On one occasion, he spotted a French frigate safely anchored near Guadeloupe but was unable to lure her into a fight. Two days later, Truxtun drew the fire of a fort at the other end of the island. He remained just beyond the fort's gun range but returned fire with double the number of shots.[29]

On 9 February, just east of Nevis, an island south of St. Kitts, the *Constellation* spotted and gave chase to a large ship. The strange ship raised American colors but, when asked, did not reply with the private signal for the day. Truxtun suspected the ship was French and was proved correct when she finally raised her French colors and "fired a Gun to the Windward (the signal of an enemy)." The ship—the "celebrated" forty-gun frigate *L'Insurgente* commanded by Captain Citizen Barreaut—carried four hundred men and was "esteemed as one of the fastest sailing ships in the French Navy." A chase ensued. The *Constellation* closed until shortly after 3 p.m., when *L'Insurgente* tried to hail her. In response, Truxtun waited until he was in range "for every Shot to do complete Execution" within a half cable's length. The *Constellation* finally opened fire with a broadside that *L'Insurgente* returned. For the next seventy-five minutes, the two warships hammered one another in a spirited and bloody exchange. The guns of the *Constellation* concentrated on the hull of *L'Insurgente,* while the French warship directed her primary fire at the sails, rigging, and masts of the American vessel. Finally, *L'Insurgente* struck her colors. The Americans suffered four casualties, including one death, but the French had seventy dead and wounded. One of the wounded Americans died later, and another lost his foot. The first American killed was a terrified young seaman who, because he had deserted his post, was actually killed by Lieutenant Andrew Sterett's sword. Clearly, Tuxtun's attention to detail, his thorough training of his crew, and his constant drilling of his men served him very well in the ultimate test of battle.[30]

A well-pleased Truxtun praised his crew for its valor and discipline. Rodgers, who had commanded five guns, was dispatched by Truxtun to board and take possession of *L'Insurgente*. Rodgers relished the moment and later reported excitedly that "the most gratifying sight any eyes ever beheld was seventy French pirates (you know I have just cause to call them such) wallowing in their gore, twenty nine of whom were killed and forty one wounded." Truxtun praised Rodgers for commanding the first division of guns and "for behaving well and being the first Lieutenant of the Constellation at the capture of the first Government Ship of any Consequence ever made by the Arms of the U.S. at Sea."[31]

Truxtun wanted to return to Bassateer Roads, St. Kitts, with his prize, but a sharp adverse wind buffeted the two ships, both of them in a "crippled State." The exchange of prisoners began immediately but was interrupted as the two ships drifted farther and farther apart. As night fell, they lost contact with each other, leaving Rodgers, Midshipman David Porter, and an eleven-man American boarding party in charge of the prize along with 173 prisoners on board. The situation on *L'Insurgente* was chaotic. Her decks had not been cleared of the dead and wounded, her "spars, sails and rigging, cut to pieces, and lying on deck." The grating had been thrown overboard, the hatches remained uncovered, and the Americans had no handcuffs or irons to shackle the prisoners on the severely damaged ship.

One later account lauded Rodgers's courage, resourcefulness, and determination in this daunting situation. He secured the small arms, ordered the prisoners below, and placed a sentinel at each hatchway with a blunderbuss, cutlass, and brace of pistols with orders to fire at any prisoner who attempted to come on deck. Rodgers and his small party restored order enough to get the ship under sail. For the next three nights, they went without sleep, maintaining a constant vigil, and slowly made their way toward St. Kitts. Finally, "after the greatest Exertions having been made," *L'Insurgente* rejoined the *Constellation* and reached Bassateer Roads, where they anchored.[32]

This stirring account of Rodgers on *L'Insurgente* appears in *The United States Naval Chronicle*, written by Charles Goldsborough, a longtime clerk in the Navy Department. Although Goldsborough's history of the early navy is generally considered to be factually reliable, there is virtually no corroboration for his description of this particular incident. None appears in the official accounts of either Truxtun or Rodgers, or in the private manuscripts of either Rodgers or Porter. Goldsborough's account has been dismissed as fanciful by some historians but accepted as reasonably accurate by others. No doubt Rodgers embellished the details of the incident when he recounted them to Goldsborough, who accepted and then further embellished them as he extolled the achievements of the navy in the *Chronicle*. At the same time, it is clear that Rodgers had performed flawlessly in his first combat action and, under challenging circumstances, had successfully navigated the American prize back to St. Kitts.[33]

Back in St. Kitts, Truxtun and his crew received a warm welcome from the inhabitants. In the next five weeks, Truxtun disposed of his prisoners and repaired his two frigates. He appointed Rodgers to command *L'Insurgente*, although Secretary Stoddert had not yet approved Rodgers's promotion to captain. In fact, the secretary considered the twenty-five-year-old Rodgers too young to receive permanent command of the prize frigate and delayed his promotion until Stoddert could also recommend to the president the promotion of two other lieutenants. Stoddert explained that he was "well satisfied" with Rodgers but wanted him to command a small ship so as not to "excite too much uneasiness with other good men."[34]

After cruising near St. Kitts for several weeks, *L'Insurgente* and the *Constellation* headed home and reached Norfolk near the end of May. There a hero's welcome awaited Truxtun, his officers, and his crew. In the weeks that followed, poems and songs were written to honor "Truxtun's Victory." Around the country, celebrations were held, toasts proposed, and resolutions adopted. Truxtun was very much the hero of the day, but his officers also basked in the spotlight. Rodgers was recognized and praised in his own right. After he returned to Baltimore during the summer, some sailors from the *Constellation* paraded him on an elaborately decorated chair through the streets of Baltimore. Rodgers welcomed his first taste of public fame and military glory. Pleased by the attention and praise, he eagerly anticipated winning greater glory on his next assignment.[35]

On 7 June 1799, Stoddert detached Rodgers from *L'Insurgente* and ordered him to Baltimore to attend to the equipment of the *Maryland*, a new sloop of war under construction there. After a hearing in which Rodgers testified to the comparative strengths of the *Constellation* and *L'Insurgente*, an admiralty court condemned the French frigate. The United States subsequently added the handsome prize to the American navy. As her first lieutenant, Rodger received $1,680, his share of the $84,500 prize money. His first naval assignment—a short but eventful one—had come to an end. Relishing his first combat experience, Rodgers had become the first lieutenant in the U.S. Navy to command, however briefly, a frigate.[36]

Captain in the Caribbean, 1799–1802

[I summoned my courage] to take a peep at the gentleman on the other side of the clock. I bent forward to do so and to my confusion, found a pair of piercing black eyes fixed on me. I withdrew my gaze very hastily.

Minerva Denison, recounting the first time she met Captain John Rodgers, 1802

On 13 June 1799, Secretary of Navy Benjamin Stoddert informed Rodgers that it was "the Presidents [*sic*] desire that you take command of the *Maryland*" and that Rodgers had been promoted to captain, effective 5 March 1799. Although Stoddert thought Rodgers "too young" to command a frigate, the secretary recommended that President John Adams appoint this "brave man and . . . good seaman" to command a smaller ship.[1]

After little more than a year as an officer but more than thirteen years of maritime experience, twenty-six-year-old Rodgers was now a full-fledged captain with the command of a handsome new warship. Embodying the leadership characteristics he had learned from Truxtun, Rodgers was well qualified to assume command of an American warship in spite of his relatively young age. And his physique fit the role. Above average in height at about five feet, ten inches tall, Rodgers was a physically powerful, stout, muscular man with an imposing presence. His rich black hair, heavy black eyebrows, thick whiskers, piercing dark eyes, and handsome face also enhanced his scowling persona, particularly when he was angry or in a bad mood. Although respected and admired by many of his junior officers, others found him to be an unpleasant, overbearing, and heavy-handed commander.

Privately built for the government by the citizens of Baltimore, the newly launched 380-ton sloop of war *Maryland* carried a complement of 180 men and was rated at twenty guns, although she actually mounted twenty-six guns. An observer described her as "a Charming Little Ship, Exceedingly well fitted with The best Materials I ever Saw—looks most Beautiful." Although he thought that the *Maryland* "is a handsome ship and I believe will sail fast," Rodgers expressed concern about her fighting potential; "she carries her guns too low, the Gun Deck at present being only eighteen inches above the surface of the water."[2]

During the summer, Rodgers completed fitting her out and recruited his 160–man crew. Following the practices he had learned from Truxtun, he took great care with the details of his preparations and the organization of his crew. Like Truxtun, Rodgers issued and posted on deck a set of forty-four regulations stressing efficiency, routine, and economy. In addition to general duties and behavior, they addressed items of dress, cleanliness, decorum, and diet. For example, the ration of "rum or spirits" was to be served twice per day in half portions "to prevent the ill effects of the whole allowance being given at once," and "special care" was to be taken to prevent "any sort of waste" of the "precious article" of freshwater. All officers and crew were to be practiced and "well skilled in the use of the great guns on shipboard, otherwise the greatest abilities in a commanding officer . . . will always be rendered abortive." After visiting the *Maryland* shortly before she sailed in September, an observer noted that the "order on Board was Great, & Probably too much a la mode L'Truxton [*sic*]—& Too distant, For Officer to Officer—& more Than I ever saw in any Ship of War before . . . & I rather Fear, that Favorite Systems may be Carried too Far. I will however hope for the Best!!!" Although this observer thought that Rodgers might have gone too far in imitating his mentor's command persona and disciplinary practices, the cruise of the *Maryland* would demonstrate Rodgers's ability to command a tightly run, efficient ship.[3]

Secretary Stoddert ordered Rodgers to cruise to the Dutch colony of Suriname, where he was to join and be subordinate to the senior officer there, Captain Daniel McNeill of the *Portsmouth*. Suriname was the location of one of four American naval stations in the West Indies, the others being in Havana, St. Kitts, and Santo Domingo. The Suriname station was also the least important and the one farthest from the United States, extending from French Guiana to the island of Curaçao along the northern coast of South America. Stoddert instructed Rodgers to provide "all possible Security to our trade by Capturing Enemy Vessels" and by "occasionally convoying our own, tho the most protection is afforded . . . by capturing the Vessels which annoy it." The secretary conveyed the president's "assurance of confidence in your activity, Zeal, & Bravery" and his own hopes for "your success and glory." In no instance was Rodgers to allow his vessel to be detained or searched or to have any of his officers or men taken from her by a foreign power "so long as you are in a capacity to repel such an outrage on the honor of the American flag."[4]

The *Maryland* sailed on 13 September 1799 and reached Suriname by 1 October. Although it was a Dutch possession, Suriname had been occupied recently by the British. As a result, the French threat to American commerce in the area had declined significantly. The French had only one frigate at French Guiana, and their privateers operated to the east in the Atlantic Ocean or south along the coast of Brazil rather than to the north toward British Guiana and Venezuela. The British also discouraged American trade by imposing new duties and custom regulations that, with the exception of molasses, applied to all items carried by American merchant ships. As a result, soon after the *Maryland* reached her station, there were almost no French privateers to hunt nor American merchant ships to protect.[5]

After a four-week cruise in November, an officer on the *Maryland* reported that the "coast appears to be perfectly clear of French privateers." Although three French frigates were rumored to be in the vicinity, they never materialized. The main activity for a time seemed to be determining the sailing speed of the *Maryland* relative to those of other American warships that appeared periodically. First, *L'Insurgente* kept company for two days and demonstrated that "she can out sail us; she is a remarkably fine frigate." Then the *Maryland* fell in with the *Portsmouth* and cruised in her company for three weeks. After a "fair trial of sailing," the *Maryland* outsailed her "shamefully, I do think we could run her nearly out of sight in 24 hours."[6]

By early December, Captain McNeill headed the *Portsmouth* for the United States, leaving Rodgers to command the station alone for the next nine months. It proved a frustrating time for him because there was virtually no action even though in January 1800, several French warships and six hundred troops had arrived at Cayenne in French Guiana, posing a potential threat for Americans to the north in the waters of Suriname. American consul Turell Tufts predicted that unless the *Maryland* was either withdrawn or reinforced with additional warships, the United States would lose "the *Maryland*—and the trade also."[7] But the station remained quiet as the French warships did not appear. In Washington, Stoddert observed that Rodgers "can do nothing there," but without direct orders to the contrary, Rodgers remained on station. In April, the *Maryland* accompanied a convoy as far as St. Kitts and then returned to Suriname. Rodgers continued to sail "windward of Suriname, in a direction which all Vessels endeavor to fall in, that are bound to any part of the Coast of Cuyanne [Cayenne]," but by 1 July he reported not "seeing or hearing of a Single Enemy" ship.[8]

On shore in Suriname, Rodgers experienced other aggravations. In December 1799 in Paramaribo, as he prepared to return to his ship from a shore visit to the commanding military officer, a guard addressed Rodgers "in a very impertinent manner" and reminded him to produce the required documents before the *Maryland* sailed "or else by Jesus Christ I should not pass." Having been insulted, Rodgers returned immediately to demand satisfaction from the commanding officer, who assured him that the offender would be punished. This assurance, reported Rodgers, "is all one officer could in such cases expect from another,—[and] perfectly satisfied me."[9]

Another dispute ended less satisfactorily. The American schooner *Ranger* arrived at the Suriname River en route to the United States with a cargo of sixty-two slaves. Responding to a recent act of Congress forbidding the importing of slaves in American ships, Rodgers requested that the governor of the colony turn the ship and its illegal cargo over to him. When the governor refused, Rodgers persisted and, in a personal meeting, asked the governor to order the ship out of the colony. The governor refused, explaining that he could not because the ship was "not seaworthy." This claim infuriated Rodgers, who could do nothing but complain that the governor has "Coats of all Colours, and he will change as often as it is his Interest to do so." Eventually the governor allowed the slaves to be sold.[10]

Adding to Rodgers's frustrations was the lack of cooperation from American consul Turell Tufts, who favored the slave trade in the West Indies and thought United States law should be changed accordingly. While he believed that slavery should not be permitted in "Northern Countries" and that "blacks should not even be allowed to be transported there," Tufts thought it foolish to legislate against the slave trade between Africa and the West Indies because the profits were "so alluring" and the laws against the trade "so easily evaded." In Tufts's view, the only crime resulted from the "inhuman treatment" of the slaves being transported, not from the slave trade or the institution of slavery itself. After all, "Blacks are of a lower degree & will from their constitution and nature of things forever remain so. . . . To ameliorate the condition of Slaves & to make them Happy is all that can be done. It is not in the power of man to make them Great . . . and as slaves they are instruments of good." Thus dealing with an evasive governor and an uncooperative consul, Rodgers failed in his only attempt to uphold this American law. Personally, Rodgers expressed no criticism of the institution of slavery or of the international slave trade. As a resident of a slave state, Rodgers's father owned slaves. In fact, Rodgers himself accepted the institution and would later own household slaves himself. At the same time, Rodgers was determined to do his duty as a naval officer by attempting to uphold the laws of the United States.[11]

Rodgers had no better fortune dealing with French privateers. On 26 July, close to Devil's Island, he recaptured the Portuguese brig *Gloria da Mar*. In French possession for only thirteen days before it met the *Maryland*, the brig mounted four guns with a crew of ten men and a cargo of rice, cotton, and leather. This was the sole prize that Rodgers took on the Suriname station. Finally, in early August, Rodgers returned to Suriname and began to collect ships for a convoy and the return trip to the United States. He sailed with twelve vessels to Martinique, where he found the brig *Eagle*, and then proceeded to St. Kitts. Now numbering thirty-two ships, the convoy then made its way to St. Thomas, which it reached on 1 September. There Rodgers captured the *Aerial*, a French ship that had been flying Swedish colors and trading between Guadeloupe and Saint Barthélemy. After being forced to wait out a hurricane for a week, Rodgers departed with a convoy that now consisted of fifty-two American ships and several British ships. As the fleet neared the United States, most of the ships scattered. The *Maryland* entered Chesapeake Bay in late September and anchored at the mouth of the Patapsco River on 30 September.[12]

Sixteen months earlier, Rodgers had returned in triumph as the *Constellation* appeared in Norfolk with her prize, *L'Insurgente*. Now he returned as a disappointed captain after his first and unproductive cruise in command of an American warship. In an area where both French privateers and American merchant ships proved scarce, Rodgers had contributed little to the naval war. In his report to Secretary Stoddert, Rodgers expressed his "unexceptionable mortification" in informing the secretary "that I did not make a single Capture except one . . . altho I can with great Justice, Say that no Ship ever cruised with more assiduity and unremitting attention than the *Maryland*." Rodgers believed that even any of "my greatest enemies who has had any knowledge of my Situation, will do me the Justice to say the Same, yet with extreme pain I am forced to Say that I never met with the smallest object of my wishes." In pleading his case, Rodgers did not explain why his prolonged lack of productivity failed to induce him to expand his cruising ground or to leave Suriname altogether to join one of the other West Indies stations.[13]

After returning to Baltimore, Rodgers discharged most of his crew and spent the winter of 1800–1801 refitting the *Maryland*. By this time, the naval war with France had ended. On 30 September 1800, France and the United States signed a treaty in Paris restoring peace. In February 1801, the Senate amended and ratified the treaty, which required the further approval of the French government. In Washington, the outgoing Adams administration selected Rodgers to convey Virginia representative John Dawson with the treaty to France in the *Maryland*. On 18 March, Stoddert instructed Rodgers to wait in France until Dawson had met with French officials and prepared his "Dispatches from Paris." Since peace had been restored with France, Stoddert reminded Rodgers to "impress on your Officers & men, the propriety [of] cultivating harmony & Friendship with the Citizens of that Nation. . . . Your own reputation as well as that of the American Navy will require that you keep up Strict Discipline on board." The *Maryland* sailed from Baltimore on 22 March and reached Havre de Grace, France, in early May. By July, Dawson was urging Rodgers to return to the United States because Napoleon had still not ratified the treaty. Although Rodgers did not return with the official ratification of the treaty, Napoleon, in fact, approved the agreement on 31 July, thus fully restoring peace between the two nations by abrogating the treaty of 1778.[14]

The American political and naval world from which Rodgers had sailed in March had changed significantly by the time he returned five months later. After ratifying the peace treaty with France, Congress had passed an act providing for the "Naval Peacetime Establishment." Actually signed by the outgoing Adams administration, the legislation severely reduced the size of the navy. It dismissed about two-thirds of the navy's officers and limited those in service to 9 captains, 36 lieutenants, and 150 midshipmen, who would receive full pay only when engaged in active service. It also authorized the president to sell all except thirteen warships; of those, only six were to retain full crews and remain ready for sea.[15]

This legislation coincided not only with the return of peace but with the naval views of incoming president Thomas Jefferson. Strongly opposed to maintaining a large, active peacetime navy, Jefferson believed that such a force was both too expensive and unnecessary for national defense. At the outset of his presidency, Jefferson faced a national debt exceeding $80 million. Rightly or wrongly, he viewed the large deficit as a dangerous threat to the new republic. Accordingly, he and his secretary of the treasury, Albert Gallatin, acted to reduce that national debt as quickly as possible. An unmistakable fiscal target was the navy, whose expenses were greater than those of the army and were exceeded only by the annual interest on the federal debt. In the 1800 fiscal year that ended on 31 December, the navy had expenses of almost $3.5 million, or 32 percent of the federal budget. In the 1801 fiscal year, the navy's expenses declined to $2.1 million but still represented 22 percent of the federal budget. If the Jefferson administration hoped to reduce the national debt, it would clearly have to cut naval expenses dramatically and use the released federal revenue to attack the deficit.[16]

In addition, Jefferson genuinely believed that a large European-style navy was unnecessary to defend the nation. The navy should be a component of unified national defense policy, not a separate diplomatic or military instrument. Rather than attempting to compete with European powers by building a large navy, Jefferson followed the concept of a passive coastal defense—using the navy in peacetime to defend American commerce when it was attacked by pirates or minor powers. In the event of a war, a few American warships could be joined by dozens of gunboats and floating batteries to defend the American coast while hundreds of privateers ravaged the enemy's commerce at sea. Jefferson specifically opposed the construction of additional large warships because they were expensive, became obsolete too soon, and might be interpreted by European nations, particularly Great Britain, as a direct threat.[17]

The Peacetime Establishment Act of 1801 and the policies of the new administration directly affected Rodgers in two ways. First, the government quickly sold the *Maryland* in October 1801 for $20,200, thus ending the brief, routine career of the beautiful ship. Second, the Navy Department informed Rodgers that he would not be one of the nine captains to be retained. On 22 October, new secretary of the navy Robert Smith explained to Rodgers that as "highly as he regards your merits," the president "cannot retain you in Commission consistently with the principles of selection that have been adopted." As a personal friend, Smith explained to Rodgers how "very painful" it was for him to convey this decision and that his own feelings had been "greatly increased by considerations resulting from a personal knowledge of your Worth."[18]

With no immediate future in the navy, Rodgers turned to a familiar activity. He became part owner and captain of the schooner *Nellie* and attempted to capitalize on the unsettled but profitable trade that existed between the United States and Santo Domingo. He sailed on 4 December and fifteen days later reached Cape Francois, where he spent the next two months selling his cargo and purchasing a new one for the return trip. Cape Francois was a small port of several thousand inhabitants located on the north coast of what is now Haiti. It was here that Rodgers met and began a close, longtime friendship with American consul Tobias Lear.

Rodgers confronted an unsettled political situation in Santo Domingo. A decade after his successful revolution there, Toussaint-Louverture retained actual political and military control of the island. The Jefferson administration continued to recognize Santo Domingo as a French province because it feared the island might become an American Algiers, that is, a pirate state in the western hemisphere. Jefferson also viewed Louverture and his state of emancipated black slaves as a potential menace to legalized slavery in America's southern states.[19] By 1801, Louverture faced internal challenges and external threats. Most serious were Napoleon's intentions in the western hemisphere. After reaching a peace agreement with the British in 1801, Napoleon began to consolidate and expand the French empire in the New World. In 1801, Spain agreed secretly to cede Louisiana to France. Then Napoleon assembled a large force to invade Santo Domingo. Under the leadership of Napoleon's brother-in law General Charles Leclerc, an armada of fifty-four ships and more than twelve thousand men sailed from Europe on 14 December 1801. In late January 1802, the French force reached Samana Bay and prepared to execute its invasion plans, which called for landings at several places on the island. Leclerc himself was to seize Cape Francois on the island's northwest coast. On 2 February, his force of twenty-three vessels and seven thousand men appeared off the harbor. Believing that rebel forces under the command of General Henri Christophe would readily surrender in the face of such a powerful enemy force, Leclerc contacted Christophe to demand that the French be allowed to occupy the town immediately. In return, the French guaranteed the freedom of the black population. The effort failed because Christophe did not trust this promise. He stalled for time and threatened to "fire the town and murder the whites" if the French tried to land. The French then landed troops outside of the town and on 4 February opened fire on one of the forts guarding the harbor of Cape Francois.[20]

True to his word, Christophe ordered his troops to withdraw and to destroy the town. A scene of fiery chaos ensued that same night. One account described a "scene of horror and destruction beyond the powers of description. . . . Many massacres took place and the brutal rape of the negroes [sic] spared neither age nor sex, or their own colour. . . . the black daemons [sic] of slaughter were seen holding up with one hand the writhing infant, and hacking off limbs with sword in the other." By the next morning, only an estimated fifty-nine of the two thousand houses in the town had been spared from fire. One American died trying to save his property. Except for a few individuals who had managed to reach American ships in the harbor, there were no inhabitants to be seen in town or on any of the plantations in the nearby area.[21]

Rodgers and Lear both spent that wild night on shore trying to save lives and property. With a small group of friendly black residents, Rodgers extinguished several fires, saved "much property," and helped local residents to escape. As he attempted to return to his ship, "a crowd of women and children flying from the negroes [sic]" overtook him and pleaded to be taken via his boat to the *Nellie*, which waited in the harbor. As hostile pursuers approached, Rodgers hastily loaded the group into his boat, but as he shoved the boat off, he fell back onto the wharf, where he was captured. In the confusion, Rodgers soon "broke away from his guard and after wandering some time went to sleep in a cave near the city." The next day he finally made his way back to his ship. Lear praised Rodgers for displaying "that dauntless spirit which he is known to possess."[22]

When General Leclerc and the French finally landed on 6 February, Leclerc personally thanked Rodgers for his efforts, gave him special permission to return to the United States in the *Nellie*, and promised him a handsome profit if he would return soon with supplies for the French troops. Agreeing to make the trip, Rodgers reached Baltimore in early March and by 1 April was back in Cape Francois, where he learned that the French forces had endured a tough time. On 24 March, Leclerc had won a major victory at Crete-a-Pierrot, but the cost of the campaign had been high—two thousand Frenchmen lost. In the face of growing Haitian resistance, immediate French prospects did not look good; Leclerc needed reinforcements, and his troops suffered from an acute shortage in supplies. At Cape Francois, Rodgers found that the previous gratitude of Leclerc had turned to an open hostility toward the Americans. Leclerc imposed new regulations on American merchant ships and refused to resolve many of the complaints that Lear registered with him. Leclerc also informed Lear that an existing agreement with France prohibited the United States from having an official consul in any French colony. On 10 April, he suspended the official duties of Lear, who left the island a week later.[23]

Rodgers's relations with Leclerc were equally poor. On 12 April, French authorities actually jailed Rodgers to his great surprise and consternation. At the prison, guards first placed Rodgers in a "wretched" stone cell little more than double the size "of a large Oven." Three hours later, they switched him to one that was "Still worse—a Dungeon surrounded by a Double wall, and totally dark except what light was afforded by the Key hole." Here the prisoner found "Lizards, Spiders and many other Insects peculiar to the Climate." Rodgers subsisted for four days and three nights "on bread and water, the latter . . . served in a dirty copper can calculated to poison in a very little time the most healthy person." On the fifth day, guards permitted Rodgers into the prison yard, where he found another American prisoner, merchant captain William Davidson of Philadelphia. Together they bribed an official with twenty-five dollars to furnish them "with a little meat and wine during our imprisonment here." They also managed to write a brief note in blood to a friend and to have it smuggled out of the prison. Five days later, the French moved the two Americans to a remote part of the prison that seemed pala- tial in comparison to their former cell because it had "the benefit of pure air" and permitted the "privilege of walking in the yard in day time." Here, several days later, Rodgers and Davidson received a smuggled note that asked what sacrifice they were prepared to make. When the Americans asked for an explanation, a disguised visitor delivered another note the next day asking how much they would pay for their liberation. Their visitor expected a large amount because, he explained, "there were many of them to share it . . . [in- cluding] the Commandant de la place." The two Americans replied that they would not pay a single dollar. Three days later, the prisoners were conducted to the quarters of a French general, who ordered the Americans to sail from Cape Francois within four days "and not to land again under the pain of Death." Rodgers and Davidson were not permitted to return to their ships but managed to obtain passage on the schooner *Pomona.* They eventually managed to recover their ships and nearly all of their personal property after reaching Baltimore on 22 May 1802.[24]

Rodgers never received a definitive explanation for his infuriating im- prisonment. He speculated later that General Leclerc had become angry when he learned that Rodgers had armed several of the black residents who assisted him on the infamous night of 4 February. A more likely explanation was tied to a meeting with a Commodore Clement, who was the French commander of the port. On 2 April, the day after Rodgers had returned to Cape Francois from Baltimore, he was called to the French commodore's office, where a stormy confrontation occurred. Rodgers claimed that Clem- ent's "language bespoke nothing but insult and contempt to my Country and my own person, as was testified by his attitude, gesture and Delivery." Clement accused Rodgers of lying about his return trip to Cape Francois and denounced the Americans' "base treatment" of the officers and crew captured when *L'Insurgente* was taken. He also charged that Rodgers had made malicious statements about the French Republic during his recent stay in Baltimore. Rodgers angrily defended his conduct and denied all of the allegations. Years later, Rodgers speculated that his imprisonment was "an act of vindictive revenge for the active part he had taken in the capture of *L'Insurgente.*"[25]

His incarceration both angered and scarred Rodgers. More than six months later, he explained to his brother-in-law William Pinkney that he had nearly recovered but would not forget. "Every nerve is carrying out ven- geance against the perpetrators of my injured constitution," wrote Rodgers.

"However, I have patience, and will philosophically be silent, until vengeance is practical. . . . as much of an Antigallican as I am; yet, I discover that I gain prudence, as my youthful faculties forsake me."[26]

Soon after returning to Baltimore, Rodgers traveled north to visit family and friends in Havre de Grace and to rest and recuperate. He soon was engaged in a round of dinners and social activities. He had not expected that a relaxed stay at home would forever change his life, but it did because there he met and quickly became enamored with Minerva Denison, a shy and softly beautiful young woman who had moved with her family to Havre de Grace in 1795. Originally from Connecticut, her parents, Gideon and Jerusha Denison, lived previously in Savannah, Georgia, and then near Philadelphia before moving to Maryland. In the early 1790s, Denison had been involved in various business activities, including the slave trade, in several states. In 1792, he had instructed his merchant captain to "keep secret" the nature of the "Business" and "to perform a voyage to the coast of Africa for the purpose of bringing about forty slaves" to Savannah.[27] Denison had also invested extensively in real estate, speculating in land in Georgia, North Carolina, Tennessee, and Maryland. Among his holdings were several farms near Havre de Grace, which he believed would develop into a large city. He was one of several real estate speculators who mistakenly believed that the village might be selected as the site of the new national capital. Three miles west of Havre de Grace on one of his farms stood a home that the previous owner had named "Sion Hill." The large, colonial-style house enjoyed a sweeping view of Chesapeake Bay, the Susquehanna River, and the surrounding countryside. It was here that he settled his family in 1795.

Born in June 1784, Minerva Denison was the second-born of four children and the eldest of three surviving daughters. A quiet and reserved child, Minerva attended a small boarding school in Philadelphia and then, after the family had moved to Maryland, another boarding school in Baltimore. Here she received a basic education and learned the rudimentary skills expected of a proper young lady, including music, literature, poetry, and dancing. She also roamed the rural countryside with her elder brother when she was home for the summer. She later spoke fondly of setting traps for the rabbits, catching snow birds, and participating in "every other innocent country pleasure" while at home.[28]

In spite of its small population, Havre de Grace included a number of wealthy families who had moved there from Baltimore or Philadelphia. Retired merchants from Baltimore and other wealthy individuals had purchased land and built large homes in the expectation of Havre de Grace's becoming "a great city." Among these individuals who provided a comfortable and lively social circle were Colonel and Mrs. Samuel Hughes, who had no children themselves but entertained other families often. At their "delightful house, with beautiful and cultivated grounds," Mrs. Hughes was an enthusiastic gardener known for growing colorful flowers and fine fruits. Years later, Minerva Denison still vividly remembered the "perfume of the violets and hyacinths" in the gardens. "I have spent many happy hours there, and was always most warmly welcomed by them . . . and [they] always called upon me to sing and play upon the piano for them."

It was here in June 1802 that Minerva Denison met John Rodgers. Colonel and Mrs. Hughes had invited Rodgers to a dinner party. Since the hosts had other guests and a full table, Mrs. Denison and her daughter Minerva were invited to come to their home after dinner for tea. Although she had never met John Rodgers, Minerva had known his mother, sisters, and brother Alexander. She was also aware that Rodgers was a naval hero whose recent adventures and imprisonment in Santo Domingo "had been much talked of and published in the papers."[29]

When Minerva and her mother entered the parlor that evening, several women were discussing Captain Rodgers. One "maiden lady . . . thought he was very rough and abrupt and did not like him. She thought he had a bad countenance, with his black and heavy eye-brows" and had "nearly fainted with horror" during dinner when Rodgers had vividly described an action that he had been engaged in "when the deck was slippery with blood." Disagreeing, another young woman described him as "very handsome." Minerva was seated at one end of a card table near a wall. A large French clock on the table "effectually concealed any one sitting behind" it. When the men came into the room, Rodgers sat down at the other end of the table from the concealed Minerva. Rodgers had been introduced to all of the other women in the room, but Mrs. Hughes forgot to introduce him to Minerva. Before she left the room to walk in the garden with other guests, Minerva summoned the courage to "take a peep at the gentleman on the other side of the clock. I bent forward to do so and to my confusion, found a pair of piercing black eyes fixed on me. I withdrew my gaze very hastily, but the gentlemen all arose and walked into the garden, the ladies remaining in the drawing room."[30]

Later, on their way home, Minerva asked her mother's opinion of Rodgers, "who seemed to be the hero of the day." Her mother responded that she "'did not like him at all.' She said his countenance was dreadful, those black and heavy eyebrows gave him such a forbidding look that it made her tremble to look at him." Minerva agreed, saying that "from the little glance which I had, I think he must be a man of violent temper, though first impressions are not always correct." Indeed, her impression was not correct in this instance. A few days later her mother returned from shopping in the village with an entirely different opinion. She informed Minerva that she had met Rodgers and now thought "him very handsome and very agreeable." He had been "exceedingly polite and friendly and had followed her into the store and assisted her to make her purchases," reported Minerva's mother; he was "in fact so very kind that she did not know to what she should ascribe it." Rodgers's "teeth and eyes were splendid and when in conversation his whole appearance was so bright that it made him very fascinating in appearance." A day or two later, Alexander Rodgers brought his brother to the Denison house and formally introduced him to Minerva. Thereafter, "his visits became frequent and his attentions to me very conspicuous."[31]

In fact, Rodgers had been smitten. This gruff, twenty-nine-year-old naval veteran and well-traveled man of the world was clearly under the spell of eighteen-year-old Minerva. Although their "love affairs made no great progress" that summer, Rodgers seems to have fallen quickly in love with Minerva and could not forget her. She was ambivalent. No doubt flattered by the attentions of a handsome, worldly naval hero, she was still initially unsure of her genuine emotions. After all, she was an inexperienced young woman who lived in a parochial and cloistered world. Their affections for each other were not allowed to develop and possibly to flower during the summer of 1802 because the professional world intruded on the temporary idyll of Rodgers when the navy recalled him to active duty.

Commodore in the Mediterranean, 1802–1806

*The Bashaw is much humiliated which he even himself confesses.
. . . I can venture to say that it is the last War the Regency
will ever wage against the U States.*

Captain John Rodgers, on the treaty of peace with Tripoli, 1805

On 25 August 1802, the Navy Department reactivated Captain John Rodgers and assigned him to command the thirty-two-gun frigate *John Adams*. He was "to proceed with all possible dispatch to join our Squadron in the Mediterranean," where he would assist in the American campaign against Tripoli and respond to threats from other Barbary powers. Commanded by Commodore Richard Morris, the squadron consisted of the frigates the *Chesapeake*, the *Constellation*, the *Adams*, the *New York*, the *John Adams*, and the schooner *Enterprise*. The six ships sailed from the United States at different times between February and October 1802, with the *John Adam* the last to depart on 22 October.[1]

In the Mediterranean, war with the Barbary powers posed very different diplomatic and military challenges than the United States had confronted in the Quasi-War with France. Together the Barbary states of Morocco, Algiers, Tunis, and Tripoli stretched along a coastline exceeding 2,000 miles from the Strait of Gibraltar to Egypt. The main seaport of Morocco, Tangiers was located almost opposite Gibraltar. Five hundred miles to the east was Algiers, the capital of the country of the same name. The distance from Algiers to the capital city Tunis was another 500 miles, and from Tunis to Tripoli yet another 350 miles. Morocco was a sovereign state ruled by an emperor, while each of the other three powers was governed by a local ruler under the nominal authority of the Ottoman Empire. The Barbary rulers controlled diverse populations of North Africans, Muslims, Berbers, Jews, and some Europeans. Since these maritime states were all economically poor, piracy on the Mediterranean constitutede their main sources of revenue. Pirate ships from the four Barbary states plundered the cargo of merchant ships and imprisoned their crews and passengers. Some prisoners were enslaved while others were held for ransom. In addition, the Barbary rulers signed tribute agreements with various European nations. In return for an annual monetary payment, the rulers agreed not to prey on the trade of a particular nation. While some European nations refused to make such agreements, other, more powerful nations such as Great Britain and France did because the bribes were relatively small and tended to reduce commercial competition by increasing the threat of Barbary piracy against those nations that did not pay a tribute.[2]

America's relations with the Barbary powers dated to the 1780s. In 1786, the United States signed a treaty of friendship with Morocco and later reached agreements with Tripoli and Algiers in 1796 and Tunis in 1797. The latter three agreements provided American payments of $56,000 to Tripoli, $992,463 to Algiers, and $107,000 to Tunis. In effect, the Federalist administrations of George Washington and John Adams had chosen cash payments over military force for two reasons. First, not created until 1794, the American navy was a small and weak force during its initial years. Second, the United States was fully occupied by its diplomatic and commercial differences with England until the Jay Treaty was ratified in 1796 and then with France during Quasi-War.

In 1801, new president Thomas Jefferson changed American policy in the Mediterranean. For several years, the rulers of Algiers, Tripoli, and Tunis had been pressing the United States to furnish naval stores as well as to increase its annual cash payments. Although intent on reducing the size and cost of the navy, the Jefferson administration preferred using military force to making tribute payments. With peace restored between the United States and France, Jefferson believed that even a reduced navy provided enough force to deal with the growing Barbary threat.

Jefferson also had the good fortune to have Robert Smith as his secretary of the navy even though the president had not made this a high-priority appointment. Smith assumed the position in July 1801 and served until 1809. Although he had no maritime background and lacked administrative experience, Robert Smith was a prominent admiralty lawyer and Baltimore politician who had served terms in the Maryland legislature and on the Baltimore city council. Energetic and capable, Smith had an easygoing manner and ingratiating personality that eased his dealings with such strong opponents of the navy as Secretary of the Treasury Albert Gallatin. Of particular importance was Smith's ability to make do with a reduced budget and still furnish American commanders in the Mediterranean with the resources they needed to wage war thousands of miles from the United States.[3]

In 1801, Jefferson sent Commodore Richard Dale with a small squadron of warships to deal with the problems in Tripoli, which was then the most troublesome of the North African states. In response to the threat of imminent war, the administration ordered Dale to blockade Tripoli and to protect American ships from Tripolitan pirates. Since the nations were not officially at war, Dale was not authorized to attack Tripoli or to take any prizes. Although Dale did not know it when he sailed on 1 June, Tripoli had declared war on the United States the previous month. During his cruise in 1801 and 1802, Dale increased American naval visibility and protected individual American merchant ships, but he lacked sufficient force to bring Tripoli to terms. In February, Congress recognized formally that a state of war existed and authorized the president to take the steps necessary to prosecute the conflict, including the taking of prizes and the outfitting of American privateers. In response, Jefferson further escalated American naval activity by dispatching the new, larger squadron under Morris to the Mediterranean.

As commander of the *John Adams*, one of the ships in Morris's squadron, Rodgers no doubt anticipated winning naval glory and fame in a decisive naval engagement or combat action. There would, however, be few of those because naval war with the Barbary states posed difficult problems for the United States Navy. From the Strait of Gibraltar to Cape Bon, the coast was first high and rocky and then low with shallow waters difficult to navigate. Most of the ports were open and exposed to the north, and the coast was beset with strong currents. From September to April, frequent and severe gales made navigation for sailing ships difficult and dangerous. Because the area was also so far removed from the United States, supplying American naval vessels posed difficulties.[4]

Naval operations also required a small number of American naval vessels to perform multiple roles. In addition to showing the flag at various ports, naval officers were expected to blockade selected Barbary ports, to find and attack pirate ships, to convoy American merchant ships, and to provide diplomatic support for American consuls in the region. Complicating matters was the fact that the Barbary powers did not employ traditional European-style battleships. Instead, they relied on small ships that were lightly armed, carried boarding parties of pirates, and could operate effectively in the shoal waters and small ports of the North African coastline. Although they employed some small warships, the American squadrons relied primarily on heavily armed frigates ranging from twenty-eight to forty-four guns. Physically impressive as these warships were, they proved to be of limited operational use.

Once he had reached the Mediterranean in 1802, Rodgers quickly got a taste of the routine duty that would dominate his cruise. Arriving at Malaga, he was ordered not into war against Tripoli but rather back to Gibraltar for a load of supplies. In fact, this logistical mission was necessary. Without a permanent supply base in the Mediterranean, American warships had to carry most of their own supplies because American supply ships refused to sail past Gibraltar and the war between France and England had made naval supplies expensive and difficult to procure in the Mediterranean. After completing her supply cruise, the *John Adams* then convoyed an American merchant ship back to Malta, where Rodgers found Commodore Morris and his flagship, the *Chesapeake*.

The Navy Department had ordered Morris to Tripoli, where it expected that a show of American naval force and the threat of a blockade would bring Tripoli to terms. But Morris proved to be a dilatory and ineffective commander. Arriving in the Mediterranean too late to begin his mission in 1802, Morris did not sail from Malta with his squadron until 13 January 1803. Once underway, he met heavy, adverse, gale-force winds from the north and west that forced him to return to Malta. Now convinced that the winter weather rendered naval operations off Tripoli treacherous if not impossible until spring, Morris decided to try instead to reduce tension in Tunis and Algiers by displaying his naval force there.

On 22 February 1803, the American squadron sailed into a hostile situation when it reached Tunis. Along with American consuls William Eaton and James Cathcart, Morris and Rodgers began negotiations with the bey of Tunis on various issues, the most important of which was the bey's demand that the Americans return Tunisian property that had been aboard a Tripolitan prize taken by the United States. After one meeting, Morris left without offering a formal farewell to the bey. For this affront, the bey's commercial agent detained Morris and demanded that he immediately pay $22,000 that Eaton had allegedly borrowed but not yet repaid. Morris was released after he promised to pay the $22,000, but negotiations had failed. Citing the bey's "declared desire of preferring war with us," Morris took no action but recommended "the necessity of encreasing [sic] the squadron in the Mediterranean" as the "only hope we can have of continuing in peace with the Barbary States."[5]

Having failed at Tunis, Morris touched at Algiers and then sailed to Gibraltar, where he switched his broad pennant to the *New York* and headed back to Malta. Since the squadron was not yet ready for action, Rodgers proceeded alone in the *John Adams* to Tripoli to establish a blockade. Once there, Rodgers moved to within three-fourths of a mile of the shore and exchanged gunfire with Tripolitan gunboats and shore batteries. After capturing the twenty-gun Tripolitan cruiser *Meshuda*, Rodgers returned to Malta with his prize on 19 May. With the *New York* and the *Enterprise* now ready to sail, the *John Adams* returned with them to Tripoli. Attempting to take the military initiative, the Americans assaulted a convoy of small coasting vessels protected by several gunboats. The vessels escaped to shallow water and the protection of shore batteries, but the next day an American party led by Lieutenant David Porter attacked. Under heavy fire, the Americans landed and set fire to the vessels. However, once the Americans had withdrawn, Tripolitan forces emerged from cover and braved steady American fire to save their boats by extinguishing the flames. Although the attack tried to make a strong point, the Americans had failed to score a telling victory while suffering a dozen casualties, including Porter, who had been wounded.[6]

On 27 May, Morris ordered three of his frigates to attack the enemy's gunboats. With the *Adams* and the *New York* following, Rodgers in the *John Adams* moved close to the city, bore up near the enemy gunboats, and opened fire. A sharp engagement followed, but American firepower was severely limited because Rodgers, in his eagerness for action, had misplaced his ship by anchoring it directly in front of the other two American warships. Unable to maneuver around Rodgers's ship because of a slack breeze, the *Adams* and the *New York* were effectively neutralized and unable to fire at the gunboats. The engagement ended when the gunboats retreated to the harbor, where shore batteries protected them. Rodgers had suffered no casualties but inflicted only light casualties on the enemy.

After these tentative and ineffective efforts to intimidate Tripoli, Morris began negotiations on 29 May. Since the American consul James Cathcart had left Tripoli after war was declared in 1801, Morris acted through the Danish consul and sent Rodgers ashore to assist with preliminaries. But Tripoli remained unmoved, and negotiations left the two sides far apart. The pasha of Tripoli demanded $200,000 plus war expenses, while Morris offered a mere $15,000. When negotiations broke off, Morris sailed for Malta on 10 June, leaving Rodgers to maintain the blockade.

After Rodgers tightened access to the harbor, a large enemy vessel attempted to run the blockade on the morning of 22 June. Carrying more than two hundred men, the polacre-rigged, twenty-two-gun Tripolitan warship was "the largest cruiser belonging to Tripoli, to appearance a very fine vessel." In response, the schooner *Enterprise*, under the command of Lieutenant Isaac Hull, intercepted the vessel and forced her into a narrow bay. There "a

vast number of cavalry and armed men on the beach" as well as nine gunboats attempted to assist the enemy ship. Rodgers shortened sail, moved the
John Adams toward the enemy ship, and opened fire shortly from "point-
blank shot." For forty-five minutes both sides exchanged a "constant" fire.
Then the enemy's guns fell silent as the Tripolitans abandoned ship. Since he
was now in less than five fathoms of water, Rodgers decided to "wear and lay
the ship's head off shore" but ordered Hull to take several boats as close to
shore as possible and open fire on the beach in order to allow the Americans
to take possession of the enemy warship. After an enemy boat reappeared
and the crew attempted to reboard their ship, Rodgers renewed his fire from
the *John Adams*. The Tripolitans hauled down their colors and fired their
broadsides, but then "a tremendous explosion . . . burst the hull to pieces and
forced the main and mizzen masts one hundred fifty or one hundred and
sixty feet perpendicularly into the air, with all the yards, shrouds, stays, etc.
belonging to them." Rodgers reported no American casualties and estimated
that everyone on the other vessel, including the captain, had been killed. He
stated that the loss of this "most valuable Cruizer [*sic*] must of course do"
Tripoli "great injury, and from appearances" he expected that "none of our
Merchant vessels will fall into their hands this Summer."[7]

Shortly after this incident, Rodgers received word that Morris was lift-
ing the blockade on Tripoli and ordering the American squadron back to
Malta. History has judged this unilateral decision a mistake. Morris needed
to maintain the pressure of the blockade, not remove it. In spite of American
attacks and the blockade, Morris had not yet secured a peace agreement
or even extracted any concessions from Tripoli. Rodgers returned with his
ships to Malta and then sailed to Messina, Naples, and Leghorn, where Morris divided his squadron. Rodgers in the *John Adams* sailed with a convoy of
five merchant ships for Gibraltar. When he touched at Malaga on 11 September and found Morris with the *New York*, Rodgers learned from government
dispatches that he was to assume immediate command of the squadron and
replace Morris, who had been suspended by the Jefferson administration.
Extremely disappointed by the inaction and ineffectiveness of Morris, the
administration later conducted a hearing and dismissed him from the navy
in 1804.

It was under this cloud that thirty-year-old John Rodgers became commander of the Mediterranean squadron. He was now officially Commodore
Rodgers, an honorary designation that allowed him to fly a broad pennant
on his ship. However, any satisfaction or pride he felt was short-lived. On
14 September, when Rodgers and Morris anchored at Gibraltar, they found
a four-ship American naval squadron commanded by Commodore Edward

Preble, who carried new orders to assume command of the Mediterranean squadron. Flying above his flagship, the *Constitution*, was Preble's own broad pennant.

This had to be an exasperating moment for the intense Rodgers, who had labored impatiently for the past nine months under the dilatory command of Morris. Now, when he might bring his penchant for action into play, renew pressure against Tripoli, and win glory for himself, Rodgers had been superceded in command. He would later write to his Baltimore friend and Navy Department superior, Secretary Robert Smith, "I shall never cease to think myself unfortunate in not knowing your intentions sooner" because it "prevented me of an opportunity of erecting a lasting monument to the zeal and regard I have for my country." Beyond his disappointment, Rodgers was offended by the sight of Preble's broad pennant. Although Rodgers was considerably younger than Preble, he outranked Preble by one spot on the navy seniority list. Naval courtesy, thought Rodgers, dictated that Preble not fly his broad pennant in the presence of a senior officer, a claim that Preble refuted. Since he commanded a squadron independent of Rodgers, Preble refused to lower his pennant.[8]

This was also a moment ripe with the potential for a heated argument and a bitter feud, for both Rodgers and Preble were ambitious officers with careers on the make. Both were also proud, difficult, stern men known for their strong tempers. As professional rivals on the rise, they instinctively disliked and could not abide one another.[9] Rodgers complained that he was offended when he saw a "Commodore's Pendant on board" the *Constitution* in a squadron that he considered to have been under his command. Responding immediately and unapologetically to Rodgers, Preble explained that he had not hoisted his broad pennant for the "purpose of injuring your feelings . . . but to designate that I command a Squadron of the United States Ships of War" so that officers commanding ships in his squadron "may know where to apply for Orders, and from whence to receive Signals for their Government, etc." Preble also quoted a portion of his command orders from the Navy Department and offered to meet with Rodgers "to consult what measures may be best calculated to keep peace with the Barbary Powers."[10]

Still piqued, Rodgers acknowledged that his "feelings as an officer" have been "most sensibly injured" by this matter of professional etiquette. However, he put his emotions aside; in deference to "the Interest of our Country I drop the subject until we have more leisure to Define what has past" and stated that he would like to meet with Preble on the *Constitution* that same day. A situation that might have provoked a violent argument soon passed as Rodgers and Preble acknowledged that their duty in the Mediterranean must supercede their personal feelings. In spite of their personal animosity, both were consummate professional officers whose good sense allowed them to patch up their differences and to work effectively together in the weeks ahead.[11]

The issue at hand was the increasingly hostile Moroccan empire, which now posed a significant threat to American commerce. In August, the twenty-two-gun cruiser *Mirboka* had seized an American merchant brig before the cruiser itself was captured by Captain William Bainbridge in the *Philadelphia*. On 16 September, Rodgers met with Preble on the *Constitution*. Joining them was Rodgers's friend Tobias Lear, who had been appointed as consul general to Algiers. Although Lear had no authority over James Simpson, the American consul in Morocco, Preble and Rodgers asked for Lear's diplomatic advice as they discussed the Moroccan situation. Preble ordered several ships in his squadron to establish a blockade of Morocco's Mediterranean ports. On 17 September, Preble in the *Constitution* and Rodgers in the *John Adams* sailed to Tangiers. The next day, Preble returned to Gibraltar, but with the *John Adams* and the *New York* Rodgers sailed into the Atlantic to patrol and protect American merchant ships on Morocco's Atlantic coast.

For the next two weeks, Preble moved between Gibraltar and Tangiers as he planned his diplomatic strategy while Rodgers patrolled in the Atlantic and warned incoming American merchant ships of the potential dangers ahead. On 4 October, Preble returned to Tangiers with the *Constitution* and the schooner *Nautilus*. The next day, the emperor of Morocco marched into the city with an army estimated at twenty thousand men who were supported by shore batteries of 105 cannons. Then, on 6 October, Rodgers arrived with his two frigates. Anchored several hundred yards from shore, the American warships cleared for action and waited. Although armed hostilities seemed possible, the emperor sent word that he harbored no hostile intentions. In the next few days, tensions eased as the Americans and Moroccans exchanged salutes and the emperor sent a goodwill gift of cattle, sheep, and fowl to the American ships. Successful negotiations followed. Although Rodgers participated in the diplomatic process, Preble, Simpson, and Lear played the lead role in reaching an agreement that reaffirmed the 1786 treaty of friendship. In addition, Preble, with Rodgers's approval, returned to Morocco two prizes, the *Meshuda* and the *Mirboka*. Although not dramatic, these breakthroughs stabilized American-Moroccan relations, thus permitting American forces in the Mediterranean to concentrate on the more serious problems with Tripoli. Situated on the Strait of Gibraltar with both an Atlantic and a Mediterranean coastline, an antagonistic Morocco would have significantly complicated American naval efforts against Tripoli.[12]

Once difficulties with Morocco had been resolved, Rodgers returned to Gibraltar and then sailed for the United States on 18 October with the *New York* and the *John Adams*. More than six weeks later, on 2 December, he reached Washington, D.C. Rodgers's timing was propitious. Within a week, President Jefferson would praise Rodgers's activities in the Mediterranean when, in a message to Congress, Jefferson announced that differences between Morocco and the United States had been settled amicably. Jefferson also lauded "the gallant enterprise of Captain Rodgers in destroying on the coast of Tripoli a corvette of that power of 22 guns."[13]

The president's kind words notwithstanding, the cruise had disappointed Rodgers. Although American naval forces had protected American commerce in the Mediterranean, they had not forced Tripoli into a peace agreement. Moreover, although he had served faithfully and conducted himself well under the commands of Morris and Preble, Rodgers had won no individual distinction. Months of inactivity, boring convoy assignments, and routine blockade duty had only infrequently been punctuated by small and indecisive combat actions. Admittedly, Rodgers had destroyed a twenty-two-gun Tripolitan corvette and taken the prize *Meshuda*, but these victories provided little personal satisfaction or public acclaim.

Thus dispirited, Rodgers had left the Mediterranean without regret. On the journey home, his thoughts turned to a more pleasing prospect. Eighteen months earlier Rodgers had met and fallen in love with Minerva Denison, but their relationship had made "no great progress" at the time.[14] There is no question, however, that the navy veteran was infatuated with this innocent woman who was eleven years his junior. After sailing for Europe, he even acted at times like a schoolboy. During the fall of 1802, he confided his feelings for Minerva to his young sister Ann Pinkney and asked her to try to ascertain Minerva's feelings for him. When approached, Minerva responded to Pinkney in a polite but noncommittal manner, explaining that Rodgers "was not sufficiently known to me to warrant the expression of any feeling for him," and that she was "too young to think of marrying any one." Although she admitted that "I so much respect—I will say admire" him, yet "it would give me pleasure to hear that he had discarded every sentiment but esteem." Attributing John's infatuation to "the force of imagination," Minerva assumed that once he met other, older women "superior in every respect" to her, they would soon "obliterate any little impression he may at present imagine he has received and enable him to see that he has rated me far above my merits." Having confided her feelings, Minerva urged Pinkney to "Have the goodness to commit this [letter] to the flames."[15]

When she received another letter from Rodgers, Pinkney reminded him that she was not a confidante of Minerva and had not even seen Minerva personally in months. Nevertheless, Pinkney assured John that when he returned he would find "your goddess" as "candid and explicit as your own honest heart could wish her. She is still the same charming girl you left here and I believe no rival in your way. Let this comfort you." Herself perplexed by Rodgers's infatuation when he had so many women available to him, Pinkney observed that "there is no accounting for taste." [16]

As soon as he had reached Washington, Rodgers wrote again to Pinkney. "Through all the storms of English, Italian and Spanish beauty," boasted Rodgers, his heart had remained true. "I have kissed and I've prattled with fifty fair maids, and changed them as oft as you see, but of all the fair maids that I've seen . . . [there is] one little girl of the ball for me. . . . I continue to love and admire your little neighbor with all the ardent feeling you have heard me express." In spite of his passionate feelings, Rodgers remained cautious and sensitive to rejection, asking Pinkney to tell him if she had any reason to suppose that his feelings might be rebuffed. "I pray you will inform me immediately as I still have pride and fortitude," admitted a lovesick Rodgers. "Do for god's sake let me hear from you." Pinkney responded that although she had seen Minerva that very day, their previous conversation had been "an age ago." Reminding him that she was not in Minerva's confidence, Pinkney told Rodgers that "the little Goddess on whom you dote" seemed very animated but could not say whether it had anything to do with Rodgers's pending visit to Havre de Grace.[17]

Fortunately for his pursuit of Minerva, Rodgers was now assigned to the Washington navy yard to superintend the construction of one of the experimental gunboats being built by the Jefferson administration.[18] This billet allowed Rodgers to visit Havre de Grace and resume courting Minerva Denison in the next few months. What were the qualities that enamored him? Minerva was admittedly beautiful in a soft, innocent, angelic way. For Rodgers, her sheltered, sensitive, and generous manner embodied an ideal of female virtue. She was also a spirited woman, one who admitted that her "natural temper is haughty and perhaps impetuous . . . traits so unbecoming my sex," which she attributed to "never having been countered by parental authority." "From my infancy," confessed Minerva, "I have been an indulged child whose foibles were almost considered as perfections." As John and Minerva worked their way through various minor quarrels and tiffs, Minerva also displayed an impish side. When John attempted to explain his love rationally, Minerva replied that "Cupid . . . had usurped the empire of reason and enveloped your eyes in a mist before he turned their tasteless gaze on the Little Heathen of Mount Zion. Since you are blinded Heaven grant you may never be restored to sight."[19]

Whatever the reasons, John fell hard for Minerva Denison. In January, he signed one of his letters "Eternally & incessantly yours" and professed his love and adoration for and devotion to her. In early February, he wrote that "to be young, and to deserve you, is the full extent of my ambition." In extolling her virtues, he confided that her "sensitivity and magnanimity . . . will ever prevent her inflicting either Spiritual, Sensual or mental punishment on a slave who always wears her chains."[20] Many years later, Minerva remembered that "This proof of devoted affection won my heart, for as he declared to me, he had in his wanderings encountered many fair and beautiful women, but not one who for a moment had caused him to forget the only woman who had enslaved his heart." By early March, the two lovers were engaged but had not set a marriage date. John asked for the consent of Minerva's mother to marry "as soon as Possible . . . between the 10th and 15th of April," but Minerva and her mother insisted that the wedding be delayed until the fall.[21]

Beyond his passionate feelings for his betrothed, John's love letters are both candid and revealing about his own professional aspirations and his intense desire to achieve public honor and fame in service of his country. As he anticipated new orders from the Navy Department, John explained to Minerva that his absence would provide the twin opportunity to "prove to my country that I merit its regard, and to you that I have no ambition beyond that of acquiring a Reputation worthy of entitling me to your confidence and love." Minerva acknowledged his "ardent spirit" and fervid desire to "inscribe your name on the Temple of Fame." For her part, Minerva pledged to "strew a few roses and soften the rugged path you must necessarily pursue." As "compensation for all my solicitude," Minerva flattered herself "that when you have attained that height . . . you may retire from the toils of life crowned with well earned laurels, to pass the evening of your days with tranquility in the bosom of your family."[22]

As John and Minerva contemplated their wedding, external events intruded again, just as they had after the two first met in 1802. The Jefferson administration had decided to expand its military efforts in North Africa. In March 1804, Congress authorized more naval vessels and established a special "Mediterranean Fund" to prosecute the war against Tripoli and any other hostile Barbary power. The administration then sent Captain Samuel Barron with a new and larger squadron to the Mediterranean. The frigates

President, Congress, Essex, and *Constellation* were to augment the existing American naval force already there, with Rodgers receiving command of the new thirty-six-gun frigate *Congress* on 2 April 1804.

During April and May, Rodgers completed his supervision of the construction of Gunboat #1, oversaw the equipping and provisioning of his own ship, and managed to secure a midshipman's warrant for his youngest brother, George Washington Rodgers. On 21 May, the *Congress* sailed from Washington and on 5 July from Hampton Roads. Thirty-seven days later, the ship reached Gibraltar.

After Rodgers had left the Mediterranean the previous October, dramatic developments had occurred in the war against Tripoli. On 31 October 1803, Preble had lost one of his frigates when the *Philadelphia* had run aground and been captured near the harbor of Tripoli. Captain William Bainbridge and his 300–man crew had surrendered and been imprisoned, as they would remain for the next nineteen months. This event immensely complicated Preble's assignment. Not only had the enemy soon refloated the *Philadelphia* and thus converted one of Preble's most powerful assets into a dangerous threat, but also Tripoli could use the American captives as a potent diplomatic pawn.

Preble decided that he needed to destroy the *Philadelphia* and selected Lieutenant Stephen Decatur to lead the mission. In a brilliant action on the night of 16 February 1804, Decatur and a force of eighty-four volunteers entered the harbor in a previously captured ketch that had been renamed the *Intrepid.* The Americans quietly approached and almost reached the *Philadelphia* before they were recognized. They then quickly boarded the vessel, routed the Tripolitans onboard, and set the frigate on fire. Returning to the *Intrepid*, the Americans escaped from the harbor under fire from Tripolitan gunboats and shore batteries. In the attack, several Tripolitans died and one was taken prisoner while only one American suffered a minor injury. This daring triumph drew great praise and made Decatur a national hero. No less a figure than Lord Nelson is supposed to have termed the feat "the most bold and daring act of the age." President Jefferson lauded Decatur and promoted him to the rank of post captain. Congress passed a resolution of commendation, authorized the presentation of a sword to Decatur, and voted two months of extra pay to each man on the mission.[23]

Decatur's mission provided the stuff of naval legend, but it did not resolve the conflict with Tripoli. When Preble opened negotiations for peace, the pasha of Tripoli refused to exchange any prisoners and demanded $500,000 as the price of peace and ransom. In response, Preble maintained the blockade, augmented his force by acquiring a number of gunboats, and prepared to attack. In August and September 1804, Preble's forces mounted five attacks on the land fortifications and naval defenses of Tripoli. Although Preble lacked sufficient land forces to attempt the capture of Tripoli, he hoped to compel the Tripolitan ruler to accept reasonable peace terms, including the release of the American prisoners.

Determined to coerce Tripoli into a peace settlement, Preble hammered away but failed to bring Tripoli to terms before his replacement, Commodore Barron, appeared in the *President* on 10 September. Eight days later, Rodgers arrived in the *Congress* after being diverted along with the *Essex* to Morocco. Although American consul James Simpson suspected that "the Intentions of the Emperor are unfriendly towards the U.States," Rodgers disagreed that the "Emperor's Conduct" or that of his ships presented reason for concern or evidence of "hostility towards our Commerce." He did concur, however, that an American warship needed to be stationed in the vicinity and left the *Essex* near Tangiers.[24]

Rodgers was anxious to get to Tripoli as soon as possible because he expected that decisive naval action as well as his opportunity for combat glory was imminent. On 30 August, Rodgers explained that he "should be greatly mortified, if the *Congress* did not share a part of the Credit to be derived, in the reduction of Tripoli by inscribing a lasting & Honorable remembrance of her name on its Walls." Furthermore, he rationalized that future relations with Morocco would "greatly depend on the kind of Peace we make with Tripoli" because they are "more closely allied than any of the other Barbary Powers."[25]

En route to Tripoli, Rodgers picked up Consul Lear and transported him to Malta before sailing to Tripoli. In fact, decisive combat action was not imminent. Commodore Barron was in such ill health that he placed the squadron temporarily under Rodgers's command on 23 September and retired to Malta. For the next month, the situation remained quiet as Rodgers patrolled and blockaded Tripoli with the *Congress*, the *Constellation*, and the *Nautilus*. Aided by good weather, the blockade prevented all but four small ships from leaving or entering the port. Impatient with the tedium of blockade duty, Rodgers decided to determine personally how close "our Ships can approach the Batteries of Tripoli with safety." On the night of 19 October, he slipped into the harbor in his ship's gig to observe the position of the shore batteries and the condition of the enemy's naval force. At one point he was in four feet of water and so close that he "could hear the People on Shore distinctly in conversation."[26]

Having concluded that the *Constellation* and the *Nautilus* were sufficient to maintain the blockade, Rodgers left for Malta for minor repairs to the

Congress. Commodore Barron had come to the same conclusion and had actually ordered Rodgers to return to Malta. Although Rodgers stopped a suspected Tripolitan xebec enroute and escorted her to Malta for further investigation, it had been a vexing time for Rodgers, who reported to the naval secretary his own regret that circumstances had prevented "the reduction of Tripoli, to Terms honorable & advantageous to our Country," but predicted success "with certainty . . . next Summer."[27]

Despite his continued poor health, Barron resumed command of the squadron in late November. After ordering Rodgers to take command of the *Constitution* in November, Barron sent Rodgers to Tangiers en route to Lisbon, where additional sailors needed to be recruited to fill an eighty-man crew shortage.[28] When he reached Lisbon on 28 December 1804, Rodgers was in a foul mood. His stop at Tangiers had gone well, but Rodgers did not like his new ship. Although his friend Lear had called the *Constitution* "as fine a Ship as swims on the Sea . . . besides being good, she will be a most fortunate Ship," Rodgers disagreed. He complained that she "is the most laboursome & uneasy Ship I have ever commanded." Making matters worse, the *Constitution* encountered heavy westerly winds that damaged her bowsprit, bower cable, and several sails.[29]

Then, once he had reached Lisbon and his ship lay quarantined in the harbor, Rodgers was further vexed not to hear from or be able to contact American consul William Jarvis. A nasty and petty quarrel between the two men commenced. On 1 January, Rodgers complained that he had still not been able to contact Jarvis. On the same day, the two began to exchange letters, a correspondence that quickly escalated into an exchange of insults. Rodgers attacked Jarvis for his lack of initiative, inattention to duty, and inability to shorten the twenty-day quarantine of the *Constitution*. Jarvis's refusal to be cowed by Rodgers's overbearing tone only fueled Rodgers's frustration and anger. Soon both men were leveling their charges against each other in writing to their respective superiors in the Navy Department and the State Department. To make matters worse, once the *Constitution* had cleared its quarantine, Rodgers found it difficult to secure the materials for the repairs his ship needed. Nor were recruits readily available in Lisbon, and those found cost more than he had expected. At one point, Rodgers mistakenly signed on several Danish deserters, whom he subsequently had to release when he learned their identity.[30]

By early February 1805, Rodgers had not recruited a full crew but had added enough men "to induce me to flatter myself, that I shall be able to give you a very fair acct of the services of the *Constitution* next Summer." After seven vexing weeks in Lisbon, Rodgers impatiently prepared to sail. "I

can scarcely describe the anxiety which I feel for the approach of Summer,"
he wrote to the secretary of navy in February; "if we do our duty, we shall
reduce Tripoli in a manner that will be particularly advantageous, and highly
honourable to our Country."[31]

On 25 February, the *Constitution* reached Malta and then, under orders
from Barron, proceeded directly to Tripoli. Once there, Rodgers maintained
the blockade of the harbor along with the *Constellation* and the *Vixen*. By 19
March, Rodgers was back in Malta, where he recommended more aggressive
action. In addition to the blockade, Rodgers urged that additional American
ships be employed to pursue those Tripolitan vessels already at sea and to
intercept any enemy ships that attempted to enter other ports such as Ben-
gazi, Derna, and Tunis.[32]

In early April, Rodgers returned to Tripoli in the *Constitution* to command the American blockade. After surveying the situation, Rodgers predicted to Lear that the pasha was not prepared to negotiate on "what you will
consider equal Terms, until he is more sensible of our Force, and demon-
stratively convinc'd of our capacity to use it." Accordingly, Rodgers awaited
the expected arrival of two gunboats and two bomb mortars that would furnish "the opportunity of negotiating a Peace perfectly to your wishes." If the
United States attacked in the next six weeks, "I will predict," wrote Rodgers,
"That we [will] succeed in the most perfect, handsome & honorable manner."[33]

But the gunboats and bomb mortars did not arrive, and the blockade did
not move the pasha. On 24 April, the *Constitution* captured an eight-gun
xebec and two Neapolitan prize ships bound for Tripoli, but such rare suc-
cesses seemed only to illustrate the necessity for direct combat operations
against Tripoli. Although the pasha's latest demand of $200,000 for peace
and the ransom of the American prisoners was "much less extravagant" than
the $500,000 he had demanded from Preble, it remained a "totally inadmis-
sible" figure. Finally, on 1 May, Barron reported to Rodgers that Barron's
health had improved enough to permit him to come and take personal
charge of upcoming offensive operations in Tripoli.[34]

However, before either Barron or Rodgers could act, unforeseen developments reduced the need for a naval attack on Tripoli. On 27 April, a motley
multinational force led by an American had captured Derna, Tripoli, in an
effort to depose and replace the pasha Yusuf with his older brother, Ahmad, the legitimate heir to the throne who had himself been overthrown
in 1795. The American leader was William Eaton from Massachusetts. A
former schoolmaster, army captain, and later American consul to Tunis, the
forty-one-year-old Eaton was talented, ambitious, charismatic, and born to

command. Eaton had studied French, Latin, and Greek at Dartmouth College, spoke several different American Indian dialects, and was fluent in at least four Arabic dialects. Unfortunately, he was also an erratic dreamer who hungered for public acclaim and loved to defy convention. Typical was a clause in his will that specified that he be buried with his horse.[35]

In 1804, Jefferson had appointed Eaton as naval agent to the Barbary states and had authorized him to restore Ahmad to power. Eaton arrived in Alexandria in November 1804. With some difficulty he located Ahmad hundreds of miles up the Nile River and then began to collect his army some forty miles west of Alexandria. The motley army of several hundred included ten American marines, thirty-eight Greeks, ninety members of Ahmad's entourage, a variety of Arab horsemen, more than one hundred camels, a few donkeys, and some military provisions. In early March 1805, Eaton's force set out from Burj el Arab for Derna, a distance of 520 miles. It was a remarkable journey that took more than a month, actually covered close to 700 miles, and required all of Eaton's energy, talents, and resourcefulness. The multinational force lacked loyalty and cohesiveness. It was short of supplies and on several occasions was without food or water. Desertions and mutiny posed a constant threat. And Ahmad himself was a weak, irresolute man who inspired little confidence. Largely because of Eaton's exceptional leadership, cleverness, and charisma, the army reached Derna in mid-April. Then, with the offshore assistance of the *Argus*, the *Nautilus*, and the *Hornet*, Eaton captured the town on 27 April. Having completed his improbable mission, Eaton now prepared to march directly to Tripoli to depose Yusuf.

Barron, Rodgers, and Lear were well aware of Eaton's plan, but they had not expected it to succeed and thus assumed that a direct naval attack on Tripoli would be needed to secure peace from the pasha. On 16 May, the *Hornet* delivered dispatches from Eaton announcing his capture of Derna. Eaton's success had altered the dynamics of the situation by making "a deep impression" on the pasha and convincing him to begin serious negotiations with the Americans.[36]

In early May, Lear conferred directly with Barron in Malta. Lear's instructions specified that he could begin negotiations once Barron, as commander of the American squadron, determined that the military situation was right. As a result of his deliberations with Lear, Barron made two decisions. First, he would immediately resign his command. Second, in accord with Lear's instructions, Barron informed Lear that "the present moment is favorable for opening a Negotiation" with Tripoli. In a letter on 22 May, Barron informed Rodgers that after a "long and painful Struggle as well as mature deliberation . . . I do hereby resign my Command of the Naval forces of the

United States in these Seas . . . to you on whom the Command devolves by the Law of Seniority." Barron explained that the pain of his decision was alleviated by his confidence in Rodgers and belief that the "present moment is eminently favorable" for Consul Lear to open negotiations with the pasha of Tripoli. Moreover, if there was one thing that would "restore me to Health as by a Charm, it would be the sight of Capt. Bainbridge and his fellow-sufferers restored at length to freedom on terms of Peace; at once honorable and advantageous to our Common Country."[37]

Barron made the decisions to relinquish command and authorize negotiations rather than fight for several reasons. First, he lacked the additional resources that he believed he needed to mount an offensive. An additional bomb ketch and gunboats had not arrived from the United States. Nor had the Neapolitan and Venetian governments agreed to loan gunboats to Barron. Second, he realized that he could not command offensive operations personally because, after a brief improvement, his health had again declined. Third, there remained the thorny issue of Bainbridge and the three hundred American prisoners in Tripoli. These men continued to be subject to the caprice of the pasha, who, if he felt threatened, might retaliate by executing some, or even all, of his American captives.

On 26 May, Captain James Barron, the brother of Samuel Barron, and Lear arrived off Tripoli in the *Essex*. After boarding the *Constitution*, they informed Rodgers that Samuel Barron had relinquished his command and had authorized Lear to begin negotiations. Rodgers assumed command immediately while Lear and Barron returned to the *Essex*, faced the town, and raised a flag of truce. With no American consul in Tripoli, negotiations began at once through European intermediaries. Lear informed the Tripolitan ruler that his previous demand of $200,000 for peace and ransom was unacceptable. When the pasha reduced his demand to $130,000, Lear responded with a counteroffer of $60,000, which the pasha accepted. Signed on 4 June, the agreement specified that the pasha would free all three hundred American prisoners in exchange for $60,000 as well as the release of the estimated one hundred Tripolitan prisoners the Americans held. The treaty formally established peace between the two countries and provided for Eaton's evacuation from Derna. It also affirmed the right of each country to maintain consuls in the territory of the other and included conventional diplomatic items such as a most-favored-nation clause and a shipwreck provision. Lear also included a secret provision that allowed the ruling pasha four years to return the wife and children of Ahmad, whom the pasha was holding as a guarantee against his brother's attempting to regain control of the throne.[38]

On 3 June, Rodgers went ashore to visit the delighted crew of the *Phila-*

delphia. The next day the prisoners were released, and the American flag, which had been cut down four years earlier, was raised again over the American consulate. Although Rodgers's role in the peace negotiations was subordinate, Lear praised Rodgers in his consul's report to Washington. Rodgers would strongly have preferred additional naval action prior to the opening of negotiations, but he willingly accepted the decisions of Barron and Lear. "I must pay a tribute to commodore Rodgers," wrote Lear, whose conduct "was mixed with that manly firmness and evident wish to continue the war . . . while he displayed the magnanimity of an American in declaring that we fought not for conquest, but to maintain our just rights and national dignity."[39] In spite of the $60,000 payment, Rodgers considered the treaty to be a significant achievement. "The Bashaw is much humiliated which he even *himself* confesses," Rodgers reported to Barron in Malta. "I can venture to say that it is the last War the Regency will ever wage against the U States."[40]

Back home the treaty with Tripoli provoked both controversy and criticism over the $60,000 paid for peace and ransom. President Jefferson did not publicly praise the agreement, while the Senate ratified the treaty amidst some criticism. Enraged by being ordered to evacuate Derna without completing his mission to overthrow the pasha, William Eaton returned to the United States, where he used his considerable rhetorical skills in a vindictive propaganda campaign against Tobias Lear and the treaty itself. Some historians have also criticized the treaty as a premature and humiliating agreement, arguing that the treaty represented a victory for Tripoli, not the United States. Critics claim that, had Eaton been allowed to continue his march across Tripoli and had Rodgers been free to assault Tripoli, the pasha would have been humiliated into signing a peace treaty that freed the American prisoners without a dollar of ransom money.[41]

This argument is plausible although hardly compelling. First, a victorious outcome of military operations was not inevitable. In Derna, Eaton had been fortunate, if not downright lucky, to capture the town. There was no guarantee that he could hold it indefinitely, much less mount another long march to Tripoli. After all, his army was a motley and unstable force. Ahmad was a very weak reed on which to base the political overthrow of a strong, if illegitimate, ruler. Second, at Tripoli, Rodgers undoubtedly would have mounted an aggressive series of naval assaults, just as Preble had done the previous year. However, there was no guarantee that Rodgers's offensive efforts would have been any more effective in forcing the pasha to terms than Preble's had been in 1804. Third, there was always the threat to the three hundred American prisoners. Rodgers later claimed that he "never thought,

COMMODORE IN THE MEDITERRANEAN, 1802–1806   47

myself, that the lives of the American prisoners were in any danger." But no one took the risk of pressuring and humiliating the pasha, who might have retaliated against the Americans he held.[42]

While the treaty can hardly be considered a national triumph worthy of patriotic chest-thumping, it did in fact achieve important American objectives at a very low cost in American dollars and American lives. The price tag of $60,000 to free the Americans was considerably smaller than the $100,000 that Preble had offered to pay the year before. The agreement also set an important precedent by protecting American commerce without requiring the payment of an annual tribute to Tripoli. The Jefferson administration could now begin to withdraw a large and expensive American naval force from the Mediterranean. In fact, the American squadron in 1805 totaled twenty-four ships—six frigates, six smaller warships, ten gunboats, and two bomb vessels—at an estimated annual cost of $1,571,66l, or approximately 15 percent of all federal government expenses for that year.[43]

With the situation in Tripoli resolved, Rodgers turned to the problem of Tunis, where the bey had been dissatisfied for some time. Sympathizing with Tripoli, the bey was alarmed by the increased American naval presence and blockade. In fact, by June 1805, the bey was demanding the return of the Tunisian xebec and two prizes captured by Rodgers earlier that spring. "He has been in the habit of threatening us with War, without any just cause," Rodgers wrote to consul George Davis in Tunis on 11 June, "but the moment is now arrived that he must acknowledge that we have done him no wrong; and . . . that *unprovoked* he never will again renew his threats." Rodgers assured Davis that Rodgers would now collect the squadron and sail to Tunis within twenty-five or thirty days. On 1 July, Rodgers informed the bey that his demand for the return of the xebec and two prizes "is totally inadmissible." In response, the bey threatened war.[44]

Rodgers now planned a full show of force. First, he sent the *Congress* and the *Vixen* to Tunis and followed on 23 July with the *Constitution*, the *Constellation*, the *John Adams*, the *Essex*, four smaller warships, and several gunboats. This formidable armada anchored in Tunis Bay on 1 August. Davis informed Rodgers that the recent behavior of the bey had been ever more threatening. If forced into war, the bey had told Davis that "I solemnly pledge myself that . . . never while I have a soldier to fire a gun will I accord peace. . . . You are the first power which has ever captured a Tunisian cruiser in full peace. . . . You are the first that has ever offered unprovoked insults. . . . If I was tamely to submit to such acts of outrage, what should I expect from nations far more powerful than yourselves?"[45]

After conferring with his senior naval officers and Davis, Rodgers reaffirmed America's peaceful intentions and asked the bey whether he had already declared or intended to declare war against the United States. If the bey did not reply within thirty-six hours, Rodgers explained that he would begin naval operations against Tunis. When Davis delivered the ultimatum, the bey explained that he could reply within thirty-six hours in the Turkish or Moorish language, but not in English since there was no "Christian clerk" available to translate his message. The bey did verbally reassure Davis, however, that the ruler intended to uphold the "letter and the spirit" of the existing treaty and to appeal directly to the president of the United States for the redress of the bey's grievances. Although he would not initiate any "hostile act," the bey would haul down the American flag if "your commodore attacks or detains any of my Vessels, Cruisers, or Merchantmen, or fires a single Gun with a hostile intention." It was then up to Rodgers "to respect the treaty made by his master, or not."[46]

When informed of this reply, Rodgers held another council and decided to require that the bey give a written guarantee of his commitment to peace to be witnessed by the British and French consuls. On 4 August, Davis informed the bey that if he refused to provide the guarantee, the American squadron would blockade Tunis. Rodgers subsequently defined his demands in a letter to be delivered by Captain Stephen Decatur. In the meantime, the bey altered his position. On 5 August, he wrote a conciliatory letter in which he offered to negotiate directly with Consul Lear, who the bey understood to be a direct representative of the president. However, the Tunisian leader refused to provide the written guarantee demanded by Rodgers and declined to receive Decatur when he appeared. Yet he did send another conciliatory note extending his compliments to Rodgers.

Rodgers renewed his demand for a written guarantee and on 8 August sent Davis with the mandate. When the bey again refused, Davis requested his papers and baggage, as previously agreed upon, and left Tunis for the *Constitution*. Rodgers now took steps to impose a blockade, an action that elicited a letter from the bey to Lear on 10 August. Reaffirming the bey's desire for peace and his willingness to negotiate directly with Lear, the bey was also prepared to send a "person of distinction" from his regime to the United States to resolve the differences between the two countries. The tone of the letter and the bey's offer provided the basis for a compromise.[47]

On 12 August, Lear began two days of negotiations ashore. Rodgers had decided to drop his demand for a written guarantee. However, when it appeared that the bey was equivocating on his offer to send an official representative to the United States, Rodgers insisted that unless the ruler did one of three things voluntarily, he would be forced to comply with all three. "He must give the guarantee already required; or he must give security for peace and send a minister to the United States; or he must make such alterations in the treaty as you [Lear] may require." Rodgers added that if the bey did not "do all that is necessary and proper . . . he shall feel the vengeance of the squadron now in this bay."[48]

The bey finally agreed to send a minister to the United States and reassured Rodgers of Tunis's peaceful intentions in accord with the treaty of 1797. On 14 August, the bey reaffirmed his promise to send an ambassador and refrain from any hostilities before the ambassador returned from his mission to the United States. On 15 August, Rodgers withdrew the ships he had positioned to begin the blockade and appointed Dr. James Dodge, the surgeon of the *Constitution*, as the new chargéd'affaires to Tunis. Rodgers also informed the bey that American naval commanders would henceforth treat Tunis as a friend. "I sincerely hope to see a Peace established between yourself & the U. States of America *on the most permanent basis*," explained Rodgers, "and at the same [time] do assure you that nothing shall ever happen on my part to prevent the same." The bey appointed a distinguished Tunisian soldier and statesman, Suliman Mellimelli, as ambassador to the United States. Mellimelli visited Rodgers on the *Constitution* on 27 August and on 5 September departed for America on board the frigate *Congress* commanded by Decatur.[49]

In fact, a basis for full friendship had not yet been established, even though Rodgers claimed that he had left "such impressions as will ever again prevent him [the bey] or his successors from daring to renew the same conduct." Rodgers boasted that the bey had "been forced to accede to reason" and predicted "almost with certainty that he never will again attempt to behave in a similar manner; as I feel satisfied this lesson has not only changed his opinion of our Maritime strength, but has caused him to discover more distinctly his own weakness in every sense." Should the administration decide to further "chastise" the bey, Rodgers asked that he be permitted the honor of bearing the standard of their Vengeance."[50]

Eleven days later, Rodgers congratulated himself in a detailed letter to the Navy Department. He boasted immoderately about his own good judgment and restraint in spite of his desire to draw the "Sword of the Nation, in defence of its honor and Interest . . . to have made him call for Mercy on his bended Knees." Rodgers claimed that "decisive measures on our part, were absolutely necessary. . . . The result is now known—. . . . In fine; I conceive that our Country has already gained, every thing that she could have promised herself, from the most successful War." Indeed, in his estimation, his success had impressed the "most powerful, and artful Nations of Europe.

The consuls . . . appear much astonished, and some of them have openly said, that no other Nation, has ever Negotiated with the present Bey, on such honorable terms as ourselves."[51]

The conduct of Rodgers had, indeed, left an impression on the bey, but it was not a favorable one. In a letter that Ambassador Mellimelli was to carry to President Jefferson, the bey affirmed his country's friendship with the United States but complained that the "many unpleasantnesses which I experienced on this occasion could quite well have been avoided were it not for the too martial temper of . . . Commodore Rodgers, very imprudently stirred up and supported by the Charge d'Affaires, George Davis."[52]

Personalities aside, the mission to Tunis had ended successfully and peacefully. Rodgers and Lear had reduced tension and the threat of hostilities and had laid the basis for subsequent stable relations between Tunis and the United States. For Rodgers this was a significant, if relatively minor, achievement for he had demonstrated effective naval diplomatic skills. Acting on his own authority in a way that he could not have in Morocco or Tripoli, Rodgers had secured a diplomatic victory without firing a shot. Showing Tunis an overwhelming naval force, he had blustered and threatened to employ it. There is no question that he personally would have preferred to use military force against a ruler he considered to be arrogant and "prevaricating," but, at the same time, Rodgers recognized that "Peace on honorable terms is always preferable to War." However much a direct attack might have satisfied him, Rodgers fully understood that he lacked specific authorization from Washington and that a military exchange would create more problems than it would resolve.[53]

After leaving Tunis, Rodgers spent the next several months reorganizing the squadron. He also sailed to Syracuse and then to Leghorn, Messina, and Naples to seek provisions and repairs needed by the squadron. A potential new Barbary crisis loomed in November when the existing ruler of Algiers was deposed. Turmoil and uncertainty brewed temporarily, but stability was soon restored. On 19 November, when Rodgers and the *Constitution* arrived in Algiers to leave Consul Lear at his diplomatic station there, the new Algerian ruler assured the Americans of his friendship.

From Algiers, Rodgers headed back to Syracuse, where he spent most of the winter and early spring. An important element of Rodgers's administration was the considerable attention he devoted to the discipline and morale of the Mediterranean squadron. He was proud of the conduct of promising young officers under his supervision. Among them were William Henry Allen, David Porter, Isaac Hull, James Lawrence, and Oliver Hazard Perry. Allen considered Rodgers to be a "second Father" and admired his "firm and decided" conduct to secure the agreement with Tunis. Rodgers was particularly impressed by the performance of Perry, who had transferred to the *Constitution*.[54]

Rodgers also dealt energetically with the details of disciplinary incidents involving rowdiness, desertion, drunkenness, and disobedience. He reminded his commanders that midshipmen should remain in the proper uniform rather than don the jackets of lieutenants, a common practice. He took a particularly hard line on the "detestable Crime of Desertion," vowing "never to suffer such an abominable crime." Accordingly, he issued to the entire squadron a decree condemning desertion and, at one point, publicly punished a deserter "alongside of the different vessels of the squadron." He also was disgusted to learn that en route from the United States to join the Mediterranean squadron, the commander of the *Spitfire*, Lieutenant McNeill, had arrived several weeks late because at times he had been "intoxicated for several days together." McNeill had allegedly also lost time "by keeping company with a merchant vessel he met with, and having her master on board to dine with him." After sending McNeill back home, Rodgers informed the Navy Department that this lieutenant's conduct provided "proof positive, that he is not (to give it no harsher name) calculated for the service."[55]

As his command neared an end, Rodgers took heart in his squadron's discipline and morale. He reported that as a result of his "most friendly" relations with British naval officers, disputes between American and British sailors on shore in various ports had virtually disappeared. In May, Rodgers informed the Navy Department that since he had taken command "the most perfect harmony has subsisted between the Officers of every denomination, added to uniform discipline on board of the respective vessels, which would not have done discredit to a much elder service, than our own."[56]

On 1 May, the squadron sailed for Gibraltar, where Rodgers finally received instructions to disperse his squadron and return home. Rodgers switched his pennant to the frigate *Essex* and on 3 June departed for home, leaving the *Constitution* behind. After two years away from home, Rodgers reached Washington, D.C., on 27 June 1806. Although he did not return home a hero, Rodgers had reason to be satisfied with his performance. Admittedly, the first nine months were discouraging ones as he labored under the indolent command of the sickly Barron, but once Rodgers had assumed command of the squadron, he acquitted himself well. He had worked well with Lear in reaching the peace treaty with Tripoli. He had effectively coerced a settlement from Tunis. If his overbearing manner had offended the bey, still he had settled a dispute with diplomacy, not force. He had also acquitted himself well as commander of the squadron. His correspondence for the year he commanded the squadron reveals a capable, energetic officer very much in control of his ships and his officers. Although his letters reveal a penchant for verbal bombast and intemperate judgments about the leaders and people of the region, he did not translate his severe opinions into personal or naval action. He also stayed in close contact with American consuls in the region and reported regularly about diplomatic and political developments there.

4

Peacetime Interlude, 1806–1808

[T]he most unpleasant piece of duty I ever performed in the course of my life; and God forbid I should ever be employed in the same way again.

Captain John Rodgers, on his role as president of
the court-martial of Captain James Barron, 1808

By the time he returned to the United States in July 1806, John Rodgers had spent most of the previous eight years at sea engaged in operations against hostile forces. During this time, he had helped to capture the French frigate *L'Insurgente*, patrolled the West Indies in search of French ships, and been imprisoned briefly in Santo Domingo. For the last four years, he had engaged in a range of military and diplomatic operations against Morocco, Algiers, Tripoli, and Tunis. Now, in 1806, Rodgers returned to a nation at peace. The Barbary War was winding down, and relations with France and England were, if not amicable, at least peaceful. Rodgers clearly expected a period of relatively routine shore assignments. Although his previous naval career had marked him as an enthusiastic naval warrior, Rodgers did not regret the coming career change. His latest two-year stint in the Mediterranean had left him unfulfilled. He had waited almost a year before Samuel Barron finally stepped aside and left Rodgers in command of the Mediterranean squadron in May 1805. When he and Tobias Lear secured a peace treaty with Tripoli shortly thereafter, William Eaton castigated the agreement because it included a ransom payment to Tripoli to release the American prisoners from the *Philadelphia*. Although he had been a successful and effective squadron commander, he was not returning to national acclaim.

Moreover, Rodgers believed that his reputation had been compromised by rumors and innuendos. On 27 May, Rodgers wrote from Gibraltar that he would not trouble Lear "with the effusions of my wounded Soul," but "my presence in America has become absolutely necessary in support of my Character which has been secretly aspersed in the most gross manner." The culprit, Rodgers assumed, was Captain James Barron, who, back in 1805, had allegedly spread rumors about Rodgers and had urged his brother, Captain

Samuel Barron, in spite of his failing health, not to relinquish command to Rodgers. On 10 July 1805, Captain William Bainbridge had informed Lieutenant David Porter of an altercation. Bainbridge reported that he had delivered a personal message from James Barron to Rodgers in which Barron accused Rodgers of speaking of Barron's brother in a "disrespectful manner." Barron planned to call on Rodgers "to answer in a proper time and place." Rodgers replied that he would expect to hear from Barron once they both were back in the United States and that if Rodgers did not, then Barron would certainly hear from Rodgers. Moreover, Rodgers instructed Porter to add that, "if I do not hear from him, I shall impute it to a want in him of— [courage] what no Gentleman who wears a uniform should be deficient in."[1]

There the matter had stood for more than a year, but Rodgers continued to be concerned that rumors back home were staining his reputation. Indeed, some had preceded him back to the United States. Appearing in some newspapers, one rumor held that Rodgers had killed Marine Captain Anthony Gale in the Mediterranean. The rumor was credible enough to require a formal contradiction by Gale in the summer of 1806. Gale attested that he was indeed alive and affirmed that Rodgers treated all his officers in a polite and respectful manner.[2]

On 24 July as his ship neared the Chesapeake, Rodgers wrote to Barron, "I shall hold myself ready to account to you at any time" in the next month. "My reason for giving you this early information is because your rank as an officer and the nature of your claim entitles you to my first consideration. I therefore must request that you will not delay." On 29 July, Barron replied that he was bedridden with a "painful indisposition," but that he would respond to the challenge of a duel as soon as his health improved. To handle the matter, Rodgers selected his close friend Commodore Thomas Tingley, while Barron selected Marine Colonel Franklin Wharton. In the next month, Tingley and Wharton attempted to make arrangements for a duel, but Barron's continued illness precluded a meeting near Washington. At one point, Wharton proposed that Rodgers proceed to Norfolk, but Wharton could not guarantee that Barron would be well enough to meet Rodgers there. The unresolved feud persisted into the fall. As weeks passed without definitive arrangements being made, the likelihood of an actual duel diminished. Fortunately, neither Rodgers nor Barron pressed for one, while Tingley and Wharton hoped to resolve the matter peacefully.[3]

Rodgers's anger gradually cooled. In Washington, he discovered that his public reputation was intact. The president had sent him a welcome-home letter and thanked him personally for two sheep that Rodgers had brought to Jefferson from the Mediterranean.[4] Now his personal attention shifted dramatically to another more sanguine matter. He would soon see his fiancé, Minerva Denison, for the first time in more than two years. Once he had reached Washington, Rodgers wrote to Minerva of "the happiness of seeing you in person, which . . . I anticipated with such pleasure as can only be equaled by the pain I experienced in being so long separated from you."[5]

Rodgers went immediately to Havre de Grace, where the two renewed their romantic relationship and set an early wedding date. When he returned to Washington, D.C., on 21 August, he wrote ecstatically to "my dear little girl" of his "unequaled happiness of seeing my such loved and much admired Minerva for whose sake alone I wish to live." "I feel more uninterrupted pleasure in contemplating the charms of the lovely little maid of Sion Hill, altho distant from her, than any or every other source of pleasure on earth is capable of affording." Eight days later, Rodgers wrote a long and joyous letter on their upcoming wedding. "To have the care of your happiness entrusted to my will is not only a honor conferred by Heaven . . . but a Divine compliment that would confer the highest obligation on a being incapable of conceiving the smallest tincture of earthly frailty," wrote the smitten commodore. "I only lament for your sake that I am not more worthy."[6]

As his wedding day approached, two positive events further buoyed Rodgers's spirits. First, he learned that he would not have to leave his bride immediately to begin duty. His next naval assignment would station him in Havre de Grace, where he was to supervise the construction of a new gunboat and to prove the naval cannons being manufactured at the nearby Cecil furnace. Second, the affair with Barron seemed close to being resolved without an actual duel. Two weeks before the wedding, and delighted that his friend's "voyage of celibacy is to terminate on the 21st," Tingley suggested that Rodgers reaffirm his desire to learn the identity of the author of the rumors against him but, at the same time, assure Barron that Rodgers had no desire to "hurt his feelings or destroy his [Barron's] reputation." One day before the wedding, Anthony Gale apologized to Rodgers for not being able to attend the event and happily acknowledged that the Barron dispute would not result in "the absurd & unfortunate mode of settling a misunderstanding."[7]

Although it took longer than expected, the quarrel between Rodgers and Barron was finally resolved in February 1807. Arguing that Rodgers would not "gain an atom by the result of such as contest as this," Tingley convinced Rodgers to make a "small and honorable acknowledgement" to Barron. A certificate was printed and distributed to friends of the two men. It carried the signatures of Tingley and Wharton and announced that the personal differences between the two men had been "amicably settled" on terms "highly honorable to both parties." The formal reconciliation notwithstanding, Rodgers and Barron continued to be rivals who carried personal animosity for each other. In fact, subsequent events would intensify their hostility. For the next three decades, the two proud officers would maintain a distant, icy, and adversarial professional relationship.[8]

On 21 October 1806, in "the green room" of her family home, Sion Hill, near Havre de Grace, Minerva Denison and John Rodgers were married. Short, blonde, and "sweet"-looking, Minerva was twenty-two years old while her husband was thirty-three. Soon after their marriage, John and Minerva moved from Sion Hill into Havre de Grace, where they lived in the "attic apartment" of the Rodgers family home at 226 Washington Street. This arrangement allowed Rodgers close proximity to his new assignment during the fall of 1806 and winter of 1807.

It was here that Rodgers would enhance his reputation for courage and daring. In the early spring, a man and a woman attempting to cross the Susquehanna River five miles upstream from Havre de Grace found themselves stranded on a large piece of ice as it drifted toward the village and nearby Chesapeake Bay. Rodgers happened to be standing on the shore as the stranded man and woman drifted helplessly toward the bay and certain death. Rodgers immediately offered a reward to anyone who would assist him in a boat, but all declined because of the danger the ice floe posed to a small boat. Rodgers then acted alone. Taking "two pieces of plank and by laying them alternatively from one piece of ice to the other, he succeeded in reaching" the frightened victims. He then took the woman under his arm and encouraged the man to follow. Finally, an estimated one mile below where he had entered the river, Rodgers and the two survivors reached shore to the great relief of gathered spectators and his own family, who had watched the entire spectacle from the windows of their home.[9]

The first eight months of his marriage provided a pleasant but uneasy interlude in Rodgers's naval career. As he supervised the construction of what became known as Gunboat #7, his professional future remained uncertain. In Washington, Rodgers had a good friend in Secretary of the Navy Robert Smith, but the Jefferson administration seemed intent on reducing the size and importance of the navy. In Europe, the war between England and Napoleon seemed ominous, but tense American relations with those two powers did not necessarily presage an expanded defense role for the American navy.

In contrast to the uncertainty of his professional future, Rodgers's marriage suited him well. As a man in his mid-thirties, Rodgers brought the same passionate intensity to his relationship with Minerva that he brought to his naval duties. In marriage, he remained as love-smitten as he had been during their courtship. He continued to idealize her and speak of her beauty and virtue in angelic terms. The two adored each other and seemed to complement one another both emotionally and physically. Within weeks of their marriage, Minerva was pregnant with the first of the eleven children she would bear over the next twenty-two years. Minerva seems to have dealt with her husband's overbearing personality by using her impish qualities to chide and humor him. At one point when he was away and she failed to write for several days, she mocked his "formidably black" look at not receiving a letter and imagined that "you lose the use of your tongue except in muttering now & then a few monosyllables in a stentorian voice."[10] Chide her as he might, Minerva would write many long, emotionally revealing love letters to him during his frequent absences in the early years of their marriage.

When Rodgers was in Washington on business, both felt the sharp pain of separation. "For gods sake, tell me when there is a probability of my seeing you," wrote Minerva; "To exist without you is a living death or [merely the] vegetation of the body." For Rodgers, his brief separation from Minerva revealed an emotional side that seemed out of character with his public persona. "I find I am a miserable devil without you," confided the gruff naval commander; "I can't sleep, eat, or drink owing to . . . the particular state of my heart—every piece of *pudding* & every glass of *wine* having the name Minerva written on it in italics."[11] Marriage had not dulled his ardor.

Rodgers's pleasant spring interlude came abruptly to an end in late June. Off Norfolk, on 22 June, the thirty-six-gun American frigate *Chesapeake* under the command of Commodore James Barron sailed for the Mediterranean, where she was to replace the *Constitution*. After sailing past two British warships in Lynnhaven Bay, the American ship was intercepted by the fifty-six-gun British warship *Leopard* about ten miles off the mouth of Chesapeake Bay. Captain S. P. Humphreys of the *Leopard* carried orders instructing any British warship that encountered the *Chesapeake* to search her for British deserters. British warships often anchored near Norfolk to secure provisions and monitor armed French ships in the area; there British sailors sometimes deserted and then reenlisted on American ships.

The British demanded that they be allowed to muster the crew and search the *Chesapeake* for British deserters. Like other American naval commanders, Barron was under standing orders not to surrender any of his men without surrendering his ship. Unfortunately, his ship was not fully prepared to resist the British demands; his gun deck was littered with baggage, lumber, sails, and cables, and his crew was not prepared for battle. He attempted to dissuade the British and stall for time, but his strategy failed when the

British opened fire at close range. In fewer than twenty minutes, the *Chesapeake* took twenty-two shots to her hull and suffered heavy damage to her main and fore masts before Barron struck his colors. The British then removed four deserters from the American ship. On the *Chesapeake*, three had been killed and eighteen wounded, including Barron, who suffered a minor wound.[12]

To make the humiliation complete, the *Chesapeake* limped back into Norfolk harbor the next day, passing ignominiously before the *Leopard* and other British warships. The attack by the *Leopard* unleashed an immediate local and then, when word spread, national outrage. In Norfolk, a mob destroyed two hundred water casks intended for the British warships, and citizens met and agreed to end all intercourse with the British. In response, the British threatened to land and take by force the water they needed. Captain Stephen Decatur, the commandant of the Norfolk navy yard, prepared his gunboat force to resist the British. The British commander then moved his squadron into Hampton Roads and threatened to take the *Chesapeake* and a French frigate undergoing repairs at Norfolk. Tensions remained high as the Americans prepared their defenses for an anticipated British attack, but none came, and gradually the tense situation cooled.

Around the nation, word of the British outrage infuriated Americans, and, along the eastern seaboard, led to widespread public demands for war. In Washington, President Jefferson was angered but intended to avoid war and took steps to resolve the matter diplomatically. His cabinet approved the gesture of sending a small warship, the *Revenge*, to England immediately with instructions for Minister James Monroe to pursue a diplomatic settlement that would include British reparation for past insults and a British guarantee to abolish the practice of impressment against American merchant ships. The Jefferson administration also mobilized part of the Virginia militia, strengthened coastal defenses, prepared plans for an invasion of Canada, recalled all American merchant and naval vessels on the high seas, and called a special session of Congress, but not until late October.[13]

Although Rodgers was not personally involved, the *Chesapeake* affair would have an immediate impact on him by ending his current naval assignment and disrupting his domestic situation at Havre de Grace. With a British attack possible and even imminent, Secretary Smith on 7 July 1807 ordered Rodgers to take immediate command of the New York naval station. He was to command the naval flotilla of gunboats and bomb vessels there with Captain Isaac Chauncey serving under him as the commandant of the New York navy yard.[14]

The crisis following the *Chesapeake* affair produced the first major test of the Jefferson administration's new defense and naval policy. Several months earlier, in February 1807, Jefferson had outlined his policy to Congress. To protect the harbors and coastline of the United States, Jefferson intended to use a combination of fixed land artillery batteries, movable artillery pieces, floating gun batteries, and small gunboats. He informed Congress that both senior army and navy officers endorsed his plan and included letters from Generals James Wilkinson and Horatio Gates as well as Commodores Samuel Barron and Thomas Tingley. Stressing the importance of small gunboats rather than large warships, the president noted that "every modern marine nation" utilized gunboats for purposes of defense and cited contemporary examples of their effective use in Algiers and near Gibraltar. Jefferson estimated that about 200 gunboats would be needed. Since 73 were already built or under construction, he recommended that an additional 127 be built in the next two years at a cost of $500,000 to $600,000.[15] Jefferson predicted that the United States would need to keep only 6 or 8 gunboats afloat when Europe was at peace, but three times that number when Europe was at war. To defend itself in time of war, the United States would mobilize its militia forces and employ its full force of 200 gunboats. Since the gunboats were small and easily preserved from the "sun and weather" under sheds, they could be put into service quickly when a crisis arose. Jefferson concluded by emphasizing that "this species of naval armament is proposed merely for defensive operation." The gunboats would neither protect American maritime commerce nor "become an excitement to engage in offensive maritime war" with the maritime nations of Europe.[16]

Jefferson's gunboat request represented an ongoing response to developments in the European war between England and France. In October 1805, the decisive British naval victory at Trafalgar had rendered the British supreme on the high seas. Then, in December 1805 and October 1806, Napoleon's victories at Austerlitz and Jena made France supreme on the European continent. As the struggle had intensified, both the French and British attempted to strengthen their military and economic positions. In 1806 and 1807, Napoleon issued the Berlin and Milan decrees, which declared it illegal for ships trading at the ports of Europe to visit or trade with England or English colonies. At the same time, the British attempted to tighten their blockade of the continent. In 1805, the British courts declared so-called "broken" voyages to be illegal. Previously, American merchant ships trading with French colonies in the West Indies had touched at an American seaport, paid the requisite duties, received new papers of clearance, and then sailed with their cargo to the continent. Now the British courts ruled such voyages illegal because, in reality, they were "continuous," not "broken" voyages. In addition, the British issued a series of orders-in-council that severely restricted American shipping with continental Europe.

Then, in November 1807, a British order-in-council prohibited trade with European continental ports from which British ships were excluded. Only vessels that had called at a British port, paid customs duties, and secured new clearance papers there were allowed to enter an open port in Europe. The British also escalated their traditional practice of impressment and insisted on their right to board American merchant ships to impress alleged English citizens and deserters from the British navy. Always a sensitive Anglo-American issue, the practice intensified to the point that it is estimated that five thousand to eight thousand individuals were impressed from American ships into the British navy from 1803 to 1812.[17]

These European developments placed President Jefferson in a difficult position. He wanted to defend American commerce, but he also sought to reduce the size of the navy and to avoid war with England. Against the Barbary powers, he had willingly employed American naval forces in the Mediterranean, but the United States could not hope to build a navy comparable to the huge British navy. Moreover, once the Barbary wars had ended, Jefferson believed that he was free to reduce the size and expense of the navy. He intended to take most warships out of commission. For national defense, he would rely primarily on the militia, naval gunboats, and shore batteries.

In Congress, supporters of Jefferson's gunboat recommendations strongly opposed building new frigates or ships of the line. They argued that large, oceangoing American warships potentially weakened the nation's defenses because they were vulnerable to capture or destruction by the huge British navy. Even if the United States doubled or tripled the number of its battleships, the American navy would still be no match for its overwhelming British counterpart.[18] Opponents of expanding the traditional navy cited two examples to make their case. First, in 1801, the British had felt threatened by the League of Armed Neutrality that included Russia, Sweden, Denmark, and Prussia. In April, without a formal declaration of war, a British squadron commanded by Sir Hyde Parker had attacked and decimated the Danish navy in the harbor of Copenhagen. Later, in September 1807, Great Britain had again felt menaced, fearing that neutral Denmark was either about to join the French alliance or have its navy seized by the French. In response, British forces laid siege to Copenhagen and seized eighteen Danish ships of the line, eight frigates, and eighteen other oceangoing warships. The Jefferson administration and its supporters in Congress predicted a similar fate would befall the United States if it attempted to enlarge its oceangoing navy.[19]

Rodgers proceeded promptly to New York to prepare the naval flotilla there for action. "War being inevitable" to Rodgers, he acted quickly.[20] In a flurry of activity, Rodgers added to his flotilla and attended to the myriad details associated with manning, provisioning, and arming his ships. By September, his forces consisted of thirty-one gunboats and three bomb vessels, which he divided into two groups of seventeen ships each, to be commanded by Lieutenants James Lawrence and Oliver Hazard Perry.[21] Although the immediate threat of hostilities faded, two minor incidents occurred. In late August, a British sloop of war fired on, stopped, and detained for one hour an American gunboat off New York. In early September, a British frigate and a large brig appeared off New York and anchored. In response, Rodgers took four gunboats and prepared to force the British warships to leave American waters. Before confronting the British, however, Rodgers conferred with Secretary of the Treasury Albert Gallatin, who explained that the gunboats should not proceed because President Jefferson wanted to avoid the use of force. As Rodgers awaited further orders before acting, any confrontation was avoided when the British warships left the area.[22]

Rodgers's move to New York separated him from Minerva, who was expecting their first child in August, and deprived her of his presence and moral support. For the first time in their marriage, the demands of naval duty conflicted with John's obligations to his wife. Still, the threat of war had unexpectedly furnished a promising opportunity for Rodgers, and he readily embraced his new assignment. On 8 July, he wrote proudly to Minerva that "This is at present considered the most important Naval command." On the way to New York, he stopped briefly in Havre de Grace before continuing north. From Philadelphia, he wrote that he already missed Minerva, but that his absence "is for the good of us both." Once in New York, he professed that "to be with you I would make any sacrifice less than my Honor and my Duty to my Country."[23]

Although Rodgers understood that duty took precedence over his marriage, Minerva was disappointed and unsettled by their separation as she approached the "dreaded hour" of delivery. "I feel and act like a spoiled child that is deprived of its mother's tender attentions when it longs to be fondled in her lap and recline its aching head on her lovely bosom." When John urged her to accept his absence, she replied: "Oh! Teach me then dear and sole possession of my affections—Teach my fond heart to forget that you are worthy of its attachment—Teach it to forget every instance I have received of your tender care and goodness." As a wife who shared her husband's ambitions, she naively hoped that he might win the fame he sought without waging war. Perhaps, reflected Minerva, the recent *Chesapeake* Affair had persuaded "all parties" that "a Navy is necessary to guard us from insult—consequently it must be increased and its officers promoted and my husband in process of time will doubtless attain the rank of admiral. You see I am an ambitious little hussy after all—but you will say I am a little coward too since I wish you to acquire rank and honor without coming to hard blows for it. To this charge indeed I shall plead guilty."[24]

The many tasks required to whip the New York flotilla into fighting order placed great demands on his time and energy but did not assuage Rodgers's own misery. He confessed that one of her letters pierced his manly facade. "I kissed it and kissed it again," admitted Rodgers; "The tenderness of its language was calculated to drain tears from eyes less accustomed to weep than my own and I am not ashamed to acknowledge, that (at the expense of every rough feature which nature has delineated in my face) for a few minutes I indulged myself in playing the woman."[25]

The last days of Minerva's pregnancy dragged on for more than two interminable weeks in August. Finally, on 15 August, Minerva's mother informed John that all had gone well and his son had been born the previous day. Like his father, John Henry Rodgers was a robust infant who was born with strong vocal cords and reddish brown hair, a fuzzy, whiskerlike feature that led him to be nicknamed "Whiskerando." Two days after the birth, an overjoyed Minerva described her son as "The living miniature of yourself—he looks indeed as if Nature has formed him in the same mould [*sic*]—his eyes—his forehead—his chin—his every feature (except his nose which you hoped would be like his mothers) are each copies of your own." She explained to her husband that through "this precious little being . . . Providence has formed a dearer and stronger tie to unite us. . . . This is a lovely boy. . . . Why should he not be perfect—Is he not the offspring of the purest and most exalted love that ever washed the heart of two mortals—Yes surely he is."[26]

When Rodgers received word of the birth, he was elated. "Oh! How happy do I feel at this point to what I did at this time yesterday." To Minerva's mother he described the anguish of not being with Minerva. "I have frequently suffered more *in one hour* on account of the delicate situation of my beloved Minerva, than I did during a confinement of three weeks in my Santo Domingo Dungeon, when I was deprived of every comfort." To Minerva he exalted, "Darling! Sweet Boy!—May he live to be as great a comfort to his dear mother as she is dear to his father." John had hoped for a quick visit to Havre de Grace, but the war scare had not yet passed, and his own overriding sense of duty precluded even a temporary absence from New York. He delayed his visit for days, then for weeks at a time, but when the demands on him did not abate, he was forced to postpone the visit indefinitely. In fact, he would not return to Havre de Grace for almost three months.[27]

For both Minerva and John, the wait was oppressive. Although she regained her health quickly, nursing was painful and troublesome. John fretted and suggested that she hire a wet nurse if necessary. With none available locally in Havre de Grace, John recommended that one be brought in from Baltimore or Philadelphia. John Henry celebrated his six-week birthday without having seen his father, and then Minerva nostalgically observed their first wedding anniversary alone. To his suggestion that she be patient, she responded: "Well! Patience is a Heavenly Virtue! Pray can you teach it [to] me? I have great need of a fresh stock—I am pining, crying, whining, dying—fretting, fuming . . . to see you." "To soften the pangs of absence," she relied on her memory of their happy moments together. "To affection like ours, if Fate is unkind Fancy is bountiful. . . . Tis true nothing can compensate for the deprivation of each other's society, but the fertile powers of Imagination render this deprivation less severe." In his letters, John agreed that his memory offered his only personal comfort. "Sometimes in Imagination when I see you running to me with a face expressive of unbounded Joy! My arms involuntarily open and every nerve and every vein appear to articulate the unbounded Joy they feel. Oh! Delightful vision." Some of his naval colleagues seem to have noticed Minerva's effect on John. "It has been remarked by some of my acquaintances here, that I either differ from all other men in disposition, or that you possess charms superior to the rest of your sex."[28]

Finally, on 12 November 1807, Secretary Smith informed Rodgers that he was "at liberty to visit your family" and to remain at Havre de Grace until he received his new orders to serve on the court-martial of James Barron for his part in the *Chesapeake* affair. Rodgers hurried to Havre de Grace, where he spent several weeks at home in November and December before leaving for Washington to prepare for the trial.[29]

The *Chesapeake* affair elicited national outrage against the British and a diplomatic crisis for President Jefferson. Worse yet, it was a disgraceful humiliation for the navy and a political embarrassment for the administration. Within miles of its home port, an unprepared American frigate had been attacked and, after offering minimal resistance, struck its colors to a British warship. For a proud, but very young, navy that had sought to build high professional standards of honorable conduct and courageous leadership, the *Chesapeake* affair was a huge blot. It seemed even more ignominious than the surrender of the *Philadelphia* in Tripoli in 1803 because the *Chesapeake* had been so close to its own shores. Nor had any revenge been exacted, in contrast to Stephen Decatur's daring mission in early 1804. In the aftermath of the affair, the *Norfolk Gazette and Publick Ledger* observed that the "*Chesapeake* is lying in Hampton Roads without any colours! And strange to tell the *Leopard* is triumphantly riding at anchor within our waters near the Capes!"[30] Clearly in this charged atmosphere, responsibility for this shameful event had to be assigned and a public scapegoat identified.

Although Captain Barron's wounds had not been serious, he lost a portion of his right calf and was bedridden for four weeks. Any hopes that his officers would close ranks behind him were mistaken. The captain of the *Chesapeake*, Charles Gordon, carried Barron's report of the incident to Washington, but his presence there allowed him to present his own story to Secretary Smith. Gordon also carried a letter signed by five of the ship's lieutenants who had turned on Barron. Acknowledging the "disgrace" of the incident, the letter requested that Barron be arrested and charged on two counts of dereliction of duty. In the aftermath of the affair, acrimony had run high. Seven duels were fought between officers of the ship in the subsequent two months. Most critical of Barron privately was Lieutenant William Allen, who, in a letter to his father, had ridiculed Barron for his conduct and cowardice.[31] Of course, because Allen had served previously under Rodgers in the Mediterranean and was considered to be Rodgers's "favorite lieutenant," Barron viewed Allen as "the most Vindictive Rascal of them all . . . he came to the Ship with all the Prejudices that his friend Comdr R [Rodgers] could inculcate."[32]

In the face of public outrage and internal dissension among the *Chesapeake's* officers, it was politically important that both the Navy Department and the openly antinavy Jefferson administration avoid being blamed for the ill-preparednessof the *Chesapeake*. The Navy Department had quickly ordered a court of inquiry to assign responsibility, but for various reasons, the court of inquiry did not convene until early October 1807. Captains Alexander Murray, Isaac Chauncey, and Isaac Hull comprised the court, with Murray serving as president. In early November, the court issued a detailed report unfavorable to Barron but not to his officers and crew. The court found Barron negligent in fitting out the *Chesapeake* on nineteen specific items. Barron had not cleared his ship soon enough for action, had improperly called his men to quarters, had used language that dispirited his men, and had surrendered his ship prematurely. Although Barron's conduct showed "great inattention to his duty, and want of decision" during the attack, the court acknowledged that during the attack he personally had not manifested "any personal fear, or want of courage."[33]

President Jefferson ordered a general court-martial for Barron, Gordon, Marine Captain John Hall, and gunner William Hook. In December, Secretary of Navy Smith met personally with Rodgers on the case. Convened on the *Chesapeake* in Norfolk on 4 January 1808, the court consisted of eleven naval officers, including five captains. As senior officer, Rodgers would preside. His fellow captains included William Bainbridge, Hugh Campbell, Stephen Decatur, and John Shaw. The composition of the court raised the issue of fairness to Barron. First, every member of the court except for Rodgers was junior to Barron in rank or seniority and thus stood "to gain a step on the ladder of promotion by the dismissal of a senior." Second, two of the captains were known to dislike Barron. In the past year, Rodgers and Barron had quarreled and Decatur had openly expressed his disgust for Barron's conduct and surrender of the *Chesapeake*. Indeed, Decatur had written to Secretary of Navy Smith and asked to be dismissed from the court for this reason, but Decatur's request was denied because the only two other captains in the navy were unavailable.[34]

As it was set up, the court-martial also included some procedural irregularities that were potentially prejudicial to Barron. Littleton Waller Tazewell was a civilian lawyer from Norfolk who had served as judge advocate for the court of inquiry and written its critical opinion of Barron. Although he preferred not to serve, Tazewell was asked to reappear as the judge advocate for the court-martial. Tazewell also read the findings of the court of inquiry into the record as the court-martial began. This was a questionable procedure, but one to which Barron's lawyer did not object. Barron also wanted several key witnesses, including navy surgeon John Bullus, Secretary of State James Madison, and Attorney General Caesar Rodney, to testify, but none of the three appeared.

For reasons that are unclear, neither Barron nor his lawyer, Robert Taylor, objected to the composition of the court or its procedures. In light of the court's findings, they may have thought any objections would be futile. Barron was, however, an experienced officer well versed in such proceedings. In fact, he had served as president of the court that tried and exonerated William Bainbridge after the capture of the *Philadelphia*. He was also a proud man who was absolutely convinced of his innocence. Whatever the court's findings, Barron also seemed convinced that a court-martial of fellow officers, including even some who were his enemies, would fully exonerate his conduct and his courage.[35]

Rodgers convened the court on 8 January 1808 in the captain's cabin on the *Chesapeake*. The court tried Barron on four charges: "for negligently performing the duty assigned him"; "for neglecting on the probability of an engagement to clear his ship for action"; for failing himself "to encourage . . . his inferior officers and men, to fight courageously"; and "for not doing his utmost to take or destroy the *Leopard*." After a long trial with detailed testimony, the court exonerated Barron on all but the second charge of neglecting to clear his ship for action, for which Barron was suspended from naval command without pay or emolument for five years dating from 8 February 1808. The court then tried the cases against the other three individuals. Officers Gordon and Hall were found guilty of negligently performing their duty and sentenced to be reprimanded by the secretary of the navy. Found guilty of insecurely mounting the guns, not filling the powder horns, and improperly reporting his work, gunner Hook was dismissed from the navy. Having completed its work, the court adjourned officially on 22 February 1808.[36]

Although Rodgers and Decatur were criticized for serving on the court, the actual proceedings were viewed as dignified and professional. Indeed, as the presiding member and an active participant in the trial, Rodgers was not called to task. He conducted the trial in an orderly and dignified manner. Although examination of witnesses was conducted primarily by the judge advocate and Barron's lawyer, members of the court also asked questions. As president, Rodgers only infrequently questioned witnesses. On the few occasions when he did, Rodgers attempted to establish precisely when the *Chesapeake* had struck her colors and whether or not the ship was capable of continued resistance. He did not press the point, but by implication, Rodgers was asking whether Barron had disgraced the honor of the navy by surrendering prematurely.[37] The main criticisms leveled against the proceedings were the wide latitude granted to Barron's accusers when they testified and the fact that some testimony that was disallowed actually remained in the official record.

In addition to questioning the fairness of the court's composition and some of its procedures, the definitive study of the affair is critical of the inconsistency in the court's sentencing. Given the dynamics of the situation, it was unlikely that Barron would be completely exonerated. However, the court judged Barron innocent of the charge of responsibility for the unprepared condition of the *Chesapeake* when it had sailed. If this was true, then logically Gordon, as captain of the ship, was accountable for the ship's unready state. Yet Gordon was not pronounced guilty of this particular charge but of another one. The court's "conclusion that 'no evil' resulted from Gordon's neglect seems inexplicable."[38]

Rodgers's absence from Havre de Grace during the trial tested Minerva's nerve once again. Although she admired her husband's dedication to duty, she could not help questioning the necessity of his absence and even the purity of his motives. "I am an advocate for Peace. What is National honor or National dignity to me, when to support them that life must be exposed on which my own depends," mused Minerva. "Self interest is the Master Spring of all our actions, and the Statesman, the Patriot and the Hero, are alike subject to be governed (almost unconsciously to themselves) by this powerful principle." Although she acknowledged that "you perhaps are an exception to this. Excuse me however if I doubt it!"[39]

By mid-January, Minerva discerned a diminishing affection in John's weekly letters. Although she understood that the "disagreeable business" and "painful task" of Barron's trial required John's time and attention, she had no intention of being "satisfied with a tame cold letter once a week—If ever you come to that I shall recur to your former epistles, filled with Cupid's flames and darts. . . . What a falling off is here." Minerva worried about the long-term effect of their separations: "Altho we sometimes continue to squeeze a little lemon juice into the sweets of matrimonial life, I believe we are not the less necessary to each other, but I am not without apprehensions that these continual separations may weaken our attachment—What think you is there no danger?"[40]

As January and then February dragged on for him in Norfolk, Rodgers also became increasingly frustrated by the trial and the tone of her letters. Her words about introducing "a little lemon juice into the sweets of matrimonial life" struck him as "too cold, and carry in them a sort of Jealousy, and an air of indifference" that was incongruous with her true nature because she had given him "indubitable proof that . . . you are too good!" But he became even more concerned when he received reports that her health was in "imminent danger." The thought of Minerva in "imminent danger" hovered "like a midnight phantom . . . over my sickened senses, and in spite of all my boasted fortitude teaches me to play the woman, by relentless agitation of the heart which timid love alone usurps over the manly voice of reason." Chagrined at having expressed such unmasculine sentiments, Rodgers apologized for "such womanish confessions." When he finally received a letter from her, Rodgers could not contain his joy. Having expected news of her death, "Judge then my adored wife of the joy I experienced at first beholding in your own handwriting that you were well!"[41]

As the trial wore on, he refused to distract himself by attending local social events. When his fellow officers gave a ball for the "Belles of Norfolk," Rodgers declined to attend because it was inconsistent with his official duties and would have been disrespectful to his absent wife "to wish to shine as the Hero of the Ball among a hundred giddy hair brained girls." By 20

February, his patience was "almost exhausted" by the trial, which he termed "the most unpleasant piece of duty I ever performed in the course of my life; and God forbid I should ever be employed in the same way again."[42] Finally, once his trial duties were completed, Rodgers headed north immediately to spend several weeks at Havre de Grace before resuming command of the New York squadron in mid-March.

To the Brink of War, 1808–1811

*I pledge my life that they can do no injury to any vessels. . . . [S]o convinced
am I of this fact, that I should consider myself as safe and sound on any
vessel experimented on, during the operation of the Torpedoes, as a Spaniard
believes himself to be in a Catholic Sanctuary during Mass—or as a Turk
does in his Mosque during the service of the alcoran [Koran].*

Captain John Rodgers, on the upcoming experimental tests
of Robert Fulton's torpedo invention, 1810

When John Rodgers returned to New York in March 1808 to resume his
duties as commander of the New York naval station, the atmosphere had
changed since his departure several months earlier. The war scare of 1807
had passed, but the *Chesapeake* affair remained unresolved diplomatically.
As their struggle in Europe intensified, the British and the French had also
tightened their respective commercial restrictions on American trade, thus
making American neutrality seem ever more tenuous.

American policy had also toughened. In response to President Thomas
Jefferson's requests, Congress had taken action in December 1807. First, it
had approved legislation that appropriated $825,000 for the construction of
188 new gunboats. When those boats were built, the United States would
have a total of 256 gunboats available for defense.[1] Second, Congress had
passed the Embargo Act.[2] The legislation interdicted virtually all trade between the United States and foreign nations. All U.S. ships were prohibited
from sailing to foreign ports while American ships engaged in the coastal
trade were required to post bond double the value of the vessel and its cargo
to guarantee that the goods would arrive at an American port. The Embargo
Act was refined by supplemental legislation in January and March 1808, but
it remained an oppressive piece of legislation to the mercantile communities
engaged in foreign trade.

Passage of the recent naval and embargo laws meant that Rodgers had
two primary responsibilities when he returned to New York. First, he needed to complete his efforts to translate Jefferson's naval defense plans into

reality. The burgeoning New York gunboat squadron needed to be molded into an effective defensive force. Second, Rodgers would have to employ his gunboats to enforce the unpopular embargo by preventing smuggling. These administrative challenges would demand all of Rodgers's energy and talents. Eventually he outfitted, armed, and equipped the new gunboats while he recruited and trained crews for twenty-three boats. As second in command and commandant of the navy yard, Captain Isaac Chauncey carried a heavy administrative load, but Rodgers remained actively involved in a wide range of details and operational issues.

Although recruiting was not a particularly difficult task, training and discipline were. Either young lieutenants or sometimes even midshipmen commanded most of the gunboats. Some lieutenants lacked command experience, and many midshipmen had neither experience at sea nor rudimentary nautical knowledge. Rodgers assigned a chaplain to instruct his young midshipmen in navigation, an activity Rodgers thought "a great acquisition to the young officers" because it would not only increase their navigational competence but also "employ their leisure hours to advantage." Four months later, however, Rodgers reported that this effort had failed because few of the midshipmen had "acquired a competent knowledge" of navigation or lunar observation due to their other duties and "want of inclination."[3]

Discipline was a recurrent issue. Rodgers's young officers required close supervision and posed predictable disciplinary problems for Rodgers. Although dueling was not a serious problem, drunkenness, insubordination, disobedience, disrespect, and sleeping on duty occurred frequently.[4] In spite of his reputation as a tough disciplinarian, Rodgers used discretion as he handled disciplinary problems on a case-by-case basis. In some instances, he demanded or readily accepted the resignation of officers, while in other cases he exercised patience and forbearance. In March 1808, he accepted the transfer of a "very gentlemanly young man and an excellent officer" so that he could return home to deal personally with his family's mismanaged estate. In another case, he accepted a resignation because the young midshipman's conduct on several occasions had deviated from that of "a gentleman and an officer." In yet another instance, Rodgers at first took "pity" on a lieutenant whose "vile habit of drinking to excess has been growing . . . for four or five years" but finally forced the man to resign because he could no longer be entrusted with command and needed to be committed to "an insane hospital."[5]

At the same time, Rodgers did not tolerate disreputable conduct. In July, the sailing master on one of his gunboats resigned after being reprimanded by Rodgers for conduct "derogatory to the character of a Gentleman" and "insulting to every sense of delicacy as well as disgraceful even to human na-ture." The sailing master had openly "kept a common prostitute onboard the gunboat he commanded." Concerned about the impact of this behavior on young officers, Rodgers wrote that he was "ready to make every reasonable allowance for the capricious follies of human nature, but, putting morality out of the question, there is a certain delicacy which every man of genteel standing in life . . . is bound by the strongest ties of honor to observe. . . . The conduct of Mr. Craft cannot be papered over in silence as he appears to be entirely insensible to every thing like self reproach, or he is ignorant of the evil consequences which naturally result from bad example." Rodgers also had contempt for officers who did not share his strong sense of patriotic duty and personal honor. In July 1808, he commented contemptuously on the resignation of a lieutenant who had "made some money" in the merchant marine but considered "the honor of holding the commission of Lieutenant in the Navy . . . of less value than his own private concerns. . . . Indeed, he has had the presumption to tell me that he has made unwarrantable sacrifices already in remaining so long in the service in the command of a gunboat."[6]

Rodgers took very seriously his responsibility as a senior officer to train and mold junior officers. He sought to weed out those whom he believed did not measure up to his demanding standards. Like other senior officers in the early navy such as his own mentor, Thomas Truxtun, and his rival Edward Preble, Rodgers believed it important to identify promising young officers and instill in them the values of patriotism and honor as well as to develop their seamanship, command, and fighting skills. He also insisted that they embrace the so-called "Rodgers system of discipline." By 1809, Rodgers had commanded many junior officers in the previous decade during his cruises in the Caribbean and the Mediterranean and his command of the New York naval station beginning in 1808. Among the most prominent of these officers were David Porter, Isaac Hull, William H. Allen, Johnston Blakeley, James Lawrence, and Oliver Hazard Perry.

Rodgers's individual relationship with each of these officers varied, and it is difficult to know the precise extent to which Rodgers personally shaped their individual values, standards, and command skills. Certainly each one of these officers later embodied Rodgers's own aggressive and combative style of command. He seems to have had a profound influence on Allen and Perry, but his direct influence on the others is unclear. Isaac Hull, for ex-ample, served under both Rodgers and Preble in the Mediterranean, but he is customarily regarded as one of "Preble's boys." Unfortunately, at least one young officer whom Rodgers trained and regarded highly developed into a poor commander. John Orde Creighton served under Rodgers in the Mediterranean on the *John Adams* and later rose to captain. A man of limited patience and nasty temper, Creighton was a martinet known for his tirades, brutal discipline, and, on occasion, physical brutality against his own crewmen.

Once Rodgers's gunboats were launched, their immediate task was to police coastal water and enforce the embargo legislation of 1807 and 1808, which prohibited American ships from carrying goods to all foreign ports but permitted them to engage in the domestic coasting trade. From the outset, the unpopular law produced numerous attempts to evade it. Enforcement fell primarily on the Treasury Department and customs collectors in various coastal ports. The administration tried to detain ships engaged in illegal trade by refusing to issue them clearance papers. However, extensive smuggling occurred, and the embargo was too often evaded. It was relatively easy to smuggle goods by land across the long, and lightly policed, Canadian-American border. On the coast, one obvious way for ships to evade the law was to exchange their overseas clearance papers for certificates allowing them to engage in the coasting trade. This practice, which required the approval of customs officials, was aggressively pursued by merchant captains. Once at sea, the ships could exchange goods with other ships in international waters or merely proceed themselves to a foreign port. Another loophole was the authority that some state governors had to issue certificates permitting the importation of enough foreign grain to avert local food shortages. This option created another opportunity for abuse as some governors granted an excessive number of permits. Finally, some ships simply ignored the law and tried to evade police detection.[7]

The U.S. Navy, then, played a significant, but not predominant, role in attempting to enforce the embargo. For the New York squadron, the initial focal point was Long Island Sound and the south coast of the island. In response to reports of "illicit" activity, Rodgers sent the schooner *Revenge* to patrol the area and deployed his gunboats between Sandy Hook and New York harbor. During 1808 and early 1809, the gunboats of the New York flotilla spoke, boarded, and, in some instances, searched almost eight hundred merchant vessels. In response to administration instructions, Rodgers also dispatched gunboats to Passamaquoddy, Newport, Nantucket, and the Massachusetts coast.[8]

In early July, the *Revenge* returned from five weeks of patrol without discovering any American vessels engaged in illicit activity. Rodgers reported confidently to Secretary of Navy Smith that "whatever may be the disposition of a few individuals (I say few because I believe the number who would violate the Embargo even in this commercial section of the United States,

very small, compared with those who would support it.)," Rodgers estimated that "the Embargo Laws have been violated in very few instances from
Newport, Rhode Island, as far south as the Delaware Bay, as the *Revenge*
and Gunboats" have regularly patrolled "all the Inlets, Bay, etc. . . . without
discovering a single vessel navigating contrary to the law."[9]

Although his ships actually detained few merchant vessels, the administration disagreed with Rodgers's sanguine assessment. Three weeks after
Rodgers's report, when Secretary Smith learned of numerous embargo violations at Newport, Nantucket, Martha's Vineyard, and Portland, he ordered
Rodgers to send additional gunboats to those places. In August, Secretary of
the Treasury Albert Gallatin traveled north to New York, where he discussed
the situation with Rodgers. As a result, Rodgers ordered the *Revenge* to Nantucket and sent a gunboat to Barnstable. A month later, Rodgers reported
that the *Revenge* had returned from a one-month cruise in which she did not
meet "with a single vessel illicitly engaged." Although Rodgers probably had
unintentionally exaggerated the level of compliance, violations of the embargo had declined sharply by the summer of 1808. Even Gallatin reported
that the embargo was functioning reasonably well, stating to Jefferson on 6
August that "no evasions can now take place worthy of notice under colour
of the coasting trade."[10]

In the midst of carrying out his duties as commander of the New York
station, Rodgers was treated to an extended visit from Minerva. Her stay
ultimately brought both joy and anguish to them both. Probably as the result of a terrifying journey during her childhood, Minerva disliked travel
and left home only when she had to. Now pregnant again with her second
child, she decided to visit her husband in New York, leaving behind their
son, John Henry, with family in Havre de Grace. Once she arrived in August,
Minerva and John joyously reunited. Almost two years of marriage had not
dimmed the intense love they expressed in their correspondence. However,
within two weeks of her arrival, word came from Havre de Grace that John
Henry had been stricken with a fever but appeared to be recovering. Then
his condition worsened as the increasingly frantic couple waited. Finally,
word arrived that John Henry had died. When he had first received news
of his son's illness, John urged that a physician from outside tiny Havre de
Grace be brought in to treat little John Henry. Then Rodgers consulted a
local naval surgeon and forwarded the surgeon's recommended remedies
for breaking the boy's fever. Rodgers's efforts having proved futile, he and
Minerva were left with their grief and their guilt. Might their son have lived
had Minerva been at home to care for him? The couple obviously discussed
this subject before John and others apparently convinced Minerva that she

had no reason to feel guilty. By October, she wrote that she was confident that everything that could have been done for the boy had been done.[11]

After Minerva returned home in November, John remained alone with his duties in New York. In December, he was called to Washington to sit on a court of inquiry, an assignment that allowed him to visit Havre de Grace. In Washington, he also observed firsthand the debates in Congress over the nation's defense policy, a discussion that disgusted him. "I am heartily tired of the bawling of congress about national honor and national disgrace without feeling . . . any disposition to place the country in a situation to guard the one and repel the other," Rodgers wrote to Minerva on 22 December. He predicted that the nation was moving to "the very brink of war with England and France, consequently to neglect preparing for war . . . is to risk the honor of the nation."[12]

In March 1809, as President-elect James Madison prepared to take office, Congress approved two pieces of legislation that affected the navy. First, the Non-Intercourse Act repealed the embargo effective 15 March 1809 and reopened trade with all nations except France and Great Britain. The act also authorized the new president to resume trade with France or Great Britain if either nation agreed to stop violating American neutral rights. After receiving assurances from the British minister to the United States, David Erskine, that British restrictions would be revoked, President Madison issued a proclamation on 19 April 1809 that reopened trade with Great Britain. Unfortunately, the British foreign office disavowed Erskine's commitment, forcing Madison later to reimpose the non-intercourse trade restriction against Great Britain.

Second, in January, Congress appropriated $1 million for the improvement of coastal fortifications and, after a contentious debate, specified that four inactive frigates were to be refitted, manned, and sent to sea. The legislation also specified that these four reactivated frigates would be used in a defensive manner. Along with warships already in service, the reactivated *John Adams*, *Essex*, *President*, and *United States* would be stationed and cruise along the American coast but presumably not overseas.[13]

President James Madison and new secretary of the navy Paul Hamilton concurred in Congress's action. Although not a proponent of a large, traditional navy, Hamilton believed that the navy needed more than gunboats to protect American commerce. The forty-six-year-old Hamilton had fought in the Revolutionary War and later had served in the legislature and as governor of South Carolina. Lacking national stature or any maritime experience, Hamilton had been an able governor who pressed for military preparedness in South Carolina. Although he was a heavy drinker, Hamilton served competently for three and one-half years as naval secretary.[14]

In June 1809, Hamilton recommended that, in the event of war, Congress consider abandoning primary reliance on gunboats and merely defensive naval operations in favor of using "a system of well armed, fast sailing, frigates, and smaller cruisers" to attack enemy trade and to convoy and protect American trade abroad. He argued that a few large warships would be preferable "on every principle" as well as "much less costly" than many small gunboats. Hamilton also acknowledged that recent naval legislation "restricted" the president "from sending our vessels equipped under that act beyond our coast" but suggested that Congress consider stationing several of the frigates in the Mediterranean, where they would not be subjected to the dangers of operating in American waters in the winter and they could readily defend the nation's "valuable trade" there against the "depredations of a lawless people."[15]

John Rodgers welcomed these developments. The end of the embargo and the imposition of the non-importation act eased the burden of policing trade. Rodgers now devoted less time to the activities of his gunboats and more time to refitting the *Constitution* for a summer cruise. The forty-four-gun frigate needed to be equipped, provisioned, and manned with a new crew. The most pressing challenge for Rodgers was the recruitment of the estimated 312 ordinary and able seamen who were needed for the *Constitution*. And he needed recruits as well to man the *John Adams* and the bomb ketches *Etna*, *Vesuvius*, and *Spitfire*. The end of the embargo in March exacerbated the recruiting situation by freeing many land-bound sailors to sign on with American merchant ships. As the demand for sailors skyrocketed, wages did too. While Rodgers offered twelve dollars per month plus a three-month advance for able seamen, merchant captains were paying twenty to twenty-five dollars per month. By the end of the year, pay on merchant ships had risen to twenty-eight to thirty-two dollars per month.[16] The recruiting problem improved a bit in April when the Navy Department ordered him to place all of the gunboats under his command in ordinary and to release their crews with the exception of two men per boat for maintenance. On occasion, resignations actually allowed Rodgers to find a better-qualified replacement. When gunner Robert Huntress resigned, a relieved Rodgers reported that in a position that depended on "ability and correct conduct, Huntress's intellectual faculties are very little superior to that of a well trained Horse.... The very reverse of what he ought to be to fill so important a station."[17]

Finally, as Rodgers prepared to sail in early August, Secretary Hamilton warned him and the captains of other ships to be prepared "for any event that may arise. Peace is the season for preparation—War, for action. As far as our means extend, we must place ourselves in an attitude for war, for we know how soon it may overtake us." Clearly in Hamilton's mind was the disgrace of the *Chesapeake* affair two years earlier as well as to the threat of war in the immediate future. The *Constitution* entered the New York Narrows on 11 August, but unfavorable tides and winds prevented her from reaching open sea until 19 August, leading Rodgers to complain formally to Secretary Hamilton about the natural obstacles that the New York rendezvous presented for large ships attempting to get to sea, particularly in wartime. Once underway, Rodgers was well pleased with his officers and crew. After a short cruise, the *Constitution* returned to New York and was then underway again in early September. The Navy Department now intended to keep its warships "in motion" to provide young officers needed experience and knowledge. The second cruise did not go well as the *Constitution* lost both "the Main, and Mizen Top-Mast" in a storm. After receiving repairs, the ship sailed to Hampton Roads in October and returned to New York in November, where she would remain for the winter.[18]

After the birth of their son Robert in 1809, Minerva visited John, but her return to Havre de Grace in December left her husband in a depressed and reflective mood. He confessed that his love for her had even begun to compromise his courage. "Before I knew you I had erected to myself a certain standard of honor, virtue and manly fortitude by which it was my ambition to have regulated all my actions; of which my honor and my virtue are I feel even more firmly established by my intercourse with the most lovely of women, but my fortitude I find has lost much of its strength in the extravagant feelings of a husband and father and which I fear I shall never recover by the force of any reasoning of my mind is capable. To love extravagantly and possess at the same time an uncommon share of fortitude is I find not possible."[19]

Rodgers spent much of the winter in New York involved in the administrative matters of his command. Never a lazy or idle man, Rodgers submitted plans for a new set of night signals and a system for masting and sparring vessels of every description. But constant activities offered an insufficient remedy for his loneliness. By April, Rodgers was both distracted and depressed. As he calculated "bearings & distances" on the *Constitution*, he confessed to Minerva that often "I so far lose myself that I forget whether I am making a chart or exploring a heart when I find I have all to do over again." Admitting that his separation from Minerva was "irksome in the extreme," a dispirited Rodgers doubted whether his country would ever "compensate me for such a personal sacrifice for its good, of the first & dearest wishes of my heart." Claiming that in any other country his sacrifices would have been fully compensated, Rodgers lamented that the United States "is a stranger to those feelings of gratitude which individual sacrifices have a claim to . . . I [have] unfortunately chosen a profession neither calculated to insure me the attainance [sic] of fame, or pecuniary independence." Rodgers was particularly disgusted that, despite "all the degrading & humiliating insults" by England, the Madison administration seemed about to settle its differences in a manner that "I despise as being unworthy of any nation possessing one single spark of laudable pride or honest resentment. . . . Oh! pitiful & contemptible country is mine, for having submitted to every degradation and injury which England & France . . . have thought proper to bestow upon her."[20]

In fact, the Madison administration had decided to deploy its warships more actively. Secretary Hamilton understood that naval legislation prevented him from sending American warships abroad, but in June 1810, he divided the navy into two squadrons and ordered them to cruise the eastern seaboard. Commodore Rodgers would command the northern division and Commodore Stephen Decatur the southern. The northern division would consist of five ships, including the frigates *Constitution* and *President*. It was to patrol from Passamaquoddy Bay to Cape Henry, while the four-ship southern division, including the frigates *United States* and *Essex*, would cruise from Cape Henry to the south.

Although the *Constitution* would become one of the most legendary warships in American history, Rodgers preferred her sister ship, the *President*, which he selected as his flagship. For the next three and one-half years, this ship would be Rodgers's home when he was at sea. Launched in 1800 and rated as a forty-four-gun frigate, the *President* was a formidable vessel that actually mounted a total of fifty-eight guns on her decks. She also was known for her elegant lines and her speed. "The ship sails fast by the wind . . . especially if the breeze is fresh," reported her first commander, Thomas Truxtun in 1801; "she is kind and good humoured in a gale of wind at sea."[21] Hamilton instructed Rodgers and Decatur to use "all the means in your power to defend & protect" American merchant vessels within a "marine league" of the coast from interference by British or French warships. The American commanders were also to seize and detain any suspicious "private armed vessels" in American coastal waters.[22]

Hamilton also reminded his senior commanders of the "injuries & insults heaped on our country by the two great Belligerents of Europe," particularly the "inhumane & dastardly attack on our frigate *Chesapeake*—an outrage which prostrated the flag of our country and has imposed on the American people cause of ceaseless mourning." It was the navy's duty "to be prepared and determined at every hazard to vindicate the injured honor of our navy and revive the drooping spirits of the nation." Accordingly, while observing "strict and upright neutrality," Rodgers was to defend "at any risk and cost the dignity of your flag; and . . . offering, yourself, no unjust aggression, you are to submit to none—not even a menace or threat from a force not materially your superior."[23]

Agreeing that the attack on the *Chesapeake* was "as Dastardly as it was Inhuman and Unjust," Rodgers assured Hamilton "that should a similar Indignity be again offered to our Flag, by any force that is not vastly our superior, England will have no just reason to triumph at the result." He intended to conduct his force "consistently with the principles of strict neutrality," but in a manner that "will give our already much injured country no cause to blush."

Rodgers sent copies of Hamilton's orders to his commanders and exhorted them to act in a manner that would make every American proud. In the event that a French or, particularly, a British warship fired shots at an American merchant vessel, Rodgers instructed Captain Isaac Hull of the *Constitution* to return them "at least" two to one. If a shot were to strike an American vessel, then "it ought to be considered an Act of Hostility, meriting chastisement to the utmost extent of all your force."[24]

The Navy Department and senior officers like Rodgers were unmistakably spoiling for a fight with the British. The humiliation of the *Chesapeake* affair still burning in their minds, they looked forward to using almost any British insult as an excuse for naval revenge. But as relations between the United States and England deteriorated during 1810, the American coastline remained quiet. Rodgers's commanders reported sighting few British ships between Passamaquoddy and Cape Henry. In July, he reported that he had not seen or heard of "a vessel of war, of any description, being on our coast, except our own." Quiet continued into the fall as Rodgers's ships spotted only an occasional English or French warship.[25]

As his squadron patrolled the coast, an unexpected development involved Rodgers in a controversy over a new weapon. Robert Fulton, an energetic and imaginative inventor, was boasting that one of his inventions would revolutionize national defense and naval warfare. Fulton's current ideas included improvements in canal navigation and the development of the steamboat, the submarine, and the marine torpedo (or mine). In late 1806, the forty-one-year-old Fulton had returned to the United States from Europe, where he had been promoting and testing his ideas. In 1807, he built and successfully tested a side paddle-wheel steamboat on the Hudson

River. In 1808, he turned his attention to promoting his ideas about marine torpedoes to the Jefferson administration. Fulton moved to Washington, D.C., where he lived at Kalorama, the estate of his close friend Joel Barlow, and sought government assistance to conduct a demonstration of models of his weapons. Although President Jefferson was both interested and supportive, Fulton met the resistance of naval secretary Smith. Then, in January 1809, both President Jefferson and President-elect James Madison attended Fulton's torpedo demonstration at Kalorama. Although Fulton thought that he had impressed Jefferson and Madison, it took more than a year to secure approval for a full-scale test of his experimental torpedoes. Although he had hoped that Congress would not approve the tests, naval secretary Paul Hamilton asked Rodgers to prepare "a plan of Opposition" to test Fulton's invention. For his part, Hamilton did not see the torpedo as a revolutionary weapon but believed that its "utmost practical effect . . . will be merely on the possible defense and not in attack."[26]

To support his project, Fulton published *Torpedo War and Submarine Explosions*, a report on his torpedo defense system and its far-reaching advantages. He also delivered an address to Congress on his proposal and displayed some components of his system, securing favorable committee support for a demonstration. In retrospect, it is clear that once proven feasible, stationary marine torpedoes or mines would be useful, but limited, military devices. But Fulton did not present his explosive torpedoes as another practical weapon to add to the navy's arsenal. Instead, he argued fervently that his torpedoes would revolutionize naval warfare, ending the need for large traditional navies and freeing the seas from the tyranny of naval warfare.

In *Torpedo War*, Fulton claimed that his invention "will be of first importance to our country . . . as part of our means of national defence" because it could be employed in various ways against enemy warships. Used against anchored enemy vessels, two submerged torpedoes could be connected by a line and chain about 100 feet long and suspended from a cork float. Several other floats could be placed on the surface to hold the chain up as the torpedo floated into contact, exploded, and destroyed the enemy warship. Against moving warships, Fulton proposed using an 18–inch-long harpoon gun connected to a 60–foot line that was attached to an explosive mine. The harpoon would be fired into the wooden hull of the enemy. A clock would detonate the mine two minutes after contact, permitting the torpedo gun crew to escape but not allowing enough time for evasive enemy action. To deal with an enemy ship turning quickly to avoid the torpedo, Fulton proposed a multipronged attack with ten boats firing torpedoes from one side and ten from the other side of the target.[27]

To protect the major American harbors of Boston, New York, Delaware Bay, Chesapeake Bay, Charleston, and New Orleans, Fulton determined that 650 small boats, 1,400 "anchoring torpedoes," and 1,300 "clockwork torpedoes" would be required. With each boat estimated to cost $336, each "anchoring" torpedo $84, and each "clockwork" torpedo $150, Fulton estimated the total cost for providing coastal defense to be $531,000, a "sum which would little more than build and fit out for sea two ships of thirty guns." Moreover, these torpedo boats "will be a better protection for six of our seaports than two ships of thirty or any other number of guns." The torpedoes could be stored indefinitely without requiring repairs, the small boats "laid up in houses" for many years and manned by a "marine militia" that would need only to "practice once a month." The visionary Fulton also claimed that "the violent explosive force of gunpowder" in mines could effectively be employed to "destroy ships of war, and give to the seas the liberty which shall secure perpetual peace between nations." He outlined different scenarios in which a British fleet of one hundred ships of the line in European waters could be effectively destroyed by a force of five thousand small gunboats, each carrying one harpoon-fired torpedo and a twelve-man crew. The total cost of this torpedo force would be $1.4 million, "or about the value of three ships of eighty guns."[28]

Finally Fulton turned to the "political economy" of his torpedo project. He reasoned that in 1800 American trade with England amounted to $14 million, or one-seventh of total British imports and exports. Estimating that British profits on their trade with America equaled $2 million, Fulton further reasoned that profits from American commerce provided approximately one-seventh of the cost of the 760–ship British navy. In other words, the American trade was providing about 2 million pounds sterling annually to support about 108 English warships. Fulton predicted that these costs would rise geometrically as the population of the United States and its trade with England skyrocketed in coming decades. In ninety years, he estimated, American trade would be furnishing more than 16 million pounds sterling annually to "support the British marine, and enable England to double her present naval establishment. Thus we are continually aiding and supporting the only tyranny which can oppress us."[29]

What, then, asked Fulton, was to be done "to arrest this enormous evil, this organizing system of oppression?" Either the United States must have a marine force "to be respected," suffer its "commerce to be as limited as the British Government may think proper," or "military marines must be destroyed, and liberty given to the seas." Since the United States could neither afford the exorbitant cost of a large navy nor possibly accept British limitations on America's commerce, the logical alternative was the extensive use of marine torpedoes to destroy "military marines" and free the seas. Fulton estimated that the United States could eventually save $250 million dollars in naval costs, which could be used for bridges, canals, and public education.

Fulton's combination of visionary boldness, energy, conviction, and persuasiveness won him political support and made his proposal seem plausible. He had the interest, if not the full support, of the Madison administration, and his proposal won congressional approval of $5,000 to conduct the torpedo experiments. The Navy Department had little choice but to cooperate and participate in the tests. Accordingly, Secretary of Navy Hamilton assigned Rodgers, as the senior officer in command of the New York naval station, to conduct the experiments.[30]

Rodgers was both astonished and infuriated by Fulton's assertions. On 16 February, after reading *Torpedo War*, Rodgers wrote two letters to Secretary Hamilton on the subject, denouncing Fulton's "extreme want of delicacy" and labeling him an appropriate target for "derision." "Oh! That mine enemy would write a Book." Noting that Fulton had lived for a number of years in France and England without any visible means of support, Rodgers questioned his "patriotism & integrity." "I find it most difficult at present to determine whether the author merits in the highest degree, the public pity, contempt, or resentment." To the extent that "such a ridiculous project may be the mere effusions of a visionary & partially deranged mind, I think he deserves pity," observed Rodgers, who also saw a sinister side to the project. "He may be the simple fool of some designing demagogues: whose vision may be to destroy, or prevent as far as possible . . . further augmentation of our little Navy: I conceive that he merits to the utmost. . . the contempt of all honest men." Rodgers claimed that Fulton might even "be the hireling instrument of some foreign power whose object is to distract the attention of those who provide the means of our national defence." Certainly Fulton's scheme was entitled to the "indignation & resentment of every individual possessing a single particle of honest American feeling." Rodgers was confident that tests on Fulton's inventions would "expose their ridiculous absurdity & wicked fallacy."[31]

Privately, Rodgers expressed equally contemptuous views. He labeled Fulton's ideas "the most visionary scheme that can be conceived to have originated in the brain of a man not actually out of his senses." What annoyed Rodgers was not the invention itself but rather the absurd claims that Fulton made for it. Possibly a stationary or timed torpedo could be put to use under certain circumstances, but Fulton did not present his invention as an incremental advance in naval warfare. Instead he argued that his mines would revolutionize maritime warfare by eliminating the need for large, traditional navies. For veteran officers such as Rodgers, this visionary assertion threatened both the nation's defense and the navy to which Rodgers had dedicated his adult life; it was a blasphemous assault on the security of the nation he had sworn to defend and the navy he had sworn to serve. Viewing Fulton as a deranged individual who might well be employed by a European enemy, Rodgers nevertheless feared that the persuasive Fulton would lead Congress to show "a greater degree of respect to such a ridiculous subject than it merited." Already Fulton had convinced "a great many learned, wise, & respected men" who agreed with or supported his opinions." To support his views, Rodgers cited the opinion of General Moreau of France, who reported during a dinner with Rodgers that the general considered Fulton's ideas to be "nonsense."[32]

Rodgers confidently set out to ensure that the test he conducted would prove the folly of Fulton's ideas. "I pledge my life that they can do no injury to any vessels. . . . [S]o convinced am I of this fact, that I should consider myself as safe and sound on any vessel experimented on, during the operation of the Torpedoes, as a Spaniard believes himself to be in a Catholic Sanctuary during Mass—or as a Turk does in his Mosque during the service of the alcoran [Koran]." As the date for the tests neared, Rodgers's confidence grew. In September, Rodgers pledged to Secretary Hamilton that he would "not only prevent the application of any Torpedoes which he has yet invented, but any which he will ever be able to invent, and this too, with very little labour & comparatively less expense."[33]

After several delays, the process began in New York on 21 September with Fulton delivering a lecture and demonstration to Commodore Rodgers, Captain Isaac Chancey, and a group of seven prominent civilians whom Secretary Hamilton had invited to observe and report on the experiment. All friends of Fulton, the group included New York governor Morgan Lewis, Robert R. Livingston, Cadwallader Colden, and Oliver Wolcott. As a result of inclement weather, the actual field tests did not begin until 26 September and continued until 1 November. Although Fulton asked that the *President* be used as the target ship, Rodgers provided the brig *Argus* instead. Captain James Lawrence protected his ship with a special net, suspended from the bow, and spars lashed together and hung from the bowsprit and yards in such a way as to prevent any boat from coming into contact with the *Argus*. The studding sail booms were weighted with kentledge (pig iron) and heavy shot and provided with grapnels to repel or sink any boat or torpedo that came within reach. Rodgers, Chauncey, and Lawrence assured the group that all the items used were readily available on any ship of war and could easily be assembled within fifteen minutes. Presented with this obstacle, Fulton "candidly admitted" that he was unprepared to attack the *Argus* "by any means which he had at that time provided."[34]

Having forfeited this first critical test, Fulton proceeded to others with negative results. His first attempt to cut an anchor cable underwater failed, and attempts to fire a harpoon into a target "did not succeed at a greater distance than fifteen feet." In an effort to demonstrate the inadequacy of such a firing distance, Chauncey conducted an experiment on 28 September in which he placed three life-sized figures upright in an old boat moored 90 yards from shore and had a 24–pound cannon loaded with canister and grapeshot fire at the figures. Seventy-three shots hit the boat, but only eighteen penetrated the first board figure, nine the second, and five the third. Finally, on 1 November, one of Fulton's devices succeeded in cutting a 14–inch cable that was submerged 6 feet underwater. Fulton also successfully placed an "anchor torpedo" underwater in the East River, where it remained for several days in "nearly a vertical position," but no test was made of its explosive capacity.[35]

The obvious results of the tests were reported separately to Secretary Hamilton by both the civilian observers and Rodgers. The civilians concluded that Fulton's system "is at present too imperfectly demonstrated to justify the Government in relying upon it as a means of public defence." Rodgers reported the tests in detail and concluded tersely that "so far from being of the importance which he had considered them, [the torpedoes] were, on a more thorough examination . . . found, to say the least, comparatively of no importance at all: consequently that they ought not to be relied on as means of national defence." In his private report to Hamilton, Rodgers stated that "as far as we have yet seen, that not a single sentence of that ever memorable book . . . 'Torpedo War' is in any degree the production of sound reasoning or even a sound mind." Rodgers repeated his earlier assertion that Fulton's exorbitant and misleading claims threatened the nation's security. "Mr. Fulton has exerted himself to impose a belief on the minds of the citizens of the United States that his project was calculated to supercede the necessity of a Navy . . . yet . . . nothing has been done farther than what serves to demonstrate that he had not only deceived himself . . . but every other individual who had placed any reliance on his scheme of offensive and defensive war." For his part, Fulton was very frustrated by the failed experiments, but in his report he recognized "the talents of Commodore Rodgers," by stating that the nets, booms, kentledge, and grapnels employed by the *Argus* made a "formidable appearance against *one torpedo boat and eight bad oarsmen.*" While vowing to refine his schemes for defense, Fulton frankly acknowledged "that Government should not rely on this, or any new invention, for defence, until its utility be fully proved."[36]

In his moment of vindication, Rodgers rendered an appropriately harsh judgment on Fulton's torpedo project. Unfortunately, like some of his naval contemporaries, Rodgers failed to recognize the potential of the "anchored torpedo." Although Rodgers admitted that Fulton's anchored torpedo had maintained its position, that test had proved nothing about the torpedo as "an engine of war" because its explosive capabilities had not been demonstrated. According to one scholar of this subject, the "anchored torpedo," or moored mine, was "the most economical and practical of all of Robert Fulton's naval inventions." It might well have been used effectively in the War of 1812 to help protect Washington, D.C., and Baltimore against British attack.[37]

Rodgers was pleased to be done with Fulton and happily returned to his duties as commanding officer. During the winter of 1810–11, Rodgers kept a number of vessels with him for the winter at New London, Connecticut. To maintain morale and discipline, he kept his officers and crews as busy as possible, conducting extensive coastal and harbor surveys. But winter duty put Rodgers in a sour mood. In spite of their unhappiness in continuing to be separated, Minerva did not join her husband for the three months the squadron wintered in New London. Indeed, word of Rodgers's gloomy mood spread. On 13 January, his friend Chauncey wrote from New York that he had learned "that the serenity of your countenance is frequently overcast and that a dark heavy cloud that look's [*sic*] very threatening has been lately barging about the quarter deck of the *President*." Rodgers's mood darkened further when the *Revenge* ran aground while surveying and was lost. A subsequent court of inquiry exonerated its commander, Oliver Hazard Perry, but the decision did not raise Rodgers's spirits.[38]

The spring of 1811 began quietly. Rodgers took the *President* to New York and then received permission to sail to Annapolis and spend several days visiting his family at Havre de Grace. From Annapolis, Rodgers reported to Hamilton that the cruise had occurred "without anything . . . worthy of remark." But, in fact, maritime tensions along the coast had worsened. On 1 May near Sandy Hook, the British frigate *Guerriere* had stopped the American merchant brig *Spitfire* and impressed one of her American crewmen. Reacting immediately, Hamilton ordered Rodgers to take the *President* as soon as possible back to New York to protect American ships and sailors there. Secretary Hamilton and Rodgers clearly expected a confrontation and possibly armed action with the *Guerriere*. Accordingly, Rodgers had the *President* fully prepared for battle.[39]

Shortly after noon on 16 May in international waters about fifty miles northeast of Cape Henry, Rodgers sighted a ship bearing toward the *President* from the east. From the "symmetry of her upper sails," Rodgers judged the ship to be a "man of war" and hoisted his "ensign and pendant." The unidentified vessel did not answer the American signals, changed course, and headed to the south. Rodgers gave chase and closed the distance quickly at first and then more slowly as the wind diminished. At about quarter after seven, or shortly after dusk, the ship changed course, presented a broadside to Rodgers, and hoisted her colors, but it was now too dark for Rodgers to identify them because he was still more than a mile and one-half away. An hour later Rodgers maneuvered within hailing distance, about 70 to 100 yards away.[40]

Rodgers asked, "What ship is that?" Out of the dark came the reply, "What ship is that?" Believing himself entitled "by the common rules of politeness to the first answer," Rodgers repeated his inquiry, "What ship is that?" Before he had "time to take the trumpet from my mouth," Rodgers was answered by a single shot into his mainmast. As Rodgers prepared to order that a shot be fired in return, the unidentified ship fired another shot, and then "three others in quick succession, and soon after the rest of his broadside and musketry." In response, Rodgers ordered his guns to open fire and then to cease firing after "four to six minutes" because the *President's* guns had "produced a partial silence of his guns." Less than four minutes later, when his adversary resumed firing, Rodgers ordered his guns to respond accordingly. Within five minutes, the unidentified ship ceased firing after suffering disabling damage and numerous casualties. When hailed again, she identified herself as HMS *Little Belt*, a twenty-one-gun British sloop of war. The next morning Rodgers sent a boat to offer assistance, which was politely declined by the British captain, Arthur Bingham. Having suffered minimal damage, the *President* resumed her cruise to New York as the seriously damaged *Little Belt* limped back to Halifax.[41]

Rodgers was disheartened to learn that his opponent had not been a British frigate but rather a single-decked warship carrying less than one-half of his armament. "I regret extremely" having to report the event, wrote a downcast Rodgers to Hamilton. "I accordingly, with that degree of repugnance incident to feeling equally determined neither to be the aggressor nor to suffer the flag of my country to be insulted with impunity, gave a general order to fire," explained Rodgers. As a man with "a humane and generous heart," he confessed that the incident "would cause me the most acute pain during the remainder of my life." His only consolation was the knowledge that he had "no alternative." Given the questionable circumstances of the incident, Rodgers asked for a formal inquiry to be conducted.

In his report, Rodgers added a postscript explaining why he had mistaken such a small ship as the *Little Belt* for an enemy frigate. "Owing to her great length, her having a poop and topgallants, forecastle, and room to mount three more guns on a side than she actually carries, her deep bulwark, and the manner of stowing her hammocks," noted Rodgers, the *Little Belt* "has the appearance of a frigate" and was taken for such from Rodgers's distant view during the chase. Only after dark did he get a view of her broadside.[42]

Rodgers's report is interesting when it is compared with his letters to Hamilton in the year prior to the incident. In some of those, he had expressed a bravado and eagerness to gain revenge for the *Chesapeake*. Now, after the initial flush of triumph, he seemed chastened. Although he never second-guessed his own conduct, he was dismayed that his victory had been against a greatly inferior opponent. He understood that however much American civilians might celebrate his action, it would undoubtedly be dismissed and possibly even ridiculed in naval circles on both sides of the Atlantic. While this encounter would not hurt his military stature, it would not add luster to his naval reputation.[43]

Indeed, when word of the incident reached the United States, the immediate reaction was positive. Individuals and most newspapers praised Rodgers's actions as just retribution for the *Chesapeake* affair. But praise was not universal. In New England, the Federalist press was critical of Rodgers. When word of the attack reached England, the English press labeled Rodgers as a cowardly bully for his shelling of the overmatched *Little Belt*. More important than the public's reaction was the response of the Madison administration, which was clearly delighted. Hamilton assured Rodgers that "you could have pursued no other course than that which you adopted consistent with your duty." He also praised Rodgers for acting in a humane manner during the incident. "You ceased your fire the moment that your country's & your own honor permitted you to do so." Hamilton also conveyed the president's "unqualified approbation" and his assurance that a court of inquiry was "unnecessary." Naval clerk Charles Goldsborough exulted that Rodgers had "acted like yourself—with true & genuine bravery tempered with magnanimous humanity. . . . Mr. Hamilton not only approves but admires your conduct."[44]

In this letter and then another the next day, Hamilton warned Rodgers that he would now undoubtedly be "marked for British" retaliation. "The chastisement you have inflicted on British insolence will mark you as an object of British vengeance," cautioned Hamilton; "your destruction will be attempted. British naval pride cannot brook the chastisement you have inflicted, even on British temerity and imprudence. You will be sought by a superior force." Rodgers immediately thanked Hamilton for his approval and that of the president, feeling the confidence of the secretary to be "truly flattering" and the "unqualified approbation of the Chief Magistrate of our country . . . highly gratifying." Rodgers also acknowledged that although he understood he might become the target for "British vengeance[,] . . . I feel pride" in it. Moreover, he assured Hamilton that Rodgers would not give the British "reason to exult" or Americans "cause to blush." "Gun to Gun & Man to Man, we have nothing to dread."[45]

As the flush of triumph faded and the threat of British naval retaliation passed, Hamilton reminded Rodgers that because the United States hoped to remain at peace with England, Rodgers should conduct himself accordingly. "Temperance & politeness belong to the real soldier as well as firmness: & you know how to exercise them: policy & humanity recommend the cultivation of peace by all means not inconsistent with national honor." In fact, Rodgers did not believe that England would risk war with the United States. Reports of recent desertions in the British navy led him to speculate that actual war would produce widespread "disaffection in the British navy & thereby effect the destruction of that Government." Nor would the British risk another naval encounter with the United States unless England had a "decidedly superior force." With an equal force, Rodgers boasted that he would "prove to the world that British Ships are not so perfectly invulnerable as British arrogance has described them. This however is not likely to happen, as it would be putting at hazard that reputation for superior skill and courage which they have acquired fighting Frenchmen & Spaniards." If an American frigate defeated a British frigate of equal force, the reputation of the British navy would be "more injured than it was elevated by the victory of the Nile." For this reason, Rodgers concluded arrogantly that "under the influence of their sober senses, they never will voluntarily attempt a game of such hazard."[46]

In Washington, D.C., the *National Intelligencer* published Rodgers's report of the *Little Belt* affair, and his version was quoted and excerpted in papers around the country. Initial response from around the country was positive. From Boston, Isaac Hull reported that "the British Commander is highly censured, even among the violent Essex Junto." In Washington, a tone of belligerent defiance emerged. On 5 July, Charles Goldsborough reported that "like good Americans we celebrated the 4th by firing of cannons, rockets—dinner, etc. etc." At the large public dinner attended by government dignitaries, Rodgers was enthusiastically honored in a toast: "Speak when you are spoken to—if you don't G-d d–m you. I will make you."

However, this version of events was to be challenged as weeks passed. Not surprisingly, Captain Arthur Bingham's account differed in important particulars. Then, in July, several newspapers reported that some sailors who had served on and later deserted from the *President* were claiming that the American ship, not the *Little Belt*, had actually fired the first shot. In response, Rodgers again asked for a formal court of inquiry, a request to which Hamilton agreed.[47]

The court of inquiry convened on the *President* in New York harbor on 30 August 1811. Commodore Stephen Decatur presided over a three-person panel, which included Captains Isaac Chauncey and Charles Stewart, who were known to be favorably predisposed to Rodgers. The court met daily for two weeks and interviewed fifty-one witnesses, including every midshipman, lieutenant, and gun captain onboard during the incident. Although the British and American accounts of it differed with respect to various particulars, three issues were key. Most important was the question of which ship had fired first. Also significant were the questions of whether the British ship had displayed her colors prior to nightfall and how long the actual exchange of guns had lasted. The account of Bingham and another filed by three of his officers claimed that Rodgers had fired the first shot, that the *Little Belt* had hoisted her colors in midafternoon, and that the engagement had lasted approximately forty-five minutes. Rodgers's account disagreed on each of these particulars. He maintained that Bingham had fired the first shot as well the first full volley. He also insisted that Bingham had not displayed his colors until it was too dark for them to be visible to the American ship and that the entire engagement had lasted only about fifteen minutes.[48]

Although the written British accounts were general recollections of the event asked of witnesses, the questions from the court of inquiry were specific and often detailed. In addition to questions from the court, Rodgers actively interrogated the witnesses, whose testimony proved very consistent. Witness after witness maintained that the *Little Belt* had fired the first shot, that she had not shown her colors until after dusk, and that the engagement had not lasted longer than fifteen to eighteen minutes. In his formal statement to the court, Rodgers also denied, as being "without any foundation whatever," the charge that he had pursued the unidentified ship "with the intention of offering menace or insult to the British flag." Given his orders from Secretary Hamilton, Rodgers claimed that he thought the ship in question must be the *Guerriere*, which he pursued in an effort to "speak her" and to get an explanation for the recent impressment of the American seaman from the *Spitfire*.[49]

As might well have been predicted, the court agreed with Rodgers's version of events and exonerated him on all counts. In fact, the day before the court convened, Secretary Hamilton ordered Rodgers to sea as "soon as the court of enquiry shall have closed." The report stated that it had been proved to the "satisfaction of the court" that the *Little Belt* had not raised her colors until it was "too dark to distinguish to what nation they belonged," that the *Little Belt* "fired the first gun," and that the action lasted about fifteen minutes. In conclusion, the court found that Rodgers's account of 23 May to the secretary of the navy "is a correct and true statement of the occurrences which took place between" the *President* and the *Little Belt*.[50] Hamilton praised the findings of the court for demonstrating "the correctness of the opinion we had previously of the honor, candor & humanity of Comm. Rodgers who richly merits & will receive the support of the Government & of every virtuous citizen in the community." Although the *Little Belt* incident was now officially closed as a naval matter, it contributed in the remaining months of 1811 to the growing public hostility to England and the deteriorating diplomatic relations between the two countries.[51]

1. Portrait of John Rodgers, artist unknown, no date.
Courtesy of U.S. Naval Institute.

2. Portrait of Commodore John Rodgers, by John Wesley Jarvis, 1814.
Courtesy of U.S. Naval Academy Museum.

3. Portrait of Commodore John Rodgers, artist unknown, no date. Courtesy of U.S. Naval Academy Museum.

4. Portrait of Minerva Denison Rodgers, artist unknown, no date.
Courtesy of U.S. Naval Academy Museum.

5. Portrait of Commodore Thomas Truxtun, by Cornelius Tiebout, no date. Courtesy of U.S. Naval Academy Museum.

6. Portrait of Edward Preble, artist unknown, no date.
Courtesy of Library of Congress.

7. Portrait of Commodore James Barron, artist unknown, no date.
Courtesy of U.S. Naval Institute.

8. Portrait of Stephen Decatur, artist unknown, no date.
Courtesy of Library of Congress.

9. *The Chace*, by Edward Chase, 1799. Depiction of the encounter between the *Constellation* and *L'Insurgente*. Courtesy of U.S. Naval Academy Museum.

10. *Action,* by Edward Savage, 1799. Depiction of the encounter between the *Constellation* and *L'Insurgente.* Courtesy of U.S. Naval Academy Museum.

11. A British view of the *Little Belt* affair, May 1811. Courtesy of Clements Library, University of Michigan.

12. A British view of the *Little Belt* affair, "elucidating the extreme disproportion of Force between the American Frigate *President* . . . and His Majesty's Sloop the *Little Belt* . . . [May 11, 1811]," by Joseph Cartwright. Courtesy of Clements Library, University of Michigan.

13. The chase of the *Belvidera*, 23 June 1812, artist unknown.
Courtesy of U.S. Naval Academy Museum, Beverly R. Robinson Collection.

14. The escape of the *Belvidera*, 23 June 1812, by Charles J. Hullmandel. Courtesy of U.S. Naval Academy Museum, Beverly R. Robinson Collection.

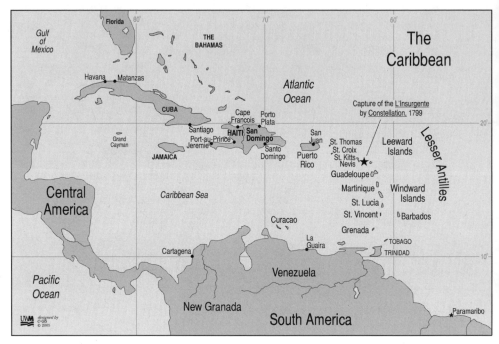

15. The Caribbean. Courtesy of University of Wisconsin–Milwaukee Cartography Laboratory.

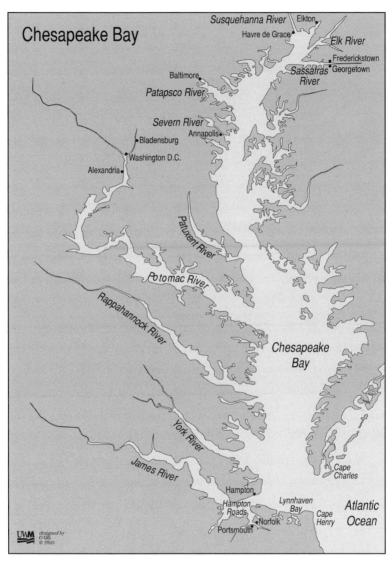

Chesapeake Bay

Susquehanna River Elkton
Havre de Grace
Elk River
Frederickstown
Baltimore Sassafras Georgetown
River
Patapsco River
Severn River
Bladensburg Annapolis
Washington D.C.
Alexandria
Patuxent River
Potomac River
Rappahannock River
Chesapeake
Bay
York River
James River
Cape
Charles
Hampton
Hampton Lynnhaven Atlantic
Roads Bay Cape
Norfolk Henry Ocean
Portsmouth

UWM designed by
C-GIS
© 2005

16. Chesapeake Bay. Courtesy of University of Wisconsin–Milwaukee
Cartography Laboratory.

17. The Mediterranean. Courtesy of University of Wisconsin–Milwaukee Cartography Laboratory

6

Commodore at Sea in the War of 1812

[My] only consolation [is that my presence] at Sea obliged the Enemy to concentrate a considerable portion of his most active force and thereby prevented his capturing an incalculable amount of American property that would otherwise have fallen a sacrifice.

Captain John Rodgers, on the results of his first cruise during the War of 1812

By the end of 1811, diplomatic efforts and economic coercion had not won America any concessions or reduced maritime harassment from either Great Britain or France. First the Non-Intercourse Act of 1809 and then Macon's Bill Number Two in 1810 had failed. President James Madison faced increasing criticism from Federalists in New England as well as escalating pressure within his own party to take decisive action. Once the inquiry into the *Little Belt* had been completed, the administration took a hard line. Secretary of State James Monroe bluntly informed the British minister that the affair represented a "violent aggression by a British on an American ship" and reminded him that reparations had not yet been made for the *Chesapeake* attack four years earlier.[1]

The president had also called the Twelfth Congress into session in November 1811 to work with him through the issues of defense, diplomacy, and possibly war. The new Congress included a group of young members who would become known as the "War Hawks." Led by thirty-four-year-old Henry Clay from Kentucky and twenty-nine-year-old John C. Calhoun from South Carolina, the group included Richard Johnson from Kentucky, William Lowndes and Langdon Cheves from South Carolina, Felix Grundy from Tennessee, and Peter Porter from western New York. All were strong nationalists under the age of forty. The War Hawks were in the minority in the House, but Clay became speaker, Cheves became chairman of the Naval Affairs Committee, and the group dominated the Foreign Affairs Committee. Although they did not represent maritime districts directly affected by neutral rights on the high seas, the War Hawks were fervent nationalists who resented British arrogance and viewed British impressment and seizure of American merchant ships as national insults that must be avenged.

Adding fuel to the tense diplomatic situation were events in the West. In early November, General William Harrison and a force of one thousand men defeated the Indian forces at Tippecanoe. The Americans recovered British weapons on the battlefield, which confirmed prior American allegations that the British were providing guns to the Indians and encouraging them to resist American settlement in the Ohio Valley. As a result, westerners increasingly demanded war with England and an invasion of Canada to remove the threat.[2]

In his message to Congress in November, President Madison presented an ominous picture. He detailed British offenses while strongly defending Commodore John Rodgers in the recent *Little Belt* affair. Because the British captain had opened fire "without cause," he "therefore is alone chargeable with the blood unfortunately shed in maintaining the honor of the American flag." Madison depicted a British government that "perseveres not only in withholding a remedy for our wrongs . . . but [also] in the execution . . . of measures which . . . have the character as well as the effect of war on our lawful commerce." In the face of Britain's "inflexible hostility in trampling on rights which no independent nation can relinquish," Madison asked Congress to place "the United States into an armor and an attitude demanded by the crisis." Madison asked Congress to strengthen the nation's defense by strengthening the regular army and increasing the militia, but he made only brief and vague reference to the navy.[3]

Congress strengthened the army but, after a spirited debate, did virtually nothing to strengthen or expand the navy. It voted to increase the number of men in the regular army to an already authorized size of 10,000; to add 20,000 more regulars; and to provide for 50,000 volunteers. Based on the recommendation of Secretary of the Navy Paul Hamilton, Congressman Cheves, chair of the House Naval Affairs Committee, recommended approval for the construction of twelve, seventy-four-gun ships of the line and a total of twenty frigates of at least thirty-eight guns each (including those already in commission). After considerable debate, this recommendation and several other attempts to add a smaller number of frigates were defeated. Eventually in this session, the navy received funds to construct its first dry dock, to purchase timber and other naval materials, and to equip and activate three frigates that were then out of commission.[4]

Rodgers spent the winter with his squadron at Newport, Rhode Island, where Minerva raised his spirits by joining him. They now had two sons: Robert was two, and Frederick had been born in 1811. Minerva was also

pregnant again and would give birth to John in August 1812. Rodgers continued to deal with the many details associated with command of the squadron
and to prepare for war. Secretary Hamilton also asked for Rodgers's assistance in establishing a "telegraphic communication" system along the coast
from New York to Washington because war would interrupt regular coastal
communications by ship. Telegraph wires not yet having been invented, the
secretary proposed a signal system that would relay visual signals from one
station to the next. Rodgers reported that various obstacles, including "numerous forests of lofty trees," made such a system impractical. Moreover, its
limited value was "inadequate to the cost & trouble attending its support."
Nevertheless, Rodgers reported that a much shorter but effective 24–mile
link might be established between New York City and Sandy Hook, New
Jersey. It could be built for $500 and maintained by only two men at each
station. To streamline the existing dictionary of telegraphic signals, Rodgers
prepared a new "regular telegraphic dictionary" to permit an individual to
send signals "with as much ease & correctness as he could do by writing" in
one-half the time.[5]

On 1 April 1812, Madison took the next step toward war when he requested Congress to approve a sixty-day embargo. His intent was twofold: first,
to keep as many ships and seamen as possible at home and protect them
from the enemy in anticipation of war; and second, to deprive the English of
American grain and other supplies that were indispensable to British forces
fighting in Spain. On 4 April, Congress approved a ninety-day embargo, but
it proved ineffective because merchant captains had already been warned
about the pending legislation, and dozens of ships had hastily cleared for
sea from Baltimore, Philadelphia, New York, and Boston. They carried an
estimated $15 million in grain and provisions.[6]

By early April, Rodgers had returned with his squadron to New York,
where he took steps to put the new signal communication line in operation and helped to enforce the new embargo. An ominous threat was the
presence of enemy warships. The British frigates *Guerriere* and *Belvidera*
were reported to be harassing American merchant ships along the coast.
Although he professed not to be "anxious for war & bloodshed," Hamilton
instructed Rodgers that "if you find proper occasion with only a tolerable
chance, you will inflict merited chastisement on foreign insolence." In response, Rodgers immediately began to patrol the coast but soon reported
that he had sighted no foreign warships.[7]

This was an emotional time for John and Minerva. Although she tried to
put on a brave face when she returned home in April, Minerva could not
dismiss her fears about war. Havre de Grace was then in the midst of the fish-

ing season and presented "quite a busy scene," but Minerva wrote to Rodgers that she took "no interest in anything that is going on, absent from you, I feel solitary and alone." She could only dream of how "happy I should be to saunter along the shore hanging on your arm with Robert laying his gambols before us." She reported that a volunteer company was being recruited; the town was "constantly greeted with the sound of the drum & fife which with two officers & 4 or 5 red feathers makes the place look quite martial. War is very generally expected here and I begin to fear it myself." As she fretted about the future, Minerva described her two small sons playing at her feet, talking of their father and pretending they were onboard his ship.[8]

Minerva was clearly torn by the prospect of war. Although it would offer her husband his chance to achieve military glory, it could also mean that she might never see him again. At one point, as rumors of war temporarily diminished in Havre de Grace, she allowed herself the luxury of thinking that "you will have it [in] your power ere long to settle yourself somewhere . . . where you can sail sticks with the boys & build them card houses without the fear of lessening your dignity—I must confess that the 'dull pursuits' of civil life are more congenial to my heart than any other and I would willingly sacrifice to them all the gay dreams of ambition which my fancy ever drew."[9]

With war imminent by late May, Minerva's anxiety grew. Once actual hostilities exposed John to grave danger, Minerva confessed that "My poor heart" would be doomed "to a tumultuous warfare between hopes & fears." As she waited in his absence, her young boys, Robert and Frederick, furnished "all my joys and all my happiness—without them life would be a blank indeed." Robert talked constantly of "you, the Ship, and the boats," while little Fred's vocabulary had not progressed "farther than 'Ship Ahoy,' which he reports on all occasions." As she closed this letter at midnight on 19 May, Minerva confessed that she would be "going to sleep to dream & hope that my head is reposing on your faithful bosom. Once more good Night!" Her anguish intensified several days later when the *President* was reported to be off Delaware Bay. "How tantalizing to have you so near & yet not see you."[10]

As he waited aboard the *President* for word of war, a confident Rodgers attempted to reassure Minerva. "I flatter myself, in the way of receiving the smiles of fortune," assured Rodgers, "without any greater risk of my person than I have been subject to for these three years past." Explaining that he would be absent for an extended period, he outlined the steps he had taken to provide for her financially. He also forewarned her that while he was at sea, she undoubtedly would hear many "idle stories," which he instructed her not to believe. Instead she "ought to suppose that I am doing well for it is probable I may not be afforded an opportunity of writing you until my return." In fact, within a week of his departure, Minerva began to receive false reports about her husband. Rodgers urged Minerva to "feel no anxiety on my account for this [is] not only the most interesting but most happy moment of my life. Be cheerful—Be composed & let no idle conjectures or rumors disturb your repose for really I shall not be" as vulnerable as "I should be were I to remain at New York during the sickly season . . . heaven has not only afforded me an opportunity of breathing pure air but at the same time the prospect of making all those who are most dear to me comfortable for life."[11]

Rodgers reassured his fearful and lonely wife that with the "return of more tranquil times," he would be able to "change the character of tiger for that of a lamb or a sheep—no not a sheep but a dove—yes a turtle dove like your old barburisser [sic]." As late as 19 June, Rodgers worried that a declaration of war might well be conditional, that is, that England might be given one final chance to rescind its orders-in-council. Rodgers reasoned wrongly that England might take such action because "without our beef & corn she can not possibly maintain her armies in the peninsula six months longer." Indeed, Rodgers judged corn and beef to be "very formidable weapons for there is nothing more shocking to any Englishman's nerves than the thought of going to bed supperless—poor John Bull would feel himself in a bad plight while the Corsican tiger has hold of his nose & the northern bear hold of his tail, if this American eagle were either to pick out his eyes or attack his corporation." For himself, Rodgers thought war would probably be "for the better, not that I love fighting but because I abhor disgrace."[12]

As war neared, Secretary Hamilton requested the recommendations of his senior captains for a "plan of operations" that would "enable our little navy to annoy in the utmost extent, the trade of G. Britain while it least exposes it[self] to the immense naval force of that Government." Hamilton understood that sustained head-to-head naval operations between the tiny American force and the mammoth British navy were out of the question, but how might the American navy be best employed to attack British commerce?[13]

Rodgers recommended a two-pronged program: first to attack the British West Indies trade, and second to menace British coastal, foreign, and East India commerce. America's smallest warships should "annoy . . . all the avenues leading to & from her West India Islands, Surinam, Berbice, & Denamara." Meanwhile, a small squadron of "two, or three of our fastest sailing frigates & a single sloop of War" should cruise along the coasts of England,

Ireland, and Scotland, and the "residue of our frigates" should "harass the enemy" by cruising British shipping lanes near Nova Scotia and Newfoundland. Rodgers also recommended that "occasionally" "all our Frigates" be united to "attack his East India Convoys." If used for the first six months and possibly the entire duration of the war, Rodgers argued, this strategy would surprise and annoy the enemy. "Menacing them in the very teeth," it would destroy "their commerce in a manner the most perplexing to their government, & in a way the least expected by the nation generally, including those belonging to the Navy: the self styled Lords of the Ocean!!"[14]

Rodgers admitted that his plan "may, at first sight, appear chimerical," given the great numerical superiority of the enemy's navy. "But this is the very reason," explained Rodgers, that "such a dispersion should be made." The enemy would be required to deploy a much larger force to protect their own commerce "than it would to annihilate ours, and our little navy with it" should that force be permitted to concentrate on the American coast. With the British Isles relatively unprotected, American warships could move constantly from point to point along the enemy's coast until they drew a large portion of its navy. American ships could then leave the British coast, move to another location, and thereby draw "the enemy off to protect his trade in some other quarter." At this time, Rodgers stood second in seniority only to Alexander Murray, who was considered too old for sea command. As a result, Rodgers was the senior naval officer in command. He understood that he would likely be entitled to command the attacking squadron, and he specifically requested that responsibility. He assured the secretary that "barring unforeseen accidents . . . I may with propriety pledge myself to make the commerce of that arrogant nation feel its effects to the very quick."[15]

Hamilton received a different set of recommendations from Rodgers's colleague, Stephen Decatur. In order to attack British commerce most effectively while exposing the tiny American navy to the least danger, Decatur urged that American warships disperse and operate "distant from our coast, & singly, or not more than two Frigates in company." Moreover, the department should not give any "specific instructions as to place or cruising but . . . rely on the enterprise of the officers." Decatur explained that two frigates cruising together would not be so easily traced by the enemy as would a larger squadron; their movements would be "infinitely more rapid," and the frigates would in most cases be "sufficiently strong" to attack a merchant convoy. In the event that disaster struck and the Americans met a "superior force" that they could not avoid, the nation would have lost two ships, not most of its navy. Since Decatur believed the greatest risk would be entering or leaving American ports, he recommended that the ships be heavily provisioned to "remain out as long as possible," thereby drawing enemy ships away from the American coast as they searched for the American vessels on the high seas.[16]

As Hamilton pondered his decision, Rodgers continued to prepare for war. Of concern was the condition of the *Essex*, which was supposed to sail with Rodgers's squadron from New York. Because she required extensive repairs to her mast and hull, the *Essex* would not be ready for sea until early July, or almost two weeks after Rodgers had sailed. Rodgers himself completed and submitted to the Navy Department two new sets of "private signals," one to be used at night and the other during the day, to eliminate irregularity in communication. He also suggested the adoption of "certain Pendants or flags, by which the Ship of a Senior Officer can be known from that of his junior, where two or more squadrons happen to meet in the same Port, or at sea." Remembering his disagreement with Preble over their broad pendants in 1803, Rodgers wanted to avoid confusion when two commodores occasionally met at sea. He recommended and the department accepted a blue, red, white hierarchy in which the senior commodore would fly a blue flag with white stars, the next in seniority a red flag with white stars, and the least senior a white flag with blue stars. The recognition of privileges of rank and seniority was a sensitive issue to Rodgers, who not coincidentally now stood second on the navy seniority list. Rodgers explained to the secretary that "the observance of a due regard to the most minute distinctions of the relative rank of officers" constituted "the first & most essential principle of a well digested system of Discipline and Government." Acknowledging his own "tenacious regard for my own rank," Rodgers emphasized that the continued absence of such a "mark of distinction might in many situations . . . be attended with serious consequences to the reputation of the service."[17]

In Washington, the president took the final step toward war. On 1 June, Congress received Madison's war message, in which he presented four main reasons why Congress should declare war. In addition to the ongoing impressment of Americans, Madison pointed to the continuing British violation of American neutrality, its blockade of American ports, and its refusal to revoke its orders-in-council. On 4 June, a divided House of Representatives voted 89 to 49 for war. Two weeks later, the Senate concurred by a much closer 19 to 13 margin. Hamilton immediately informed Rodgers that war had been declared and that his warships were "entitled to every belligerent right, as well of attack as defense." Although he advised Rodgers to remain in the vicinity of New York to receive "more extensive, and more particular orders," Hamilton authorized his senior commander "to strike . . . capture or destroy" any British frigates in the area.[18]

These instructions reached Rodgers about 3 p.m. on 21 June. Hamilton followed these instructions with more detailed ones dated 22 June. The latter dispatch represented Hamilton's response to the earlier recommendations from Rodgers and Decatur regarding the best way to deploy American naval forces to harass British commerce. The secretary emphasized that the protection and safe return of American merchant ships at sea, not the harassment of enemy shipping, was now "of the highest importance." Accordingly, he divided American naval forces into two squadrons. Rodgers would command a force of five ships and cruise eastward from the "Capes of the Chesapeake"; Decatur would lead a three-ship squadron and patrol from Sandy Hook south along the coast. Should an opportunity of "sufficient importance" present itself, the two squadrons could unite. Although Hamilton thought "that it may not be prudent, for the vessels to sail singly," he authorized Rodgers and Decatur to detach one or two ships from their main force when "a different arrangement may promise more success." In any event, American naval forces were not to flee from an equal enemy force nor voluntarily confront a force "superior to your own. . . . nor need I remind you of the precious effects, which victory will procure." Hamilton admonished Rodgers to "go forth" with the assurance that Hamilton had full confidence in Rodgers's "valor & discretion . . . may the God of battles be with you." Although Hamilton did not specifically authorize either of his senior officers to range widely across the Atlantic Ocean, he had essentially concurred with Rodgers that America's main naval forces should be joined and used in concert rather than operate singly or in pairs.[19]

American strategic options were restricted to a great extent by the disparate sizes of the two nations' navies. When war was declared, the British boasted a navy of about 1,000 ships, including 124 ships of the line, all carrying at least sixty guns and all outclassing the single largest American warship. Although the British were concerned primarily with the struggle against Napoleon in Europe, the British navy in the western Atlantic and Caribbean still comprised 111 ships assigned to four different commands, including 2 in the West Indies, 1 at Newfoundland, and 1 off the coast of the United States with bases in Halifax and Bermuda. In sharp contrast, with no warships then under construction, the United States Navy consisted of no ships of the line, 6 frigates, 9 lesser warships rated at ten to sixteen guns, and 165 gunboats. An additional 5 frigates were "laid up in Ordinary," requiring six months to repair and place into commission. In the estimation of one prominent naval historian, "the wonder is that she [the American navy] accomplished anything at sea."[20]

With their navy vastly outnumbered and outgunned, American naval commanders were constrained to harassing and raiding enemy commerce. Whether cruising singly, in pairs, or in a larger squadron, they could not engage England's larger squadrons directly. As they subsequently did, American captains might pick propitious moments to engage an enemy battleship, but such occasions had to be carefully chosen. From the outset, American naval strategy was to attack or make prizes of British merchant vessels wherever possible in an effort to distract the British navy from concentrating on a few major American seaports. Aiding American warships in their efforts were hundreds of American privateers that operated in the waters of the Atlantic and the Caribbean.[21]

As it turned out, Hamilton's second set of instructions proved academic because Rodgers was already at sea by the time the letter arrived in New York. Within ten minutes of having received Hamilton's initial instructions on the afternoon of 21 June in Sandy Hook Bay, Rodgers had sailed in the *President*, which was joined by the frigates *United States* and *Congress*, the brig *Hornet*, and the schooner *Argus*. His "principle object" was to find a "large West Indies convoy, which from the information I have received, is now about S.E. of us, on the outer edge of the Gulf Stream." The convoy reportedly numbered more than one hundred vessels but was lightly escorted as it made its way from Jamaica to England.[22]

"We are all in high spirits, and hope to give our Country a good account of this cruise," reported Rodgers. He announced that he had "never seen the *President* in more efficient order, neither has she ever had a better crew." Although Rodgers knew that his ships would be far outnumbered, he boasted that it was "not impossible that we may be able to cripple & reduce their force, in detail, to such an extent as to place our own upon a footing until their loss could be" replaced from England.[23]

At 3 a.m. on 23 June, an American merchant ship inbound from Madeira to New York informed Rodgers that it had passed the British convoy four days earlier. Rodgers shaped his course to the east, and three hours later, when the *President* was about one hundred miles southwest of Nantucket Shoals, he sighted a sail to the northeast. The ship proved to be the thirty-two-gun British frigate *Belvidera*. A daylong chase ensued. By noon, the *President* was within three miles of the *Belvidera*. As the fastest American ship, the *President* gradually reduced the distance, but when the breeze lightened, it was unable to come close enough to open a direct broadside assault, which would distinctly favor the more heavily armed *President*. Fearing that the *Belvidera* was about to open fire with its stern guns in an effort to injure the

President's rigging and spars, Rodgers opened fire with his bow guns at 4:20 p.m.

Rodgers himself fired the first shot as his bow chase guns attempted to cripple the enemy's "spars and rigging" and allow the *President* "to get alongside." The initial shots struck the stern of the *Belvidera*, killing or wounding nine men. The enemy responded with her stern guns as both ships exchanged fire until 4:30, when one of the *President's* bow guns exploded, shattering her own forecastle and main deck. The explosion killed one man and wounded fourteen others, including young midshipman Matthew C. Perry and John Rodgers himself. Blown into the air, Rodgers fractured a leg when he landed on the deck, but he had himself propped up and continued the fight undaunted.

Although the *Belvidera's* steady "galling" fire damaged the *President* and killed or wounded six more Americans, the *President* pursued the *Belvidera* into the evening. In an effort to bring his heavy guns to bear, Rodgers yawed the *President* to port or starboard and fired broadsides on several occasions, but this tactic failed to cripple the sailing capacity of the *Belvidera* or close the distance on her. In a final effort to escape, Richard Byron lightened the *Belvidera* by jettisoning her boats, waist anchors, 14 tons of water, and other nonessential equipment while her crew quickly repaired her sails and rigging. As the evening passed, the distance between the two ships gradually widened until Rodgers finally abandoned his chase shortly before midnight.[24]

Although he had lost a golden opportunity for the first naval victory of the war, Rogers expressed no regret. After all, the *President* was the only ship that had come in contact with and engaged the *Belvidera* in hostile action. Moreover, the war was still less than one week old, and the squadron was fewer than three days into what was planned to be a long and productive cruise against enemy commerce. However, Rodgers had lost his best chance of the entire War of 1812 to win the military glory he so keenly desired. In retrospect, it is clear that his failure to capture or destroy the *Belvidera* resulted from an unfortunate combination of his personal impatience, bad luck, and the skill and bravery of his British adversary. Rodgers's stated determination to strike a blow at the enemy induced him to be more impetuous in opening fire than a more deliberate commander might have been. In and of itself, his eagerness to strike as quickly as possible was not decisive, but the explosion of one of his bow guns that injured Rodgers was a stroke of very bad luck. The explosion created a chaos on the deck that allowed the *Belvidera* a chance to escape, a situation on which Byron readily capitalized. Rodgers has been criticized for losing ground in the subsequent chase by attempting unsuccessfully to bring his broadsides to bear by yawing his ship to port and starboard. Byron himself made this assertion, and it has been repeated by some naval historians, although others hold Rodgers blameless in this regard. For example, Captain Isaac Hull sent an account of the chase to Secretary Hamilton in August; Hull claimed the evidence "clearly proved that she [*Belvidera*] only escaped, the commodore by superior sailing after having lightened her and the *President* being very deep."[25]

Having repaired his own spars and rigging, Rodgers in the *President* and the other ships in company continued their pursuit of the large British merchant convoy. But Rodgers had lost valuable time and may well have missed his chance to catch to convoy. Five days later, the American squadron spoke a westbound American schooner, whose captain reported that he had passed the British convoy two days earlier. Three days later, the *President* "fell in with quantities of Cocoa Nut Shells, Orange peels &c &c which indicated that the Convoy was not far distant and we pursued it with zeal." But the American force was frequently diverted by having to chase other vessels, including the armed British brig *Dolphin*, which it captured on 9 July. Rodgers finally abandoned his unsuccessful pursuit on 13 July when he was "within 18 or 20 hours sail of the British Channel." From here, Rodgers turned his squadron south to pass Madeira, then the Azores, and sailed back across the Atlantic toward the banks of Newfoundland. From there, the presence on his ships of "that wretched disease the scurvey [*sic*]" forced him to head for Boston, which he reached on 31 August.

Although he had reached home safely and with his squadron intact, the cruise had disappointed Rodgers. The eastward leg across the Atlantic had been plagued with dense fog "at least 6 days out of 7 so to obscure" every vessel that was not within a four- to -five mile range. Indeed, for several days, "the fog was so thick that it prevented "our seeing each other, even at a cable's length assunder [*sic*], more than twice or thrice in 24 hours." In spite of the distance covered, the tangible results of the cruise were minimal. His squadron had chased every vessel it spotted and "brought to" all but four it had pursued. Nevertheless, it had encountered surprisingly few ships and only "made seven Captures & one recapture." Rodgers immediately informed Hamilton that "our cruise has not been as successful as I had anticipated." In his official summary, Rodgers admitted his "unpleasant task" of making a report "thus barren of benefit to our country." His "only consolation" was that his presence "at Sea obliged the Enemy to concentrate a considerable portion of his most active force and thereby prevented his capturing an incalculable amount of American property that would otherwise have fallen a sacrifice."[26]

Intensifying Rodgers's disappointment, on the day before Rodgers arrived, Captain Isaac Hull and the *Constitution* had reached Boston with news that on 19 August the American frigate had engaged and destroyed the British frigate *Guerriere*. Rodgers congratulated Hull on his "brilliant victory," but with envy. Hull had won the naval glory that Rodgers so desperately sought.[27]

Rodgers lifted his spirits with redoubled activity. His leg was "nearly well," he assured Secretary Hamilton, only a "stiff ankle remained." "I am extremely anxious to make up for time lost, at the first of the War," wrote Rodgers on 4 September. Since the men with scurvy were "recovering very rapidly," Rodgers expected to be ready to sail within twenty days. He suggested that his entire squadron sail from Boston and then separate once it reached open sea. "By this means the Enemy will for a considerable time be kept in ignorance of the disposition of our vessels," wrote Rodgers, "and, in consequence, concentrate his forces, to the advantage of our commerce." Once at sea, the squadron's frigates would cruise singly in an attempt to locate single enemy frigates "to our advantage," Rodgers assuming that the British would never attack "without a decidedly superior force."[28] As he hastened to return to action, Rodgers rationalized his previous efforts. Admittedly, his last cruise had not added "any lustre" to the American navy, but at least it had rendered "essential service to our commerce." Even "enemies of the administration" now admitted that his cruise had "been attended with infinite benefit to our returning Commerce."[29]

On 9 September, Hamilton divided the American force into three small squadrons. The squadrons would be led by Rodgers in the *President*, Decatur in the *United States*, and William Bainbridge in the *Constitution*. Hamilton authorized each commander to pursue the course most likely "to afford protection to our trade & to annoy the enemy; returning into ports, as speedily as circumstances will permit." The secretary also reaffirmed his confidence in Rodgers. Although Rodgers commanded only a small force, "yet we hope, that the acknowledged skill, vigilance & valor of our commanders will enable them seriously to annoy the Enemy. . . . with you, I am persuaded that with only half their number, of equal force, they would soon be made heartily sick of our Coast."[30]

Although Hamilton authorized each of the three commanding officers to sail separately, Rodgers and Decatur were ready for sea at about the same time and left Boston together on 8 October. Rodgers's force consisted of the *President* and the frigate *Congress*, while Decatur commanded the *United States* and the brig *Argus*. On 11 October, the two small squadrons separated from each other as Rodgers headed eastward in search of British merchant vessels. Once at sea, Rodgers also separated from the *Congress* in an effort to deceive the enemy. Believing that the two squadrons had undoubtedly been spotted by the enemy as they sailed from Boston together, Rodgers reasoned that the British would assume Americans intended to keep the squadrons together close to the American coast. Accordingly, Rodgers divided his two ships to afford his force "the greatest scope for harassing his Commerce, and . . . perplexing the Commanders of his Public Vessels."[31]

Prior to his departure, Rodgers had advised Hamilton that the commodore could not predict a "definite course of proceeding" until he was actually at sea. Clearly, the enemy's superior forces would require "me frequently to act as well on the defensive as offensive." Once at sea, Rodgers thought it "probable I may find it prudent to leave the coast and assail his commerce wherever I may hear of it . . . and after drawing his ships off our coast to its protection, return again with a more certain prospect of meeting him on equal terms." Although he intended to avoid concentrations of enemy frigates, he expected only two British frigates to be stationed off the Delaware and Chesapeake bays. If he could confirm this situation, he planned to head for one of those places "in the hope that God in his infinite goodness will permit us to get for once fairly alongside of them, ship to ship."

Rodgers was determined "not to encounter a decidedly superior force . . . or, in any way to risk action where I have not the prospect of success, as the like would be rashness in the extreme." Instead, by exercising a more unpredictable approach, "I feel confident, even with the few vessels we have, that we shall, barring unforeseen accidents, not only annoy their commerce, but embarrass and perplex the commanders of their public ships equally to the advantage of our own commerce and disadvantage of theirs." Rodgers knew that the British had recently enlarged their already superior naval force at Halifax, but he doubted that the enemy could maintain such large naval force indefinitely on "this side of the Atlantic; and at any rate, if such a one do [sic] appear, it will be only with a view to bullying us into a peace as best accords with their own interests, but which I trust" the United States would "reject with disdain." Rodgers had outlined a sound, thoughtful, and flexible plan that took into full account the enemy's superior force. His approach promised to menace British commerce, "perplex" their naval commanders, and provide the opportunity for a single ship encounter that Rodgers was obviously very confident that he would win.[32]

Initially, the cruise went well. Only a week after leaving Boston, the *President* and the *Congress* captured the British packet ship *Swallow* near the Grand Banks. It carried no cargo, but it held eighty-one boxes of gold and silver worth an estimated $150,000 to $200,000. After assisting an American schooner that had lost her mast, Rodgers dispatched both ships to the United States, but his efforts prevented him from pursuing an enemy ship in the vicinity, the thirty-eight-gun *Galatea*, which was then almost one hundred men short of her crew complement.[33] Two weeks later, Rodgers captured a British whaler returning to England with a full cargo of whale oil. Still Rodgers's luck had not turned in that he subsequently sighted few other vessels and captured none. His cruising ground took him across the Atlantic in a southeasterly direction toward the Cape Verde Islands into an area where he hoped to intercept merchant traffic bound to England from the East Indies and South America. He then sailed toward the Caribbean and eventually returned to Boston by passing east of Bermuda. After encountering rough weather, he reached Boston on 31 December, having captured only two ships and having sent an American merchant ship trading under a British license back to the United States.[34]

"It will appear somewhat extraordinary when I inform you," reported Rodgers to Hamilton on 2 January 1813, "that in our late cruise we have sailed by our log nearly 11,000 Miles, that we chased every thing we saw, yet that we would have seen so few Enemies [*sic*] Vessels." Reluctant to return home without "adding additional reputation to our little Navy," Rodgers had even cruised between Halifax and Bermuda for the past three weeks "without seeing a single Enemy's Vessel. Although he was "anxious to get to Sea again," a winter cruise was out of the question. In addition to necessary work on her spars, sails, and rigging, the *President* would require a main mast and considerable repairs to her coppering. Rodgers would be forced to endure a winter of disappointment in Boston before he could once again pursue the elusive enemy.[35]

In fact, it would be early May before the *President* was back at sea. In winter months unduly harsh even for Boston, snow and very cold temperatures slowed work on the *President*. In early March, Rodgers reported that the ground was still covered with ice and snow and the mercury hovered just above zero. Rodgers also had to adjust to a new naval secretary. Paul Hamilton, who had resigned on 31 December, was replaced by William Jones on 19 January 1813. The new secretary was a successful merchant and former sea captain from Philadelphia. In his early forties when he became secretary, Jones had been born in Pennsylvania, fought in a militia company during the Revolutionary War, been taken prisoner while he served in the Continental Navy, and eventually was promoted to first lieutenant for gallantry. He spent several years as a merchant in Charleston before returning to Philadelphia in 1793. There he prospered financially, became an active Republican, served one term in Congress, and sailed around the world on his own merchant ship. An excellent choice for secretary, Jones was a hardworking, able, imaginative person who understood naval and defense issues. He also opposed engaging the British navy in single-ship encounters because, he believed, they had little effect even when they were successful. As a result, he was prepared to praise commanders like Rodgers who spent months at sea menacing British commerce without engaging in naval battles.[36]

Shortly after assuming his new duties, Jones asked his five senior commanders for their recommendations for cruises during 1813. Jones expected the British to increase its naval force on the American coast in an effort to "blockade our Ships of War in our own harbors" while harassing American ships in coastal waters. Although "our great inferiority in naval strength" did not permit the American navy to challenge the enemy directly, Jones hoped to create a "powerful diversion" and turn "the Scale of annoyance against the enemy." By quickly sending American warships to sea and dispersing them singly into the sea lanes of the entire Atlantic Ocean, Jones sought to avoid direct encounters, instead drawing the enemy's naval forces away from "the annoyance of our own coast" in order to protect "his [England's] own, rich & exposed commercial fleets." Such a strategy would also "afford our gallant Commanders, a fair opportunity of displaying distinctly their Judgement, skill & enterprise, and of reaping the laurel of Fame . . . which so extended a field of Capture . . . cannot fail to produce." In response to Jones, Rodgers recommended that five different cruising grounds be maintained between the equator and the coast of Norway. He offered to cruise along the American coast off Chesapeake Bay in an effort to draw the blocking British forces there far enough away to enable the two American frigates then blockaded at Norfolk to get to sea.[37]

Because repairs and preparations proceeded slowly, it was not until 22 April that Rodgers left Boston and not until early May that the *President*, in company with the *Congress*, actually got to sea. The delay frustrated Rodgers, but he received encouragement from old friend Tobias Lear, who counseled that "as we used to say in the Barbary, Patience, and . . . the occasion as much wished for may arrive." Rodgers had planned a long and ambitious cruise that would take him first to the Grand Banks to harass enemy supply ships, to the Azores for three to four weeks, then to the coast of Portugal for ten to fifteen days, and north to the coasts of northern Ireland and Scotland. From there, Rodgers expected to sail into the Baltic Sea, stop for provisions in a Danish port, and then head for the "China Seas" before returning home. In selecting such a wide area, Rodgers predicted "that I shall be enabled on my return to give you a pleasing account of my cruise." Although he agreed with Rodgers's general plans, Secretary Jones rejected Rodgers plans to enter the "China Seas" by instructing the commodore not to go beyond the Cape of Good Hope.[38]

Rodgers's skills as a commander are reflected in the fact that the *President* was one of only six American warships to escape the tight British blockade and get to sea in 1813. The others were the *Congress*, the *Chesapeake*, the *Enterprise*, and the *Argus*. The *Constitution* did not get to sea until December, and the *Constellation* spent the entire year blockaded at Norfolk. Meanwhile, in attempting to put to sea from New York, the *United States*, the *Macedonian*, and the *Hornet* eluded the British blockade only by escaping to New London, where they remained indefinitely.

About six hundred miles east of Delaware Bay, the *President* separated from the *Congress* and headed north to the banks of Newfoundland, hoping to intercept a convoy of supply vessels heading toward Halifax or the St. Lawrence River. Making no contacts, Rodgers then steered toward the Azores with similar lack of result. Having learned that a convoy in the vicinity was headed for England, Rodgers gave chase unsuccessfully. In June, however, he did capture four vessels in quick succession. Three of the ships carried codfish while the fourth was a packet, which Rodgers sent to England as a cartel carrying prisoners.

Having missed the convoy, Rodgers decided to head to the North Sea. En route he hoped to intercept ships engaged in trade with Newfoundland. He found none and, in fact, did not even spot another ship until he reached the Shetland Islands. Even then, the ships he located were Danish vessels trading under British licenses. The *President* remained in the North Sea, where his fortunes improved but only slightly. In a nine-day period from 24 July to 2 August, Rodgers captured three British ships: the whalers *Eliza Swan* and *Lion*, and the brig *Alert*, carrying naval stores of pitch and tar. He ransomed the whalers for $5,000 and $3,000 respectively, burned the *Alert*, and required the *Lion* to take the prisoners from the *Alert* to Liverpool as a cartel. Although he did not know it at the time, even these modest prizes were tainted because Rodgers and his men never received the ransom money from the two whalers. Rodgers then touched at Bergen, Norway, to replenish his water and provisions but learned that only water was available. Norway was suffering from "an unusual scarcity of Bread," which limited the supply to "Not more in Bergen than a bare sufficiency for its inhabitants for Four or Five weeks."[39] At one point, as he pursued a convoy, Rodgers mistook two enemy warships to be a British ship of the line and frigate. After a nearly eighty-hour chase, he made his escape. But, in fact, Rodgers had missed a chance to engage the enemy on favorable terms because the two vessels were not a ship of the line and a frigate but only the thirty-two-gun frigate *Alexandria* and the sixteen-gun schooner *Scourge*. In fact, Rodgers had exaggerated the size of the two ships. Rodgers then headed west, made three captures off the north coast of Ireland, and captured two more cargo vessels as he steered back toward the United States.[40]

The high point of the disheartening cruise came near its end. On 23 September near Nantucket Shoals, Rodgers captured the five-gun British schooner *High Flyer* commanded by Lieutenant George Hutchinson. After the two ships had spotted each other at an estimated distance of six to seven miles, Rodgers "decoyed" the British ship. Rodgers hoisted an English ensign to which Hutchinson responded with its complement. Rodgers then signaled that his ship was the English frigate *Sea Horse*. The *High Flyer* then bore down and hove to under the stern of the *President*, where one of Rodgers's lieutenants informed Hutchinson that he should board the frigate to receive a revised signal book.

Still unaware of his plight and pending capture, Hutchinson entered Rodgers's cabin and informed him that "the main object of the British naval commander-in-chief on the American station . . . Was the capture or destruction of the *President*, which had been greatly annoying British commerce, and spreading alarm throughout British waters." After describing Rodgers himself as "an odd fish, and hard to catch," Hutchinson finally learned of his embarrassing plight and then was forced to listen to a spirited rendition of Yankee Doodle from the ship's band. Coincidentally, Hutchinson had participated in a raid the previous spring on Havre de Grace during which Rodgers's family home had been burned. Hutchinson had in his possession a sword taken from the home.[41]

From information he obtained from Hutchinson, Rodgers determined that Boston was likely to be more heavily blockaded than Newport, Rhode Island. Three days later, on 26 September, he entered Narragansett Bay without incident. Although Rodgers had covered thousands of miles in the nearly five months that he had been gone, this cruise was no less disheartening than the previous two. The weather had often been difficult and conditions on board arduous. Although they returned healthy, his officers and crew had "experienced great privations," surviving the last three months on "a Scanty allowance of the roughest fare." A total of twelve captures, most of them of little value, was small compensation for a long, difficult cruise." Once again acknowledging that his cruise had not added "any additional lustre to the character of our little Navy," Rodgers believed that at least he had "rendered essential Service to my country, I hope, by harassing the Enemies [*sic*] Commerce and employing, to his disadvantage, more than a dozen times the force of a single Frigate."[42]

Since Secretary Jones was more interested in disrupting the enemy's commerce than he was in winning isolated, single-ship victories, he congratulated Rodgers on his safe return after "an active vigilant and useful Cruize" even without the opportunity to engage an enemy warship. "The effects of your Cruize however, is [sic] not the less felt by the enemy either in his Commercial or Military Marine," commented Jones. "While you have harassed and enhanced the dangers of the one, you provoked the pursuit & abstracted the attention of the other . . . which will not cease until his astonishment shall be excited by the Account of your [safe] arrival." Rodgers also received praise from other sources. Given the "multitude of Blood Hounds" pursuing him, wrote George Blakley, Rodgers's cruise was "a most bold and brilliant one . . . it has struck with more terror than would have done the capture of half dozen of their frigates."[43]

Although Jones ordered Rodgers back to sea quickly, it was not until mid-November that the *President* sailed again, and then adverse weather prevented Rodgers from actually getting to sea until early December. Rodgers was no more successful in his fourth cruise than he had been in the previous three. In a period of seventy-six days, he recaptured one American schooner and took four British vessels. A severe gale carried the *President* far into the Atlantic before it could turn back toward the West Indies. Rodgers steered along Cayenne, down the coast of Suriname, and then turned toward the south coast of Puerto Rico. He continued along the north side of the Bahamas to the Florida coast, and then made his way north along the American coast until he reached Sandy Hook Bay on 18 February 1814. Along the way, Rodgers had spotted a number of enemy vessels that he evaded when he believed them to be part of a superior force. On other occasions, he tried unsuccessfully to engage vessels he estimated to be of equal force.

Rodgers's final opportunity to win a ship-to-ship engagement came on the last day of his cruise as he approached Sandy Hook. There, on 18 February, Rodgers discovered two British warships. When the larger of the two approached him, he prepared for battle and twice attempted to approach. Each time the unidentified vessel retreated. A revenue cutter then informed Rodgers that the vessel in question was actually a British ship of the line. When a third sail appeared, Rodgers concluded that he was overmatched and crossed the Sandy Hook bar. Rodgers did not realize that the large British ship had been mistakenly identified. She was actually the thirty-eight-gun frigate *Loire* in company with two smaller consorts. Had Rodgers known the true identity of the enemy ship, he undoubtedly would have attacked.[44]

As he had on each of his previous three cruises, Rodgers admitted to the Secretary Jones that he was "disappointed, for altho I excited the enemies [*sic*] fear, I did not do him the injury I had anticipated." In Washington, however, Jones was pleased to learn of Rodgers's safe return. Although the cruise had admittedly been "less successful than might have been expected," still Rodgers had provided "another proof of the exaggerated power and fictitious omnipresence of the British flag."[45]

Although he received some criticism, Rodgers's efforts also received public praise. On 7 March, a sell-out crowd of three hundred, including many shipmasters, jammed Tammany Hall in New York City to fete the commodore. During the entertainment, eighteen cheers responded to Rodgers's toast to "Peace—if it can be obtained without the sacrifice of national honor, or the abandonment of maritime rights; otherwise, war, until peace shall be secured, without the sacrifice of either." An eight-stanza ode to Rodgers entitled "The Warrior's Return" was also sung and included the lines:

> Then here's to the heroes high-sounding in story,
> Who're gallantly *met*, and have conquer'd the foe;
> And *Rodgers*, brave *Rodgers*, coeval in glory,
> Who's "ready, and steady," to give him a blow
>
> . . . .
>
> Then join the glad song, worth and valor commending,
> Fan the flame which in each patriot bosom should burn,
> And all honest hearts, in true sympathy blending,
> United in a toast to *the warrior's return*.

Three weeks later, a public dinner in Baltimore, presided over by the mayor, honored Rodgers and toasted him as a man "hated and feared by the enemy—revered and beloved by his countrymen."[46]

Rodgers graciously accepted and was no doubt flattered by such public expressions of gratitude, but he still had not realized the glory in battle that he sought so passionately. No doubt adding to his frustration were the dramatic victories of Isaac Hull, Stephen Decatur, William Bainbridge, Oliver Hazard Perry, and other American naval commanders. He had won for himself no personal glory, earned no fortune in prize money, and added little "luster" to the American navy. For all of the months at sea covering thousands of miles of ocean, Rodgers had achieved meager success. Four cruises produced nine ships sunk or destroyed, thirteen ships captured or recaptured, and one small British warship taken. Rodgers had not engaged a comparable enemy warship in a gun-to-gun battle after his initial unsuccessful chase of the *Belvidera*. In spite of all his bravado, a combination of plain poor luck, mistaken judgment, and admirable caution in confronting enemy forces accounted for this combat void.[47]

Still, his efforts had produced very positive, if unspectacular, results. Against wartime blockades he had gotten to sea three times, spent months ranging across thousands of miles of the Atlantic and Caribbean, harassed British sea lanes, and distracted the British navy by his efforts. Over the twenty months he spent at sea, Rodgers was reported by the British to have been in widely separated parts of the Atlantic. As a result, the British were forced to withdraw some of their naval forces from the American coast on several occasions to hunt for him. Moreover, Rodgers had avoided losing any of his ships to the British. In spite of all his boasts and personal desire for a ship-to-ship shoot-out with a British frigate, Rodgers had remained a mature and prudent commander, one who had refused to blunder into an unequal, albeit glorious engagement. The tiny American navy could ill afford to lose one of its frigates; his ship contributed far more at sea than it would in a valiant defeat to the British navy. His decisions would not play well in the annals of naval glory.[48] They made him the target of public criticism at the time and of some historical criticism since, but his war record confirmed his good judgment. In addition to the American warships that the British kept blockaded in American ports, the ten warships that the United States lost at sea during the war significantly weakened the American navy. At the same time, the few, but dramatic, American single-ship naval victories that had elated public opinion had virtually no strategic or military impact on the British navy.[49]

Rodgers personally engaged in little actual combat, but junior officers whom he had trained or commanded played a major role in naval combat. In fact, while Rodgers proved after the *Little Belt* and *Belvidera* engagements to be a prudent and cautious wartime commander, his protégés did not. During the war, they typically manifested the bravado they had previously observed in him as they aggressively challenged the enemy.

Although not an overbearing and aggressive man, Isaac Hull demonstrated extraordinary seamanship and resourcefulness as commander of the *Constitution* as he first eluded a British squadron in 1812, and then great skill and courage as he defeated the British frigate *Guerriere* in August of that year. In command of the brig *Argus*, William Allen unsuccessfully engaged the British brig *Pelican* in June 1813, a battle in which he was killed and his ship forced to surrender. In 1813, after defeating the British brig *Peacock* in his sloop, *Hornet*, James Lawrence took command of the frigate *Chesapeake*. In a hasty and ill-advised move, Lawrence challenged the British *Shannon* off the Massachusetts coast in June 1813. In the action, Lawrence lost his life and the British destroyed his ship. As commander of the sloop *Wasp*, Johnston Blakeley preyed aggressively on British merchant ships, captured the sloop

Reindeer, and sank the brig *Avon*. Although it took heavy damage, the *Wasp* continued its cruise into the South Atlantic, where it disappeared in 1814. Finally, David Porter commanded the frigate *Essex* during a legendary cruise into the Pacific, where he wreaked havoc on the British whaling industry near the Galapagos Islands before he was eventually cornered and defeated by the British warships *Phoebe* and *Cherub* in March 1814 off of Valparaiso.

In addition to Hull, the Rodgers protégé who won the greatest combat acclaim was Oliver Hazard Perry, who had served in Rodgers's New York squadron as commander of the schooner *Revenge* in the two years before the war. Although Rodgers admired Perry's courage and confidence, he was miffed when Perry lost the *Revenge* while surveying in early 1811. Cleared of charges and later transferred to the Great Lakes, Perry led an American squadron to victory in the Battle of Lake Erie, a triumph with important strategic implications for American military forces in the western theater of the war.

Although unnoticed at the time, Rodgers also continued to shape the careers of young junior officers during the war. Two of the most noteworthy were Robert F. Stockton and Matthew Calbraith Perry. Midshipman Stockton served under and impressed Rodgers on the *President* and later in the defense of Baltimore in 1814. Perry served under Rodgers on the *President* as a midshipman and then a lieutenant from 1810 to 1813, thus beginning a long relationship in which Perry first became an in-law, when Rodger's younger brother George Washington Rodgers married Perry's sister Anna Marie in 1815. After the war, Perry became a leading protégé and ally of Rodgers.

The Defense of the Chesapeake, 1814

Your name is worth a thousand Men to us and the animating influence
of your presence a thousand more.

Commander Robert Spence to John Rodgers, after the Battle of Baltimore, September 1814

When he returned safely to the United States in February 1814, John Rodgers remained an imposing military presence. An admiring contemporary writer described Rodgers as "a man of few words, and not conspicuous for the love or parade or dress," but the appearance, order, and elegance of his ship would "vie with any that floats on the ocean." The "perfect" discipline of his crew explained his reputation as "distant and very reserved to those under him; but his reserve in company carries the air of the reserve of the studious man," and his "great attention to the care of the youth under his command is a pleasing trait in this brave man's character." Given his "most cordial hatred" of the enemy, Rodgers wanted to get to sea again as soon as possible. Unfortunately, after four extensive cruises during the war, the *President* first needed extensive repairs, including new coppering, a "new suit of sail," new fore and main masts, and other time-consuming refitting. From Washington, Secretary of Navy William Jones offered Rodgers his choice of four assignments. He could retain command of the *President* or take command of one of three new ships still under construction, the frigate *Guerriere*, the frigate *Java*, or a seventy-four-gun ship of the line.[1]

Rodgers chose to take command of the *Guerriere*, which was then nearing completion in Philadelphia. After a reunion with Minerva and his three small children and an interview in Washington, Rodgers received word in mid-April that he was to transfer command of the *President* to Commodore Stephen Decatur and proceed to Philadelphia along with the officers and crew of the *President* to take command of the *Guerriere*. The Navy Department also instructed Rodgers to take command of the naval "flotilla on the Delaware."[2]

Although he hoped to sail soon, Rodgers unexpectedly would spend the rest of the war in Philadelphia and in the Chesapeake Bay area for two reasons. First, it took much longer than anticipated to prepare the *Guerriere* for sea. Second, and more important, the nature of the war itself had changed; military developments required Rodgers's presence stateside. Beginning in 1813, the British stationed additional ships along the American coast and clamped a tight blockade on the United States, targeting New Orleans, Charleston, Savannah, Philadelphia, New York, and, later in the year, New London and Newport. Only swift privateers or merchant vessels had any hope of escaping capture; American warships entered or left the blockaded ports with great difficulty. The enemy also stationed a large squadron in lower Chesapeake Bay. Under the command of Admiral Sir John Borlase Warren, it controlled access to the bay, destroyed small American ships, and kept the *Constellation* blockaded at Norfolk for the entire year. Warren also dispatched a small flotilla under the command of Rear Admiral Sir George Cockburn to the head of Chesapeake Bay to interrupt shore communication and to destroy any American military resources. Cockburn was a tough and energetic commander who relished his work; his activities in 1813 would make him a detested figure in the United States for decades to come.

Cockburn stationed his force of one light frigate, two brigs, several schooners, and four hundred to five hundred men near the mouth of the Susquehanna River in late April 1813 and began to pillage the countryside. First, he took possession of several islands from which he extracted ample supplies of fresh food. Then he moved into the Elk River to Frenchtown, a small village on the route between Baltimore and Philadelphia. Here the British dispersed light American resistance and burned property, provisions, cavalry equipment, and five small vessels.

Next the British moved on to Havre de Grace to destroy a small battery that had recently been erected there. In spite of the obvious threat posed by the British, the town of approximately sixty houses was virtually unprepared. Except for a few men on sentry duty, the local militia had dispersed before the alarm sounded at daybreak on 3 May. As the panicked residents struggled from their beds to their windows, they beheld enemy barges advancing rapidly toward the town. As the guns of the shore battery and the enemy began to exchange fire, great confusion ensued. Attempts to rally the militia failed. As fiery enemy Congreve rockets began to land, women and children scrambled for the neighboring hills and woods.[3]

Easily evading the shore battery, British troops overran it and turned its guns on the town. The sun had barely risen by the time several hundred enemy troops were ashore and assembled in the town center. Divided into groups of thirty to forty, they began to burn and plunder every house in town while a detachment of fifty men unsuccessfully pursued what remained of the militia into the countryside. The looting and destruction of property was extensive. In the midst of the action, Admiral Cockburn came ashore and, in response to the pleas of several distraught women, countermanded his initial orders. As a result, one observer estimated that only about forty of the sixty homes in Havre de Grace were burned to the ground, although every one was plundered or damaged.

Of course, Commodore Rodgers, hundreds of miles away at sea, was completely unaware that the war had struck directly at his family and his home. Minerva had been in town that morning with her sons but had scrambled to safety. On Washington Street, the Rodgers family home was looted and burned. British officers took furniture and a number of John's prized possessions as mementos. Two of John's sisters played a courageous role in preventing even greater damage to Havre de Grace. Along with a number of other citizens, the Rodgers sisters took refuge near the village in the large house of Mark Pringle. When a British detachment appeared and prepared to burn the house, the two women appealed to the officer in command to spare the house because it sheltered only children and women, including Mr. Pringle's elderly mother. Although the officer reversed his order, the house was set on fire but was saved by the extraordinary efforts of those present.[4]

After their four-hour rampage at Havre de Grace, the British force located a small foundry several miles away. Owned by Colonel Hughes, the foundry contained dozens of cannons as well as several stands of small arms, all of which were destroyed or captured by the enemy. Two days later, Cockburn's forces entered the Sassafras River, where, despite sharp resistance, they destroyed the towns of Fredericktown and Georgetown. The British flotilla then rejoined the main British squadron on the lower Chesapeake. In one week and at the cost of only a few injuries to his men, Cockburn had destroyed resistance in the upper Chesapeake, struck fear and anger into the area's residents, and created panic in Baltimore.

In the lower Chesapeake, the British continued to blockade the *Constellation*, which lay five miles up the Elizabeth River at the Portsmouth navy yard. At the mouth of the river, two strong forts protected Norfolk; five miles below these forts a battery on Craney Island provided a further line of defense. In June 1813, Admiral Warren prepared to attack Norfolk. From Bermuda, he added 2,650 marines and soldiers, including 250 French chasseurs (French prisoners of war who had entered British service). On 22 June, the British launched a two-pronged attack against the heavily outnumbered American battery on Craney Island. But as a result of poor planning, flawed leadership, and shoddy execution, the attack failed and the British were forced to retreat to their ships.[5]

Having failed at Craney Island, the British now determined to attack the small and strategically unimportant town of Hampton ten miles north on the James River. On 25 June, British forces captured the town after meeting sharp but brief resistance from American militiamen. Once they entered the town, British forces proceeded not only to plunder and loot property but also to assault a number of residents and to beat and rape several women. British officers subsequently denied any responsibility for the outrages to civilians, instead attributing them to the French chasseurs who had participated in the attack. Making no attempt to occupy the town, British forces returned to their ships two days later. News of the outrage spread fear throughout the Chesapeake and inflamed American opinion.[6]

Although the British squadron controlled the entire Chesapeake, it was not until the following year, 1814, that the enemy launched a major offensive in the area. In Europe, the overthrow of Napoleon in April now enabled the British to concentrate on the war in North America. In addition to tightening their blockade of the American coast, the British sent an additional fourteen thousand troops to the American front, where they planned coordinated land and naval operations against Lake Champlain, the Chesapeake, and New Orleans during the summer and fall.

By early May 1814, Rodgers was back in Philadelphia undertaking his new duties of outfitting the *Guerriere* and commanding the Delaware flotilla. The officers and crew of the *President* had been transferred with Rodgers to the *Guerriere*; now as they awaited the launching of the new ship, they were assigned to the Delaware flotilla. In Newcastle, Delaware, Lieutenant C. W. Morgan took direct operational command of the flotilla as it anticipated enemy incursions into the bay. Consisting of nine gunboats, three galleys, and one schooner, the flotilla under Morgan was deployed to keep any British warships in the bay at check and to "prevent depredations on the vessels trading in the Bay, as well as injury to the inhabitants residing" nearby. Rodgers instructed Morgan to station officers at Cape May and at Lewiston as lookouts to provide early intelligence of enemy ships approaching the Delaware. In typical fashion, Rodgers took steps to assure a high level of discipline, ordering Morgan to take every precaution to preserve the health of the men and the readiness of the force. Officers were not to sleep on shore. Guard patrols were to be rowed regularly. Each ship was to be supplied with shot and powder and to be exercised daily. Morgan was also to use caution in employing his small force to engage enemy ships. "The flotilla must never be exposed to an attack by the enemy disadvantageous to yourself," ordered Rodgers. Accordingly, Morgan should always avoid enemy contact and make a harbor if possible and, once there, anchor his ships "in such order as will best concentrate your forces."[7]

Although Rodgers received periodic reports of sightings of British warships, no incursion or attack developed. The most serious incident occurred on 19 June, when Rodgers's old nemesis, the British frigate *Belvidera*, entered the bay and captured a small trading vessel. Morgan responded quickly and alerted Rodgers, who prepared to proceed with reinforcements to the scene of the attack. But the *Belvidera* quickly ransomed the American vessels and disappeared before the American forces could make contact.[8]

On 20 June 1814, the *Guerriere* was launched in the presence of an estimated fifty thousand spectators. Rodgers now intended to concentrate on outfitting the new frigate and getting it to sea as quickly as possible. The 175–foot-long vessel would carry a crew of two hundred men and was rated at forty-four guns, although, when launched, she would actually mount fifty-three. During the summer, work on the *Guerriere* proceeded slowly as military events distracted Rodgers's attention. On 11 July, Admiral Cockburn resumed his marauding in the upper Chesapeake with an attack on the town of Elkton. Expecting the British to return the following night, Rodgers sent Lieutenant Morgan, 250 men, and two pieces of "Traveling Artillery" to the town, which was about twenty miles away. Marching through a rainy night over muddy and "excessively bad" roads, the American force reached Elkton in an amazing time of "three hours and forty seven minutes" but faced disappointment when the British did not reappear. Having organized, trained, and disciplined the men of his flotilla well, Rodgers lauded their "alacrity and zeal" in his report to the Navy Department. Rodgers had also sent a detachment of men to protect the Cecil furnace located near Havre de Grace.[9]

Secretary Jones praised Rodgers's direction of the flotilla as "very judicious and executed with a zeal and promptitude highly honorable," but British intentions rendered moot Rodgers's plans to protect the upper Chesapeake. Back in London, British officials had decided to invade the United States from three different points in Canada while effecting a diversion along the American coast by harassing and attacking American ports. The main diversionary activity was to come in the Chesapeake, where the British increased their already large flotilla by adding dozens of ships and several thousand men. Admiral Cochrane and Major General Ross, who was fresh from battle against Napoleon in Europe, were placed in joint command and given discretion on the details and specific objectives of their attack. Cochrane and Ross settled on three objectives. First, they would destroy the

American gunboat flotilla commanded by Joshua Barney and blockaded in the Patuxent River. Then, having destroyed all American naval forces in the area, British forces would occupy Washington and destroy Baltimore. Although it held little strategic or economic importance, the nation's capital held great symbolic value; Baltimore represented a valuable commercial center and key base of privateering activity. After sailing up the Chesapeake, the British entered the Patuxent and landed more than four thousand troops at Benedict on 19 August. The next day British warships sought Barney's gunboats while British land forces began their march toward Washington. With no route of escape open, Barney destroyed his gunboats on 23 August to prevent their capture as the British continued their march.[10]

Meanwhile, on 19 August, Secretary Jones had informed Rodgers that the British had "entered the Patuxent with a very large force" with the intention of marching on either Washington or Baltimore. Jones ordered Rodgers to proceed "with the least possible delay" to Baltimore with three hundred officers and men as well as the marines guarding the Cecil furnace. Although these orders reached Philadelphia on the morning of 22 August, Rodgers did not receive them until late that evening because he was then inspecting his flotilla at Reedy Island some fifteen miles below Newcastle. With his force of several hundred, Rodgers began a forced march south. En route on 23 August, a confident Rodgers wrote to Minerva that he expected to reach Havre de Grace tomorrow and that he did not think Washington or Baltimore was in danger because the enemy's "force is very inferior to what has been represented." Rodgers soon learned, however, that his optimism had been misplaced. On the evening of 25 August, Rodgers reached Baltimore, where new orders instructed Rodgers to march "with the utmost celerity" to Bladensburg to try to "preserve the National Capitol." But these orders proved meaningless because, as Rodgers soon learned, the British had already occupied Washington.[11]

The day before, on 24 August at Bladensburg, British invaders had routed a numerically superior but poorly organized and incompetently led American army comprised primarily of inexperienced militiamen and commanded by General William Winder. While terrified American militiamen scattered from Bladensburg and American government officials fled, General Robert Ross led British forces into the capital. They then proceeded to torch the White House, the Capitol, other government buildings, a number of private residences, and the office of the *National Intelligencer*. On orders from Secretary Jones, the navy yard and newly constructed warships there were burned by the Americans. On the evening of 25 August, the British marched out of Washington and had returned to Benedict by 29 August.

In the meantime, a small British force had sailed up the Potomac River to Fort Washington, which was just below Alexandria. Consisting of two frigates, two bomb ships, two rocket ships, and a dispatch vessel, the force occupied the fort and then, without resistance, the town on 28 August. After the town sued for terms, the British commander agreed to spare Alexandria in return for all of its naval supplies, ordnance, merchandise, and ships. The enemy received twenty-one ships as well as significant quantities of tobacco, flour, and cotton before departing on 1 September.[12]

Back in Baltimore, Rodgers awaited new orders from the Navy Department and immediately began to assist with preparations for the defense of Baltimore. He also received a panic-stricken letter from Minerva. Word of the disaster at Bladensburg had reached Havre de Grace. Having just heard that Washington was in ashes and that her brother-in-law, William Pinkney, had either been killed or seriously wounded, a terrified Minerva was afraid to ask for news of Rodgers. "Oh My Husband. Dearest of men. All other evils seem light when compared to the danger which threatens your precious safety," she confided. "When I think of the perils to which your courage will expose you I am half distracted. Yet I would not have you different from what you are but if I am permitted to behold you again in safety I shall think myself the happiest of created beings." In fact, Rodgers probably knew that Pinkney was alive but had been seriously wounded in the arm. In any event, he took a few minutes to reassure Minerva that there was "no serious cause for alarm. . . . I do not think the enemy dare attack us."[13]

From Baltimore on 27 August, Commodore David Porter reported that after news of the Bladensburg disaster had arrived, the people initially were "much disheartened and showing no disposition to defend the place," but they had quickly "recovered." On the same day, Rodgers reported that he had united his seamen and marines with those under Porter into a combined brigade of between eight hundred and nine hundred men that Rodgers would command. Intending to use them in concert with the army or onboard a flotilla, Rodgers divided the force into two regiments, one under Porter and the other under Captain Oliver Hazard Perry. Two days later, Rodgers ordered Porter and one hundred of his men to march to Washington "more with a view to Guard the Executive than anything else."[14]

Although he was ready "to march with all my strength at a moment" when deemed necessary, Rodgers intended to remain briefly in Baltimore until it could be "better fortified" in anticipation of a widely expected enemy attack. Fortunately, the "people now begin to show something like a patriotic spirit." Rodgers observed to Secretary Jones that its citizens were fortifying the town "by all the means in their power" and that their leaders "are pledged to me to defend the place to the last extremity, otherwise I should have been at Washington before this could reach you." Rodgers reported to Minerva his satisfaction that "our little band of seamen coming here at the moment they did has changed the complexion of things very much."[15]

Rodgers then marched with 650 seamen and marines to Bladensburg, where he met with Secretary Jones. The two agreed upon a plan to harass enemy forces as they retreated from Alexandria down the Potomac River. Porter was to man batteries on the Virginia side of the Potomac at a place named White House, a few miles below Mount Vernon, while Perry was to attack the enemy from Indian Head, on the Maryland side of the Potomac about ten miles below Porter's position. In the Potomac, Rodgers was to harass the retreating British flotilla from its rear with fireships.

On 3 September, Rodgers headed down the Potomac from Washington with three fireships, four barges, and sixty armed seamen. At Alexandria, he met no enemy presence and hoisted the American flag. Locating the enemy downstream near Fort Washington, he ignited his fireships and set them adrift toward the enemy's ships, but British rowboats prevented their making contact with the main force, and no damage was done. Rodgers then returned and occupied Alexandria. Since he believed that the enemy might return to retrieve a significant quantity of supplies they had left behind, Rodgers fashioned a hasty defense by mounting cannons on the wharf and organizing a company comprised of his seamen and some Virginia militiamen. Having secured Alexandria, Rodgers renewed his efforts against the British flotilla for the next two days, but his forces inflicted no damage on the British. Downstream American forces under Porter engaged the retreating British in an artillery duel, which inflicted several dozen casualties on each side. Finally, at Indian Head, Perry's detachment engaged the enemy in a one-hour exchange before being forced to retreat. All told, seven British men were killed and thirty-five wounded.[16]

On 6 September, Rodgers arrived back in Baltimore, where his temporary absence had created a minor panic. "We deplore your absence, as you were looked upon the Bulwark of the City," wrote Lieutenant Robert Spence, whom Rodgers had left in temporary command of the small navy contingent. Irritated by Rodgers's pursuit of the British on the Potomac, an uneasy Samuel Smith admitted that "I am persuaded you can do no good where you are." With Rodgers's sloops on the Patapsco River unprepared, "we are not defended [there], it is a weak point."[17] But in spite of Smith's misgivings, defensive preparations had continued in full anticipation of an imminent enemy attack. Although the enemy force was formidable, the situation in Baltimore was much different from that in Washington the previous month.

The nation's capital had been largely unfortified and unprepared. In spite of the impunity with which British naval forces had raided and marauded in the Chesapeake in 1813, Secretary of War John Armstrong had not believed that Washington would be attacked and had failed to fortify or prepare lines of defense along approaches to the city. Military command of the city was given to General William Winder from Maryland, but the appointment was made only over the objection of Secretary Armstrong, a situation that precluded their active cooperation. Winder also proved to be a poor planner, an uninspiring leader, and an inept field commander. The result was the debacle that came to be derisively labeled the Bladensburg Races.

In contrast, Baltimore had begun preparing its defenses in the spring of 1813 after Cockburn's marauding forces in the upper Chesapeake had created fear and panic in the city. General Samuel Smith took command of Baltimore's defensive preparations. As a veteran of the Revolutionary War and the commander of the Baltimore militia since then, Smith brought military experience to the task. A capable and talented leader, he understood how important basic military tactics, planning, and careful attention to detail were to success on the battlefield. A longtime resident of Baltimore, Smith was a successful merchant and an influential politician. One of Maryland's U.S. senators at this time, Smith was well connected in both local and national political circles. He not only had access to the city's business and political elite but also commanded the respect of the city's many rank-and-file Jeffersonian Republicans. As his biographer observed, a "unique blending of institutional and personal authority, of official and unofficial power, of local and national influence made Samuel Smith Baltimore's most effective leader."[18]

With Cockburn's forces nearby, the mayor and the city council created a special governmental unit known first as the Committee of Public Safety and later as the Committee of Vigilance and Safety. Comprised of the mayor and other leading citizens, the committee worked closely with Smith to take whatever measures were necessary for the city's defense. It provided support to Smith, raised large amounts of money, and scrupulously carried out his recommendations to fortify the town, recruit additional militiamen, drill and equip the militia, and seek whatever limited federal resources were available.

Most pressing in 1813 was the poor condition of the city's existing fortifications. Baltimore was located twelve miles from the mouth of the Patapsco River. As the river approached the city, it split into two branches: the right fork, named the Northwest Branch, led directly to the main waterfront, while the left fork, named the Ferry Branch, veered to the west but at one point still came within a mile of the city. Between the two branches was Whetstone Point. Here stood Fort McHenry, which guarded both branches and served as the critical defensive obstacle to a British assault on Baltimore. To strengthen the fort, two massive fortifications were rebuilt, sixty large guns added, and the size of the garrison increased. Opposite the fort, across the Northwest Branch, stood a lazaretto that Smith armed with a three-gun battery and backed up with a line of armed barges. To protect Fort McHenry from a rear attack from the Ferry Branch, Smith constructed two small batteries, named Fort Covington and Fort Babcock, a mile up the river to the west. Smith also began the construction of gunboats and prepared to sink hulks in the river to impede a British advance up the river. The British would menace and blockade Baltimore for almost a month in the spring of 1813 and returned later, but they did not attack and finally withdrew in late August 1813.[19]

These preparations during 1813 had placed the fortifications guarding the water approach to Baltimore in reasonably good condition by the time the British reappeared in 1814. The main defensive problem was now the roads approaching the city from the east. Smith believed that the British forces would land fifteen miles east of Baltimore at North Point near the mouth of the Patapsco River and then march up the peninsula formed by the Patapsco and Back rivers, approaching Baltimore from the east. Expecting as many as seven thousand enemy ground troops, Smith ordered extensive trench and ground work done at Hampstead Hill on the edge of the city. There, during the last days of August, hundreds of citizens worked with picks and shovels. Whites and African Americans, both free and slave, labored away to create what became formidable groundworks. At the same time, Baltimore's defensive force grew dramatically as thousands of militiamen appeared from Pennsylvania, Virginia, and Delaware. Expecting a force of only five thousand, Smith ended up commanding about fifteen thousand men.

When Rodgers arrived back in Baltimore on 6 September, he immediately threw himself into the final defensive preparations there. In cooperation with General Smith and Major George Armistead, the commander of Fort McHenry, Rodgers worked tirelessly. He deployed and drilled his naval forces, helped build land fortifications, prepared gun batteries, and sunk old hulks in the channel on both sides of Fort McHenry. Most of Rodgers's troops were stationed on the Patapsco River, where their main mission was to help defend the fort and to prevent British ships from entering the harbor and bombarding the city. Although Fort McHenry was well fortified, plenty remained to be done as Rodgers took primary operational command of the Patapsco River defense. He and Smith agreed where additional vessels should be sunk, where the gunboats should be deployed, and where various small batteries should be placed. In addition, Rodgers divided and deployed his navy seamen and marines. About one thousand men from the navy manned the battery on the lazaretto, the water battery of the fort, as well as the guns at Forts Covington and Babcock. Included were some two hundred seamen and marines under the command of Lieutenant Thomas Gamble, who manned gun batteries at a crucial point on the main road near Hampstead Hill. They came to be known as the "Rodgers Bastion." Although Rodgers rode constantly between the widely separated naval detachments, he maintained his headquarters near those of General Smith on Hampstead Hill.[20]

He may have contributed little to the defensive strategy and tactics, which had already been devised, but Rodgers did bring an important presence and resources to a critical situation. First, he added several hundred well-disciplined veteran seamen, marines, and gunners to the defensive force. Second, his readiness to work cooperatively with and, in effect, serve under the command of General Smith avoided any of the distractions that had surfaced previously when Smith's authority had been challenged by others. On numerous questions such as the placement of guns, the use of gunboats, or the locations for sinking hulks, Smith and Rodgers agreed. Third, Rodgers's extensive naval experience and expertise was an invaluable resource to Smith. Fourth, Rodgers's illustrious national reputation and his standing as a senior naval officer in the prime of his career added credibility to and increased public confidence in Smith's strategic plans.

The British had settled on precisely the two-pronged land and water assault that the Americans had anticipated. A land force of approximately 4,500 men would be led by Major General Robert Ross and accompanied by Rear Admiral Cockburn. Admiral Cochrane would sail a naval flotilla of frigates, bomb ships, sloops, and rocket ships up the Patapsco toward Fort McHenry. On the morning of 12 September, British land forces disembarked at North Point and began their fifteen-mile march up the peninsula toward Baltimore. The British encountered little resistance until they approached the narrowest point of the peninsula between Bear Creek on the south and Back River on the north. There they met an advance force of three thousand American militiamen commanded by General John Stricker. An extended afternoon artillery duel ensued before the Americans were forced to retreat. The inexperienced Americans had fought well, but they lost 163 killed and wounded in inflicting significant losses on their enemy. The British lost forty-six killed, including their commander, Ross, and 295 wounded. The next morning, the British resumed their march and by midmorning reached a point about one and one-half miles from Baltimore. Here their new commander, Colonel Arthur Brooke, studied the defenses and decided that, with the assistance of the British flotilla, he would attempt a night attack on the American entrenchments.[21]

Meanwhile, the sixteen-ship British flotilla had moved up the Patapsco on 12 September and was in position to attack Fort McHenry the next morning. In order to enter the harbor, Cochrane needed to destroy the cannons at Fort McHenry and the guns at the lazaretto. Since his huge ships of the line could not enter the Patapsco, Cochrane had to rely on his frigates and bomb ships. Under the command of Major George Armistead, one thousand regulars, sailors, militiamen, and volunteers manned the fort. In addition, booms and twenty-four sunken hulks blocked the river between the fort and the lazaretto with its small battery. Inside the harbor, American gunboats awaited any British ships able to pass the sunken ships. The British attack began at sunrise from bomb ships that were out of the range of American guns. After firing a few initial rounds, the American guns desisted. For the next several hours, the bomb ships assaulted the fort as the defenders and their guns waited inside. At about 2 p.m., the British frigates advanced on several occasions, but each time the American cannons forced their retreat. Whenever the British attempted to close the range, American guns drove them back. The shelling continued throughout the day and night.

Eventually the British fired more than 1,500 rounds at Fort McHenry but inflicted only light damage and never seriously threatened the fort. Watching the shelling was Francis Scott Key, an American militiaman who had gone aboard a British ship to secure the release of a local physician being held prisoner. The British also detained Key onboard until after the battle had ended. There Key witnessed the spectacular attack firsthand as he paced the deck of the ship. On the morning of 14 September, he penned his timeless lines describing how "the star-spangled banner" had withstood "the rocket's red glare" and "the bombs bursting in air." Key's simple poem was quickly printed and put to music, becoming wildly popular, but it was not until 1931 that Congress would officially designate the "Star-Spangled Banner" as the national anthem.

Finally, at 1 a.m. on 14 September, the British sent twenty armed vessels and two hundred men up the Ferry Branch. The cover of a rainy and exceedingly dark night allowed them to pass Fort McHenry undetected. The British intended to land troops behind the fort and capture it. Once past the fort, however, they were detected by Americans at Fort Covington. In the exchange that followed, Rodgers's experienced naval gunners at Forts Covington and Babcock, assisted by the guns of Fort McHenry, forced the enemy ships to retire. One British barge was destroyed, and all of her men killed. Although enemy boats were forced to withdraw, the British maintained its increasingly futile fire until 7 a.m. The previous evening, Admiral Cochrane had decided that a naval assault on Baltimore was futile and so informed Colonel Brooke, who had himself determined that a continued land attack would also be too dangerous and costly to mount. Accordingly, on 14 September, both British land and naval forces began their withdrawal as Rodgers reported to Secretary Jones that the "enemy has been severely drubbed as well his Army as his navy and is now retiring down the river.[22]

Although the Battle of Baltimore was not as bloody as that at Lundy's Lane had been in July, as strategically important as the Battle of Lake Champlain on 11 September, or as decisive as the Battle of New Orleans four months later, the defense of Baltimore represented a major American victory. Coming as it did in the immediate aftermath of the defeat at Bladensburg and the burning of Washington, Baltimore furnished a success story in which the American public rejoiced. With many Americans expecting Baltimore to be overwhelmed, the British retreat came as a most welcome surprise. Well-organized and courageous American naval and land forces had defended the nation's third-largest city. As it turned out, similar positive news soon arrived from Plattsburg and Lake Champlain in upstate New York, where Americans had just defeated a British invasion force on 11 September.

Baltimore had been saved through a combination of careful planning, sound strategy, widespread cooperation, exceptional leadership, and hard work. Although many individuals had played essential roles in the success, the well-deserved hero of the day was General Samuel Smith. Indeed, "he was the chief architect of victory, the man whose energy, stature and personal prestige made Baltimore capable of resisting the British. From first to last it was his triumph."[23] But Smith readily acknowledged "the great aid I have derived from Comr. Rodgers. He was ever present & ever ready to afford his counsel and to render his important services. His presence with that of his gallant officers & seamen gave confidence to everyone." At the same time, Rodgers distinguished himself at Baltimore in the critical days of September, when he served as a confidence builder and source of critical expertise. "Your name is worth a thousand Men to us," observed Lieutenant Spence, "and the animating influence of your presence a thousand more."[24] Once the battle began, Rodgers and his well-trained men performed admirably. From his headquarters at Hempstead Hill at one point, Rodgers actually directed a militia unit that was formed behind his naval batteries on the hill. Rodgers communicated with his widely scattered detachments through his aides, who moved under fire back and forth between headquarters and his units. These men and the batteries that Rodgers had created on the lazaretto, in the water battery at Fort McHenry, at Forts Covington and Babcock, and on barges in the river between Fort McHenry and the shore all worked effectively and courageously.

After the British had retreated, Rodgers briefly assumed command of Fort McHenry, where he reported proudly that the "Navy and everything connected with it in this quarter has done well and stands preeminently high in the estimation of all who have witnessed its exertions." Rodgers commended the men at Forts Covington and Babcock for performing "the duty assigned to them to admiration" and the lazaretto battery for its "constant and animated fire . . . during the whole bombardment, altho placed in a very exposed situation to Rockets and Shells." Likewise the battery at Fort McHenry had served exceptionally well, and the men of the barges deserved special praise for firmly maintaining their position under enemy rocket and shell fire. "In a word, every Officer, seaman and marine belonging as well to the Navy as to the Flotilla performed his duty in a manner worthy of the corps to which he belonged."[25]

Local papers praised Rodgers, and the citizens of Baltimore would later honor him, but he and his men did not linger. By 23 September, they had returned to Newcastle, Delaware, expecting another British attack. Rodgers went about the business of preparing to defend Philadelphia, but the anticipated British attack never came. In late November, Rodgers began to dismantle the Delaware flotilla for the winter after reporting that all trace of the enemy was gone. In the meantime, he had resumed preparing the *Guerriere* for a winter cruise, but progress was slow.[26] The new frigate would not be ready until the new year, and the department had not provided a consort. Rodgers unsuccessfully requested that an existing naval vessel be assigned and finally received permission to purchase a merchant ship, which he refitted in late December.[27]

In the meantime, President James Madison had asked Rodgers to become secretary of the navy after Secretary Jones resigned. Rodgers replied that although the offer was "flattering to my pride . . . my abilities are not of a kind to justify my acceptance. . . . No, sir, neither my habits, temper, or education" were suited to the position. Nevertheless, he would accept the position "for a limited time" on the condition that the appointment not be done "at the expense of interfering with any rank or further pretensions as an officer of the Navy." Because the retention of Rodgers's rank represented a "legal incompatibility," Madison looked elsewhere for a new secretary.[28]

Rodgers remained in Philadelphia, where Minerva visited him in early December. Although the war was close to its end, John and Minerva did not expect hostilities to cease soon. As John continued to outfit the *Guerriere*, Minerva worried about what the new year might bring. Almost overcome with anxiety, she departed for Havre de Grace in mid-December, leaving John to spend the holidays alone. Once she reached home safely, she wrote to John that she had "commenced her journey with severe mental pangs which there was some cause to apprehend would produce bodily ones not less acute. . . . [I]t took all my best attempts at fortitude as the carriage drove off & deprived me of the sight of your beloved countenance . . . I was ready to exclaim the trial was too great to endure." For his part, John returned to his busy schedule and by Christmas Eve had settled comfortably into his new cabin on the *Guerriere*. He apologized for not sending her a gift and for writing such a "milk & water kind of letter, but it is now eleven o'clock & I have no time to devote to the little God for fear of falling into a train of thinking that might disturb my repose." A bit perturbed, Minerva responded that her husband seemed too comfortable without her. "Me thinks you bear my absence with too much philosophy & you have not" told me that "your slumbers are less profound, that your appetite has decreased or that you look & feel like a picture of melancholy! In short I begin to find that my presence is not of so much consequence as I have been flattering myself it was."[29] As a turbulent year ended, both John and Minerva expected another one in 1815.

President of the Board of Navy
Commissioners, 1815–1824

*The navy will never again I fear present such a field for the acquirement
of glory as it has done as war with no other nation can afford such a field—
The peace, particularly at this moment, has deranged all my plans, & [were]
it not for the ardor of my love for you, I think [I] should nearly grow crazy.*

Captain John Rodgers to Minerva, February 1815

The new year began seamless with the old one as an anxious Minerva continued to fret back in Havre de Grace and John Rodgers readied the *Guerriere* for sea. He had purchased a merchant brig, which he renamed the *Prometheus* and armed to serve as a consort. However, by early February, just as he was finally ready to sail, news of a peace arrived from Europe. In fact, the United States and Great Britain had signed a peace treaty on Christmas Eve at Ghent. The new secretary of the navy, Benjamin Crowninshield, ordered Rodgers to Washington for a different assignment.

The United States had reached a major historical turning point that would strongly impact the navy and its officers. The War of 1812 was over, and peace had returned to Europe. In the Mediterranean, where Algiers had renewed hostilities during the War of 1812, an American squadron under Commodore Stephen Decatur extracted a peace treaty in 1815, followed by guarantees of peace from Tunis and Tripoli. The United States would not fight a major war again for three decades. After 1815, the United States would disengage itself from European affairs as it focused on its own economic development and territorial expansion in North America.

This new epoch created a new peacetime role for the republic's navy. Since 1798, the navy had been almost continuously involved in the defense of American commerce or in hostile operations against France, the Barbary powers, or Great Britain. After 1815, the threat to American commerce came not from enemy warships but from scores of privateers and pirate vessels operating in the waters of the Caribbean and elsewhere. The navy's primary peacetime role now became the protection of American commerce overseas. Specifically, the navy would not only fight privateers and pirates but would also police smuggling, show the flag in various ports around the world, perform limited diplomatic duties, and maintain a continuous presence on various distant overseas stations.[1]

For veteran naval officers, this new mandate changed and reshaped their careers. No longer called upon to be warriors who engaged in battle with the warships of other nations, naval commanders rarely made dramatic headlines or become instant national heroes in the decades after 1815. Instead, their peacetime assignments usually required them to be well connected politically; career advancement favored capable administrators, careful planners, and patient negotiators in quasi-diplomatic roles.

Although he had not achieved dramatic battle victories, John Rodgers was a naval warrior by inclination, training, and reputation. But he was also well suited to excel in this postwar peacetime navy. Well connected to influential politicians and government officials, he was known as a capable administrator who had mastered the demanding details of naval command. He was also by nature a thorough and careful planner. It was undoubtedly these attributes that had led President Madison to offer Rodgers the position of secretary of the navy the previous fall.

In February 1815, the direction of Rodgers's career changed dramatically when he was offered the position of president of the newly created three-man Board of Navy Commissioners. The board represented an important attempt by Congress and the Madison administration to reform the administration of the Navy Department, which consisted of a civilian secretary of the navy, an accountant, and several clerks. From the field, the commanders of the navy yards, various navy agents, and the commanders of all ships had considerable latitude but reported directly to the secretary. He, in turn, made all major decisions, authorized all administrative actions, and wrote instructions to each commanding officer.[2]

Quite understandably, the exigencies created by the War of 1812 overwhelmed the department and exposed its administrative deficiencies. Secretary William Jones had worked tirelessly to deal with the myriad details of supplying, arming, provisioning, and manning the navy while attempting to provide some strategic direction to American naval forces. Inundated with duties, Jones reported in early 1813 that he was burdened "with the cognizance of details and with the execution of duties which divert his attention from the sound direction of the great and efficient objects" of the navy. As a result, he asked that Congress create a naval purveyor's office and give him two additional clerks.[3]

In November 1814, Jones submitted an extensive reorganization plan to Congress. In addition to requesting additional battleships, the secretary proposed that naval construction be standardized, that a permanent career naval service be created, and that a naval academy be established. Jones also pinpointed administrative changes needed in the department. Most important was the creation of a "board of inspectors," consisting of three naval officers and two civilians with naval expertise. The new board would be located outside of Washington at a major seaport. The secretary of the navy would assign each of the inspectors individual responsibilities divided as follows: general correspondence and the preparation of reports; naval personnel; ordnance and transportation; provisioning and medicine; and equipping of naval vessels. In addition, Jones suggested the appointment of a chief and two assistant naval constructors and a navy paymaster. Ironically, Jones's proposal would have seriously weakened the secretary of the navy by stripping the position of most of its duties.

In response, a committee of the House of Representatives sent Jones's report to every captain in the navy for comment. Although the congressional committee received numerous differing opinions and recommendations, general agreement on several changes emerged. The naval officers wanted civilians excluded from the board; they wanted the inspectors to act collectively, not individually; and they wanted more power left with the secretary than he himself had recommended.[4] Although Rodgers's response was not included in the congressional report, he had expressed his views directly to President Madison in November 1814, when he declined the position of secretary of the navy. Recognizing that the requisite naval expertise and "scholastic education" needed for the position were rarely to be found in one person, Rodgers suggested a combined board of navy "directors." The "duties of the navy office" would be executed by a three- to five-man board of naval officers whose presiding officer would be the civilian secretary. The board would serve as the "organ of communication" between the Navy Department and the executive branch, would control all "the fiscal duties" of the department, and would manage the department's other responsibilities.[5]

In January, a House committee proposed the creation of a board of navy commissioners. The accompanying report claimed that three factors necessitated the reorganization: the "excessive and laborious duties" of the secretary; the lack of sufficient checks on naval agents in the field; and the excessive "latitude allowed commanders in altering, repairing, and furnishing their ships." After prompt consideration, both houses approved the bill, and President Madison signed it on 7 February 1815. The principal feature of the act was the establishment of the Board of Navy Commissioners. Attached to the office of the secretary of the navy, the board would consist of three navy captains to be appointed by the president and confirmed by the Senate. Under the secretary's supervision, the board would discharge all the "ministerial duties" of the department relative to the "procurement of naval stores and materials, and the construction, armament, equipment, and employment of vessels of war, as well as all other matters connected with the naval establishment of the United States." The act specified that nothing was to be so construed as "to take from the Secretary of the Navy his control and direction of the naval forces of the United States, as now by law possessed." With the ranking member serving as president, each board member would receive a $3,500 annual salary in lieu of rations and other fringe benefits. The board was authorized to adopt its own operating rules as well as to hire a secretary and two clerks to assist with its work.[6]

Secretary Crowninshield immediately asked Rodgers for advice on who should be appointed to the new board. In a memo that briefly, but candidly, assessed the strengths and weaknesses of his fellow captains, Rodgers recommended a combination of either William Bainbridge, Isaac Hull, and Charles Morris or of Hull, Morris, and David Porter. President Madison offered Rodgers, Hull, and Porter positions as the first navy commissioners. If he accepted, Rodgers would also serve as president of the board because he was the senior officer of the three.[7]

When Secretary Crowninshield formally extended the offer on 8 February 1815, Rodgers was forced to make a major career decision. Although the Senate ratified the peace treaty with England on 17 February, Congress was also expected to authorize war and naval action against Algiers. The question for Rodgers was whether he should pursue command of a naval squadron or accept the desk job in Washington. As he hastily prepared to leave Philadelphia for Washington, he informed Minerva of the offer and asked for her "wishes on the subject & what figure you think [I] should make attending to the 'dull pursuits of domestic life.'" Rodgers confessed that "the navy will never again I fear present such a field for the acquirement of glory as it has done as war with no other nation can afford such a field—The peace, particularly at this moment, has deranged all my plans, & [were] it not for the ardor of my love for you, I think [I] should nearly grow crazy."[8]

Obviously delighted by this turn of events, Minerva immediately replied that "no earthly advantage could outweigh the happiness which would result from having you at home in perfect security. . . . Therefore I trust you will have nothing to do with an Algerine war & yet I am far from being insensible to the voice of Fame nor am I so contracted in my ideas as to think that your life should be devoted to me and my children." Acknowledging that her husband was destined to play his part on a "scale of more extensive use," nevertheless she argued that the naval mission to Algiers would not add to his "reputation." Concurring that peace with England meant that "the navy will no longer present such an ample field for glory as it has hitherto done," she reassured her husband that he had much to "exult in altho you have not like some others excited the clamoring and unmeaning voice of popular applause, you know that there are some valuable hearts which duly appreciate the value of your services." In her judgment, his "exertions" for his country "will ever" provide a "pleasing retrospect" and "like a vernal sunshine gild the remainder" of his life.[9]

At age forty-two, Rodgers still hungered for naval glory and was hardly ready to leave sea duty behind, but he thanked Minerva "for her affectionate solicitude," announced that he had accepted the presidency of the board, and asked that she prepare to move to Washington. He immediately began the daunting task of looking for a home, confessing his inadequacy to Minerva: "this is the only thing in which I feel much dread of being able to suit your taste."[10] In the spring of 1815, Rodgers acquired a home for his family in Bellevue on the heights of Georgetown.

Whatever misgivings Rodgers might have had about his decision were assuaged by the encouragement of friends like Isaac Hull, who would be one of his new colleagues on the board. Hull assured Rodgers that he would be happier in Washington living "with your charming family." Hull admitted that the new squadron offered a "very handsome command, but whether much honour and glory is to be acquired is to be uncertain—I fear much that the expectations of our country could not be realized [by] sending our ships alone." Also helping to ease his transition was a letter from Samuel Smith announcing that a citizens' committee from Baltimore was planning to honor Rodgers's role in the defense of Baltimore by presenting him with a formal plate service worth $4,000.[11]

In 1815, Washington was still little more than a village in a rural setting. Board secretary James K. Paulding referred to it as a "rather dull place" in the fall when Congress was not in session, except to "sportsmen, who find excellent shooting about the centre of the city. I have seen a great number of quail, plover, and snipe within a couple or three hundred yards of the President's mansion." In spite of its rural attributes, Washington was very different from a place like Havre de Grace. First, it was a political town. Paulding described it as an "odd place" where "everybody and every thing seems to hang on the Government. There is a regular gradation from the President downward. Did you every see a basket of crabs, lifted up body and soul, by taking hold of the top one? Just so it is here—take hold of the President and you raise the whole city, one hanging at the tail of the other." Second, it was a town where Paulding found social gossip pervasive. As a bachelor, he estimated that there "are at least a thousand women, who being too lazy to work and too stupid to read, 'have no delight to pass away their hours' but by attending to the affairs of other people." Washington, then, was not a place that would be readily embraced by sheltered and family-oriented Minerva.[12]

Rodgers's decision to become president of the board affected both his professional career and his personal life. Since they had married in October 1806, John and Minerva had never had their own home or a separate life of their own. They had lived together only for brief periods in the Rodgers family home in Havre de Grace or during brief sojourns together when Minerva visited John at one of his posts. Now, in 1815, Rodgers would be both a full-time husband and father. For the first time, John and Minerva could fashion their life together as husband and wife while they raised their family together. The family now consisted of Robert, age six; Frederick, age four; John, age three; and infant Elizabeth, who was born in 1815. In the next seven years, the Rodgers family would continue to grow as Minerva gave birth to four more children: Louisa in 1817; Jerusha Carolina in 1819; William Pinkney in 1821; and Henry, or Hal, in 1822. Along with the eight children, the Rodgers household included a retinue of domestic slaves. By the early 1820s, Rodgers owned approximately ten slaves, including a body servant, a coachman, a nurse, a cook, a maid, a gardener, and two table waiters. In late 1822, Rodgers arranged for the gradual manumission of four of his youngest slaves. Twenty-two-year-old Maria would be freed at age twenty-five, but three young male slaves ages three, five, and nine would not be freed until they reached age thirty. Rodgers was clearly doing well financially despite having failed to make his fortune in prize money. Nevertheless, he had earned $19,743 in prize money during the war, a figure roughly equivalent to $174,000 in 2005 dollars. By 1823, not including his $3,500 salary as board president, Rodgers listed assets of more than $36,000, including real estate in Washington and Havre de Grace, $3,500 in Bank of the United States stock, $3,200 in Columbia Manufactory stock, and a $5,000 interest in a lumber business located in Havre de Grace.[13]

The Rodgers family soon needed a larger residence to accommodate their growing numbers. In 1820, John purchased extensive grounds and two houses at Greenleaf Point, which is located at the apex of the land between the Potomac River and its Eastern Branch. Renovations connected the two houses that had their address on P Street. By then Washington was a small but growing town of about twelve to thirteen thousand residents who lived in different clusters around the White House, the Capitol, the navy yard, and the post office, all at least a mile from one another. Farther removed across Rock Creek was Georgetown, then a town of some seven thousand. In effect, the Greenleaf Point residence placed the Rodgers family in a rural setting with few close neighbors. John was about two miles from the board's offices in the old Navy Department building and about a mile and a half from Congress.[14]

There is every reason to believe that Rodgers adjusted readily to his new life. He seems to have spent and enjoyed a great deal of time at home. For example, he did not use his new navy position as an excuse or pretext to leave Washington for extended periods of time. On the few occasions when an assignment did take him away from home, he complained about his absence in his letters to Minerva. Unfortunately for posterity, his almost continuous presence in Washington for the decade after 1815 meant that he rarely had reason to exchange personal letters with Minerva.

Rodgers would spend virtually all of the next ten years in Washington as a desk captain, not a ship or squadron commander. Unlike other officers like Hull, who served briefly on the board and then resigned in preference for a field command, Rodgers seemed quite comfortable with his administrative position. The only temptation to leave the board came in 1818, when President James Monroe offered Rodgers the position of secretary of navy. Although more favorably inclined to take the position than he had been in 1814, Rodgers again declined when the administration affirmed that he would have to resign his naval commission. Whatever attractions the secretaryship might have held for him, they palled in comparison to the prestige, prerogatives, and financial security of his commission as a senior navy captain. A minor flap followed his decision when colleague David Porter sent an item to the *National Intelligencer* on Rodgers's behalf. The article denied that Rodgers had been offered the position, an assertion to which Secretary of State John Quincy Adams took offense. As men of "honor," asked Adams, how could Porter and Rodgers "justify themselves for passing this deliberate falsehood on the public?" Apparently, Porter's submission had been a misguided attempt to avoid diminishing the stature of Smith Thompson, who was offered the position when Rodgers declined it.[15]

The Board of Navy Commissioners convened for its first meeting on 25 April 1815, with David Porter and Isaac Hull present and Rodgers sitting as president. They selected a secretary and two clerks to assist with the board's business. When L. W. Tazewell of Virginia declined the position of secretary, the board appointed James K. Paulding, who served until 1823. A particularly important appointment as one of two clerks was C. W. Goldsborough, who had served previously as a clerk in the Navy Department, brought solid experience to his position, and was a loyal friend of Rodgers. Subsequently replacing Paulding as board secretary in 1823, Goldsborough served until the board was replaced in 1842.

The board's operating rules specified that its office would be open daily, except Sundays, from 10 a.m. until 3 p.m. All business was to be submitted in writing; correspondence would be opened only by the board and would be handled on a first-come, first-served basis unless extraordinary circumstances dictated otherwise. Attesting to the serious intent of its members, board rules specified that no member was to leave Washington without the consent of the other two.[16]

Almost immediately, an authority dispute arose between the board and new secretary of the navy, Benjamin Crowninshield, who had assumed his duties the previous January. A native of Massachusetts, Crowninshield was an experienced sea captain whose family had earned a fortune in the East Indies trade. He had served briefly in the Massachusetts legislature and then been elected to the U.S. Senate in 1812. Although he would prove to be a weak administrator, the new secretary vigorously defended his civilian authority from board encroachment.[17]

The initial legislative proposal of the previous naval secretary, William Jones, had transferred important powers from the secretary to the board and had not addressed the details of specific administrative authority. Although the actual legislation significantly modified the initial plan, the bill had been hastily considered and passed and, as a result, did not address in detail the relationship between the board and the secretary and their respective spheres of authority. Specifically at issue were the "ministerial" powers granted to the board and the extent to which those powers were to be exercised independent of the secretary. When the board asserted that the secretary was required to communicate to it the destination of a squadron, Crowninshield demurred, claiming the transmission of such information was his prerogative. At stake was whether the board or the secretary would control information on the movement of naval forces and the disposition of navy personnel. The board claimed that its "ministerial duties" required such information. If the secretary could reserve to himself the execution of any part of the board's duties, then "the object of the Law would be defeated and the powers of the Board completely nullified."[18]

When Crowninshield refused to concede, the board appealed directly to President Madison. Although they continued to meet daily, the commissioners conducted no business for more than three weeks in May and June as they waited for a reply.[19] Finally, Madison resolved the dispute with a letter on 12 June 1815. The president pointed out that the secretary of the navy was the "regular organ of the President" for the business of the Navy Department. Accordingly, no direct relationship existed between the board and the president. The board was attached to the office of the secretary, and its "ministerial duties" were to be discharged "under his superintendence." "The ministerial duties to be performed by the Board are the ministerial part of the duties of the office of the Secretary." To say that its authority in discharging these duties provided it with "an independent power" would, if taken "in a literal and absolute sense," make the board independent of both the president and the secretary. Such independence "could not be contemplated by the Legislature."

At the same time, Madison emphasized that while the board was required to discharge its duties subject to the "superintendence" of the secretary, in executing his responsibilities the secretary was "restricted to the intermediary functions of the Board" and was not to employ any separate officers to discharge its duties. In Madison's opinion, "with the consent of the Secretary" and the approval of the president, the board was specifically authorized to prepare rules and regulations for "securing uniformity in the several classes of vessels and their equipments, and for repairing and refitting them, and for securing responsibility in the subordinate officers and agents."[20]

Madison's authoritative statement ended the controversy. Although the board's correspondence seemed to indicate that it sought to supercede the authority of the secretary, that seems not to have been the case. Its subsequent actions indicate that the board was less concerned with expanding its authority than it was in clarifying its powers. The board did not have a specific set of powers that it was determined to control, but it did seek total authority over those "ministerial duties" that had been delegated to it. The board readily accepted the president's decision. At a meeting on 15 June, Crowninshield and the board resolved their differences by clarifying the meaning of "ministerial duties" and identifying those matters on which the secretary would consult with the board.

The board would control the building, repairing, and outfitting of ships and superintend the navy's yards, stations, and dry docks. The secretary would control the appointment and assignment of officers, the movements of ships, and naval discipline. The board could advise the secretary on personnel matters and other unspecified naval matters. In effect, the controversy had relegated the board to acting as a technical body that dealt almost entirely with issues of construction, equipment, armament, naval contracts, and personnel rules. Apparently it had very little close day-to-day interaction with the secretary, although the official correspondence indicates that the board and secretary kept each other well informed of their respective activities.

The new board performed its duties with great energy and expertise. After Stephen Decatur replaced Hull in November, the board benefited from stable membership until 1820. Laboring to make the new administrative entity a success, Rodgers, Porter, and Decatur worked and met every day except Sunday. Other than for periodic visits and annual inspection tours of naval facilities around the country, board members rarely missed the daily meetings or left Washington. From the outset, Rodgers dominated the board and its proceedings for several reasons. First, he set high standards of competence and efficiency for the board in addition to presiding at all meetings and signing virtually every letter and document sent by the board. Second, he was also the board's senior officer, which meant that other board members, all of whom were friends or former subordinates, deferred to him.[21] Third, Rodgers proved to be an extremely capable administrator with a dominant personality, an energetic man who worked tirelessly and mastered technical details easily. Finally, Rodgers displayed important interpersonal skills. Since they were a small group in a close working relationship, the personal feelings of the three commissioners about one another mattered. On a number of occasions in his first years as president, Rodgers had to mediate between Decatur and Porter as the two sparred on their respective duties.[22]

The records of the board indicate that the commissioners reviewed and took action on hundreds of administrative items each year, bringing improved order, efficiency, and system to the administration of the navy. The commissioners improved the department's financial system and instituted the practice of procuring supplies by contract. They approved supply and service contracts, scrutinized innumerable supply purchases, and collected information on naval facilities and personnel. They pushed for the establishment of naval hospitals, attempted unsuccessfully to reduce the number of navy yards, insisted on public construction of new battleships, and recommended the establishment of a naval academy. In addition to improving the naval accounting methods and making various estimates, the board instituted important checks against fraud and misuse of public funds by navy agents, pursers, and contractors.[23]

Rodgers and the board took a particular interest in improving naval ordnance. On a number of occasions during the War of 1812, guns on American warships had accidentally exploded. Chauncey had lost twenty-two men when a gun exploded on the *General Pike*, and Decatur had lost forty-nine men to an explosion on the *Guerriere*. And, of course, Rodgers himself had been wounded and had lost fifteen men when one of his deck guns on the *President* blew up in 1812. To address the problem, the board provided funds to three foundries to improve their works, funneled all contracts for naval contracts to these firms, and appointed an ordnance officer to visit and inspect the factories. To systematize armament on large warships in 1820, the board specified that frigates and ships of the line were to carry 32–pound guns on the gun deck and 42–pound carronades on the spar decks.[24]

Rodgers and the board also brought uniformity to navy personnel regulations. Early regulations written as early as the Revolution by John Adams and revised in 1798 needed to be updated because the size of the navy and the complexity of its duties had increased. In 1800, Congress had adopted the navy's disciplinary code, or Articles of War, but many practices and rules had never been codified. In 1818, under Rodgers's leadership, the board completed a comprehensive revision of the "Rules, Regulations, and Instructions, for the Naval Service," which outlined standard naval practice and remained in effect for half a century. The new set of rules showed the board at its very best. The rules reflected not only the expertise and command experience of three very capable and committed senior officers but also the high standards of performance and conduct to which they themselves had adhered during their careers. Containing thirty-eight sections, the new regulations outlined in great detail the duties and expectations of commissioned officers, noncommissioned officers, and various naval specialists. Specific regulations governed the administration of the navy yards, including the duties of a yard's commander, master shipwright, storekeeper, and purser. General instructions for officers required that they set "an example of morality, regularity, and good order" and that they maintain the ship or ships under their command in a condition of "order, discipline, and attention to cleanliness" while preserving the health of their men and ensuring that naval regulations were enforced. Also addressed were issues of rank and command, military honors, naval ceremonies, formal salutes, and even the specific duties of minor positions such as chaplain and cook.[25]

The commissioners sought to codify what had become known as the "Rodgers system of discipline." Ships were to be maintained in top condition. Officers were to engage their crews in constant activities to exercise the guns, keep the ship clean, maintain the sails and rigging, and maintain a current inventory of stores and provisions. An officer should be "constant in his attention to detail, never absenting himself, except on public service, without the consent of his commander." And, except in very special circumstances, officers were not to be absent from their ship overnight, for more than twenty-four hours, or "after the setting of the watch."[26]

The new regulations devoted considerable detail to the promotion of health, discipline, and cleanliness among the crews. Men were to "wash themselves frequently," bathe three times a week in summer, change their linen at least twice a week, and never sleep in wet clothes or wet beds. To ensure "cleanliness, dryness, and pure air," the upper decks were to be washed every morning; the lower decks were to be washed, swept, and ventilated as often as necessary; and the ship was to be pumped out daily. The new rules even specified the daily rations and clothing items, or "slops," to be provided to crewmen. On Tuesdays, for example, each ration would consist of 2 pounds of cheese, 1 pound of beef, 14 ounces of bread, and 1 ounce of sugar. On Thursdays, the ration would be 4 ounces of suet, 20 ounces of beef, 8 ounces of flour, 14 ounces of bread, and 1 ounce of sugar. Beef was to be cut and stored in 10–pound pieces, pork in 8–pound pieces. The daily grog ration was set at 8 ounces. The 1818 regulations make very tedious bureaucratic reading, but they represent a significant achievement in bringing professional naval expertise to the administration of the Navy Department and guiding the service with high professional standards for decades to come.[27]

Although one might have predicted that the volume of naval technical and administrative activity might have decreased after the War of l812, just the opposite was true. Having achieved noteworthy success in battle during the war, the navy benefited directly from the public upsurge in patriotism and an increased support in Congress. In the immediate aftermath of the war, the Madison administration strengthened the nation's economy and defense. In 1816, in addition to approving a new protective tariff and establishing the second Bank of the United States, Congress authorized an expanded peacetime navy. "An act for the gradual increase of the navy of the United States" provided $1 million annually for eight years to build 9 seventy-four-gun ships of the line and 12 new forty-four-gun frigates. The act also authorized the president to acquire the equipment for three steam batteries.

This act ranks as one of the most important in American naval history. For the first time, the United States had committed itself to a program of peacetime naval expansion, one whose purpose was to establish a navy comparable to those of Europe. Between 1816 and 1822, construction began under board supervision on the nine ships of the line. Construction of the first ship, the seventy-four-gun *Columbus*, was started at the Washington navy yard in 1816, and it was launched in 1819. For various reasons, progress on the other ships was slow. As late as 1842, four had still not been launched. Upon the recommendation of the board and the secretary, Congress approved another act in 1820 that authorized the construction of five small warships of not more than twelve guns each for service in the waters of the West Indies and West Africa. The construction of new ships ensured that the board would be fully employed with the details that accompanied the building, arming, outfitting, and launching of the new warships. By 1818, in typical bureaucratic fashion, the board was complaining that it was understaffed and asking for additional personnel.[28]

Although constituted as a technical, not a policy, body, the board played an influential advisory role on various policy issues for two reasons. First, Rodgers and his fellow commissioners furnished a ready source of expert advice for Congress and the administration. Second, from 1815 to 1823, both Benjamin Crowninshield and his successor, Smith Thompson, proved to be weak secretaries of the navy. Both were poor administrators with minimal expertise on naval and defense matters who, furthermore, absented themselves frequently from the department. Crowninshield remained in Washington only for the few months each year when Congress was actually in session, thus leaving his chief clerk to conduct most naval business. Also known for his absenteeism, Thompson was once away from his office for eight consecutive months in 1819. The board stepped readily into this vacuum to offer advice and opinions on an array of naval issues. Even when Crowninshield or Thompson were present, the two secretaries routinely referred technical and policy questions from congressional committees to the board.[29]

On occasion, the opinion of the board significantly influenced the legislative process. The 1816 naval expansion act seemed to signal a new national policy of long-term naval expansion. In fact, the new policy and the act itself were being criticized within several years for two reasons. First, the act that authorized the construction of large seventy-four-gun ships of the line and forty-four-gun frigates did not suit the postwar naval needs of the nation. In order to protect widely spread American commerce overseas, combat piracy in the West Indies, and police the illegal slave trade in West Africa, the navy needed small, fast ships that could operate in shallow coastal waters as well as on the high seas. In accord with traditional naval policy, the new battleships were designed primarily to deter potential aggressors and to demonstrate the nation's naval might overseas. But President Monroe did not believe that a fleet of active battleships was necessary in peacetime. Instead, he wanted battleships that would remain in ordinary in peacetime but could quickly be launched and manned with volunteers in a crisis. In Congress, antinavy politicians questioned the need for and utility of new large warships.[30]

Second, the Panic of 1819 and ensuing economic crisis led to congressional calls for government retrenchment. An obvious target was the Naval

Expansion Act of 1816 and its annual $1 million price tag. By 1820, only one of the new ships of the line, the *Columbus*, had been launched and only one other battleship was on active duty. In January, in an effort to reduce military spending, Kentucky congressman Tunstall Quarles moved for suspension for a limited time of the $1 million annual appropriation for naval construction, arguing that suspension was merited by the nation's severe financial problems and by the current peaceful state of foreign relations. "Does not prudence dictate that we pause awhile and inquire whether the nation had not better omit so much of the appropriation as applies to building the vessels?"[31]

The motion was referred first to the Naval Affairs Committee, then to the secretary, and finally to the board. Speaking for the board, Rodgers answered ten questions and supplied detailed information about the total costs, future contractual obligations, and construction status of four ships of the line and one frigate then in progress. With respect to suspending ongoing contracts, the board recommended that the financial savings would be outweighed by the potential long-range negative impact. For example, the continuing contracts with American ordnance manufacturers were designed not only to meet immediate needs but also to ensure the development of domestic producers of the high-quality ordnance that had been a serious deficiency for the navy in the War of 1812. Likewise, the ongoing contracts with American canvas factories were designed to eliminate existing American naval dependence on foreign suppliers.

In response to the question of whether construction could be stopped for a limited time "without material injury to the ships now building," Rodgers argued that suspending construction would damage those warships. Moreover, Rodgers warned, the 1816 act had provided the means to achieve "Certain great national objects." "To render the means adequate" to these "objects . . . the expediency of progressing [with construction], particularly when so great a portion of the means has already been applied . . . is a consideration of no little weight."[32] In a report that temporarily buttressed the naval construction program, the board strongly recommended that the nation's belated attempt to build a first-class navy not be abandoned. Congress took no action in 1820 to suspend the program but renewed debate on the issue during its next session because the economy had not improved. Even then, Congress decided not to suspend the naval construction program but rather to reduce the annual cost by one-half while extending the program for three additional years.[33]

As a resident of Washington and an active naval officer, Rodgers became involved in various personal situations and naval duties not associated with his official position. The most tragic of these was the duel between Stephen Decatur and James Barron on 22 March 1820. The origins of their feud dated at least to the *Chesapeake* affair in 1807. The court-martial that tried Barron in 1808 had included Decatur as one of its members even though Decatur had announced that he was already prejudiced against Barron. When Barron's counsel did not object, Decatur continued as a member of the court that subsequently cleared Barron of the most serious charges but found him guilty of neglecting to clear the *Chesapeake* for action and sentenced him to a humiliating five-year suspension without pay from the navy. To earn a living, Barron spent the next decade working in the carrying trade in Europe. When his suspension ended in 1813, he became eligible for a naval assignment in the War of 1812, but he did not return to the United States until 1818, claiming that personal poverty had prevented him from returning earlier. Once back, Barron requested restoration to active service, a request that, if granted, would have placed him second only to Rodgers on the naval seniority list by 1821. The findings of a court of enquiry in 1821 did nothing to resolve the matter. Composed of Captains Samuel Evans, Charles Morris and Charles Stewart, the court acknowledged Barron's "sincere and earnest desire to return to the United States" during the war but concluded that since the evidence of his "inability to return sooner than he did, is not satisfactory . . . his absence from the United States, without permission of the government, was contrary to his duty as an officer in the Navy of the United States." Although the commissioners and every captain in the navy, except for Richard Dale and Jesse Elliott, opposed Barron's request, an extended personal campaign and support in the Monroe administration eventually restored Barron to active duty in 1824.[34]

Barron faced a difficult situation in 1818 in that he remained a disgraced outcast with most of his fellow naval officers, while Decatur's fortunes and stature had soared. A combination of his naval exploits, exemplary character, and charismatic personal qualities had catapulted his stature to that of the preeminent naval hero of his day. Serving under Barron as a young officer during the Barbary War, Decatur had first become a national hero following his daring mission to destroy the *Philadelphia* in 1804. Then, in 1812, Decatur's brilliant victory over the *Macedonian* brought him into the limelight once again. Finally, in 1815, his naval and diplomatic mission to Algiers, Tunis, and Tripoli added more luster to Decatur's fame. Even though he had earlier surrendered his warship, the *President*, to British frigates off Long Island in January 1815, the rapid end of the War of 1812 and his subsequent mission to the Mediterranean left Decatur's reputation largely unscathed.

Although he publicly manifested a heroic ideal, Decatur had fatal character flaws. His exaggerated sense of honor and acute sensitivity to slights against himself, his uniform, and his country had involved him in a series of affairs of honor and played an important role in the dispute with Barron. After Barron had applied to be restored to active status, in several conversations (some of which were reported back to Barron), Decatur openly and sharply criticized Barron's fitness for active service. Direct correspondence between Decatur and Barron began in June 1819, escalated in October and November, and led to a formal challenge from Barron in January 1820. Fueling Barron's resentment was his belief that he had been unjustly blamed for the *Chesapeake* affair while Decatur had been completely exonerated for surrendering the *President* to the British. Once challenged, Decatur readily accepted it over the objections of both Commodore Charles Morris and Rodgers, who along with Porter declined to serve as Decatur's second. Rodgers urged Decatur to decline the challenge because his unparalleled naval combat record placed his personal courage and honor above reproach. Unmoved, Decatur finally convinced William Bainbridge to serve as his second.[35]

Barron selected as his second Captain Jesse Elliott, who had served under Barron on the *Chesapeake*. A difficult and controversial man, Elliott readily fomented dissension in the service and had a sharp enmity for Decatur. This hostility dated from the postwar controversy between Oliver Hazard Perry and Elliott over the latter's role in the Battle of Lake Erie and the question of whether Elliot had kept his ship out of the battle while enemy fire was battering Perry's ship. Because Decatur had sided with Perry in the dispute, Decatur became a logical target for Elliott's scorn after Perry died in 1819. The festering enmity between Decatur and Barron suited Elliott's troublemaking talents perfectly.[36]

The duel was set for 22 March 1820 at Bladensburg, Maryland. The two met with pistols at the deadly range of eight paces, or only about twenty-four feet, on a cold, damp morning. At the time, dueling involving American naval officers at home and abroad was a relatively common practice. But these duels almost invariably involved young, hot-headed, prideful midshipmen and lieutenants. The duel between Decatur and Barron represented a sharp departure because the two participants were experienced, middle-aged, senior captains.[37]

Once on the field, the two men presented a sharp contrast: the forty-one-year-old Decatur a medium-height, dark, handsome man in the prime of his life, and the fifty-one-year-old Barron a tall, paunchy figure with red, puffy facial features. According to accounts of the duel, while final arrangements were being made, Barron called out, "Now Decatur, if we meet in another world, let us hope that we will be better friends." Decatur replied, "I was never your enemy." Although the seconds could have taken this exchange as an opportunity to stop the duel, Bainbridge said nothing, and Elliott quickly hurried the antagonists to their places. The two men stood sideways at their positions. They were to aim at first command and then fire between the second and third. Both men fired simultaneously, staggered, and fell. Each had been hit in the hip. Decatur's shot glanced off Barron's femur and inflicted a painful wound in the thigh, but Barron's shot deflected from Decatur's hip into his abdomen—a mortal wound.[38]

Within minutes Rodgers and Porter anxiously appeared from nearby, previously aware of the scheduled duel. As the two wounded and bleeding men lay on the ground awaiting medical attention, a strange scene developed. In a panic, Jesse Elliott left the field and fled toward Washington. Porter pursued him, overtook him, and finally persuaded him to return to the scene to assist Barron. In the meantime, Rodgers had ridden up, dismounted, and glared at the fallen Barron briefly before turning to assist Decatur. According to Barron, when Rodgers came back later to ask if Barron was hurt, Barron responded that the last time the two had met, Barron had tipped his hat to Rodgers, who had not returned the compliment. Now Barron told Rodgers that "you must apologize for that, before any question of yours will receive an answer from me." A potentially ugly exchange between the two was averted by the reappearance of Porter.[39]

Decatur was taken back to his home on Lafayette Square in Washington, where he was helped inside by Rodgers; Decatur would die in great pain that night. Barron was moved to a friend's home, where he remained in seclusion. The senselessness of the tragedy was heightened by the fact that it might well have been prevented. The role of Decatur's board colleagues, Rodgers and Porter, might have been proper but it was certainly not admirable. Admittedly both Rodgers and Porter had advised Decatur not to participate, but neither had taken the initiative to actually prevent the duel.

News of Decatur's death stunned the nation. In Washington, the inexplicable loss of a beloved hero in his prime created an outpouring of grief as Congress adjourned on the day of Decatur's funeral. With Rodgers serving as a pallbearer, the services were attended by all of official Washington, including the president and the chief justice. Saddened by the death of his friend, Rodgers also seethed over what he considered to be Barron's insulting comments to him in the immediate aftermath of the duel. Accordingly, on 23 March, he sent Porter to Barron's bedside to demand a satisfactory explanation or possibly another duel. In great pain and with a high fever, Barron was in no condition to make a thoughtful response. Fortunately, the matter went no further after intermediaries carefully drafted a statement that both Rodgers and Barron signed. Each man disavowed his hostility and affirmed kind and friendly feelings for the other.[40]

More than two years later, Rodgers found himself involved in another feud between naval officers, this time in his official capacity. After he had left the board in 1815, Isaac Hull resumed command of the Boston navy yard. There a series of disputes arose between Hull, as commandant of the yard, and William Bainbridge, as commander afloat at the station. Later, Hull clashed with Captain John Shaw and Lieutenant Joel Abbot. The ugly result was a series of trials in 1822. First, Shaw received a six-month suspension, then Abbot received a two-year suspension. Finally, to clear his own name against accusations of fraud and mismanagement, Hull asked for his own court hearing in the summer of 1822.

Since they were then conveniently in New York en route to Boston on an inspection tour of navy yards, Rodgers and Captain Isaac Chauncey were logical choices for the court. They were joined on the court by Captain Charles Morris. Since there were no specific formal charges against Hull, the court conducted an inquiry to determine whether formal charges should be brought. Rodgers expected the proceedings to take about two weeks, but they proved to be a long and unpleasant process. Convening on 12 August 1822, the court met for nine weeks before adjourning on 15 October. The court took 244 pages of testimony from seventy-six witnesses, some of whom testified several times. In spite of the allegations of mismanagement and fraud against Hull, the few concrete charges leveled were ultimately discredited.

In fact, Hull had been careless and imprudent in some of his actions. For example, when the navy declined to purchase a piece of land adjacent to the navy yard, Hull bought it himself and later sold it to the navy at a small profit. On other occasions, he had personally employed workmen from the yard to work on his own property and paid them in an irregular manner. Eventually, the court found that though Hull had lacked discretion in some of his actions, there was insufficient evidence to charge him with fraud or misconduct in office.[41]

With his friend exonerated, Rodgers happily left Boston to return to his family and his regular work routine. The senior officer in the navy since 1821, Rodgers worked smoothly with new commissioners Isaac Chauncey and Charles Morris. Then, in September 1823, after Rodgers had served briefly as the interim secretary of the navy, the Navy Department ordered Rodgers to south Florida on an unhealthy mission. In December 1822, the department had appointed David Porter to command the West Indies squadron in an effort to attack rampant piracy against American merchant ships in the Caribbean. Although Porter had pursued his mission zealously, he received a serious setback in August 1823, when yellow fever struck his squadron at the naval rendezvous at Thompson's Island, or Key West. Dozens of men, including twenty-five officers and Porter himself, were stricken.[42]

When word of the contagion had reached Washington, the new secretary of the navy, Samuel Southard, acted quickly and proposed to President Monroe that one of the navy's "oldest and most experienced officers," along with three skilled surgeons, be sent "as speedily as possible" to investigate the "origin, causes, and progress of the disease" on the island. In fact, Rodgers had already agreed to lead the mission, which, as Southard explained, would provide immediate medical assistance to the sick at Key West, quiet "the public mind" about the situation, and avoid complete evacuation of this important base. His orders instructed Rodgers to proceed with three surgeons as quickly as possible from New York in the schooner *Shark*. Once they reached Key West, they were to attend to the sick and investigate the contagion on the island. Rodgers was also to form a "correct opinion" on the "propriety of continuing the vessels" at Key West and of using the base thereafter "during the sickly season." Having completed the investigation, Rodgers was to either leave the squadron in place or order its removal to a safer location. In the event that Porter's health required him to leave, Rodgers was to place someone else in command.[43]

Yellow fever was a little understood and lethal disease at this time. Although he could have easily dodged this potentially dangerous assignment, Rodgers readily agreed to investigate personally at the height of the epidemic at Key West. When John Randolph of Roanoke learned of the mission, he expressed his hope that Rodgers would "escape [the dangers of the climate] and every other danger & may speedily return to your country & Family." Rodgers's decision reflected his typical unwavering sense of duty and characteristic disregard for his own personal safety even if he had misgivings about his danger. He later admitted that when he sailed, "it was not, I must confess, without some little apprehension that I might never return, but the service to be rendered . . . was mentioned to me in such a way . . . as impelled me as well from a sense of honor, as of duty to undertake it without hesitation."[44]

The *Shark* left New York on 6 October and reached Key West seventeen days later after a rough, disagreeable passage. When he arrived, Rodgers learned that Porter had already left along with all but one of the ships of his squadron. Rodgers also found that 59 of the 140 officers, seamen, and marines who remained on the island were sick. Rodgers paid ten dollars per person to have the sick men transported to Norfolk. Since the disease had assumed a much milder form in the previous three weeks, Rodgers predicted that the remaining force would be sufficient to man the island. Four days later, Rodgers reported no new cases and predicted that as the weather cooled, the health of the men there would continue to improve.[45]

By 29 October, the team of surgeons accompanying Rodgers had completed its report on the likely causes of the disease. About half of the island's area consisted of shallow salt and freshwater ponds that receded during the dry season and exposed a mass of vegetable and animal matter . . . to give miasma its most powerful effect on the human frame." Beyond these "miasmatic causes of disease," the surgeons cited other causes. They noted the negative effect on men of a sudden and sharp exposure "of northern constitutions to a tropical climate," the "fatigue and exposure" of officers and crews on active duty, the lack of fresh and wholesome food, the constant annoyance of mosquitoes and sand flies, and the lack of restful accommodations.[46]

Despite these findings, Rodgers recommended that Key West be retained as a naval rendezvous. Although the island generated "bilious, and probably malignant fevers," Rodgers entertained his own "doubts whether those causes" were decisive ones and noted that the surgeons' report did not attribute the disease "entirely to any one cause." From his own experience, Rodgers found the climate of Key West generally similar to that of the islands of the West Indies. It was "perhaps less salubrious than some, more so than others." Still its excellent harbor and strategic position on the map made Key West "too important an object in a political and commercial point of view, to be suffered to remain unoccupied and unregarded." Perhaps it should be used only as an auxiliary station to a permanent and large base at another location such as Pensacola, but Key West should not be abandoned. For the United States, it served not only as "the advance post, from which to watch and guard our commerce passing to and from the Mississippi" but also as "the most certain key to the commerce of Havana, to that of the whole Gulf of Mexico, and to the returning trade of Jamaica." Rodgers also predicted that "the first important naval contest in which this country shall be engaged will be in the neighborhood of this very island."[47] Based on his report, the navy continued to use Key West as a rendezvous, although it never attained the strategic importance that Rodgers assigned to it. After spending ten days there, Rodgers departed, reached Hampton Roads by 16 November, and returned to Washington one week later.

Although Rodgers soon settled back into his desk job, his term as president of the board would end the next year. On 22 July 1824, a large dinner honored Rodgers as he prepared to leave the board to lead a major naval and diplomatic mission to the Mediterranean. In attendance at Gadsby's Hotel were Secretary of State John Quincy Adams, Secretary of the Navy Southard, Secretary of War John Calhoun as well as other government officials, naval and army officers, and assorted dignitaries. The marine band played and vocal music was sung, including a specially written and entirely forgettable song in honor of Rodgers. The guests drank forty toasts, which kept them late into the evening and no doubt challenged their sobriety. Rodgers himself toasted the Union and gave a "neat Address" in response to the toast in his honor: "Commodore Rodgers—As distinguished in his professional character, as he is estimable in private life."[48] As he basked in this moment of public recognition, Rodgers had good reason to feel great pride, but he also knew that a difficult assignment loomed ahead.

Commodore of the Mediterranean
Squadron, 1825–1827

*I think about scenes which live only on the page of memory—when the ardent
feelings and romantic anticipations of youth lent a charm to every object—
"Dim are the long past days. Yet they still please, like sounds half heard,
borne on the inconstant breeze."*

Minerva Rodgers in 1827, contemplating her husband's return after his two-year absence

On 15 December 1824, John Rodgers announced his resignation from the
Board of Navy Commissioners. The fifty-one-year-old captain had agreed
to hoist his "broad pendant on board the *North Carolina*" to command the
Mediterranean squadron. Although this assignment was the most presti-
gious command in the navy, Rodgers had been reluctant to accept it. The
board presidency clearly suited him well, and he saw the work of the board
as important. Excelling in this desk job, Rodgers also enjoyed the distinction
that accompanied the position and the praise that he received for his work.
For example, even President James Monroe directed Secretary of the Navy
Samuel Southard to convey the "high sense entertained by the Executive of
the zeal, intelligence and skill at all times manifested by you" in the discharge
of your duties as a commissioner.[1]

Rodgers had also settled happily into the life of a family man. While keeping him in close proximity to his job, the Rodgers's home at Greenleaf Point
kept John and Minerva away from the swirl of the capital's social politics. By
the beginning of 1825, Rodgers and Minerva had produced ten children, nine
of whom still lived. Of these, Robert Smith at age fifteen, Frederick at age
thirteen, and John at age twelve were the oldest. The others were all under
ten years old: Elizabeth age nine, Louisa age seven, Jerusha Carolina age five,
William Pinkney age three, Henry (or Hal) age two, and Ann Minerva (or
Nannie) not yet one year old. With six of them under age ten, the Rodgers
children were a demanding brood. Even with considerable help from several
domestic slaves and servants, Minerva had her hands full and her time spo-

ken for. The prospect of her husband's extended absence seemed daunting and promised to load a myriad of additional family responsibilities on Minerva. In addition to keeping the family's financial accounts, she would have to deal with the condition of the house, the adequacy of the wood supply, and the management of their slaves and servants.

Accepting command of the Mediterranean squadron also required a significant sacrifice from Rodgers. He could expect to be gone for at least two years and probably longer. At first, Rodgers resisted. Secretary of State John Quincy Adams noted in his diary in May 1824 that Rodgers was reluctant. In addition to wanting the flagship to be the *Columbus*, not the *North Carolina*, Rodgers explained that there "are difficulties of economic and domestic arrangements—deficiency of pay, and some question of additional expense which a meeting with the Capitan Pasha may render necessary."[2]

Rodgers probably would have turned down the assignment had it been a routine one. But command of the squadron in 1825 promised a difficult and complex challenge. As commander-in-chief of the Mediterranean squadron during the Greek war for independence, Rodgers would be expected to protect American commerce in the Levant from Greek pirates and privateers. His actions and words there would need to maintain the neutrality of the American flag, convincing the Turkish of the American government's impartiality in spite of the American people's vocal sympathy for the Greek cause. This would also be a sensitive diplomatic mission to Turkey, where he would try to meet with the grand admiral (or Capudan Pasha) of the Turkish fleet to convey the terms on which the United States hoped to conclude a formal commercial treaty with Turkey.

In addition, the department expected Rodgers to help revitalize the sagging image of the American navy by restoring discipline and order to its Mediterranean squadron. By the mid-1820s, the public stature of the navy had deteriorated as personal disputes and animosities among naval officers played out publicly in the press or in naval trials. The restoration of peace in 1815 and then, four years later, the Panic of 1819 had combined to provoke renewed calls for a smaller and much less expensive navy. Although construction continued on new warships, few had actually been launched and fewer still placed in active service. Hundreds of officers were either unemployed or underemployed on watch duty at half pay. Midshipmen, lieutenants, and master commandants saw little hope for positive change or promotions. Tensions grew between junior officers seeking opportunity and senior officers clogging the promotion channels. "In this climate, aggressions formerly expended on the national foe turned inward," one historian has observed, "and the navy seethed with quarrels between officers—with accusations, courts-martial, and duels—reaching a kind of crescendo of acrimony in 1825 and gradually declining thereafter."[3]

The new secretary of the navy, thirty-six-year-old lawyer and newspaper editor Samuel Southard, seemed to lack the stature to deal with these thorny problems. Even though he would emerge as an outstanding secretary, Southard seemed a poor choice at the outset of his six-year term in 1823. Appointed to the Senate from New Jersey in 1821, Southard lacked maritime background, extensive national political experience, or demonstrated administrative talents. Indeed, one of Southard's friends bluntly advised him to decline the appointment: "'stick to your law and to politics about which you know something; but let alone the navy about which you know nothing.'" Another asked Southard, do "you know the bow from the stern of a frigate?" Once in the position, Southard dispelled doubts about his capacity to head the department. As a result, newly elected president John Quincy Adams asked Southard to continue as secretary in 1825. While he won respect for his administrative ability, Southard was still unable to quell the growing acrimony among officers. In 1825, the secretary wrote to Rodgers of Southard's concern for senior officers in the department. "I feel some anxiety for the present state of the service—every weapon is in motion . . . [and] produces towards the *older officers* much feeling & prejudice."[4]

Key to the navy's image problem was the poor condition of the Mediterranean squadron. As the most internationally conspicuous squadron, the Mediterranean fleet symbolized the nation's naval power. Its ships were visible to many European naval officers, government officials, and diplomats. On shore, the conduct of American naval officers and sailors embodied the character of the American republic to a monarchical Europe. By the 1820s, American misconduct and rowdiness had increased as brawls among sailors as well as duels between officers became more common. Gambling and public drunkenness were rife. As discipline in the squadron had declined, national and international respect for the American navy suffered. You will find the service "much changed since you were at sea and I apprehend that you will be good deal annoyed and perplexed aft first," warned Isaac Chauncey in early 1825, "but by a steady strict forward course you will soon bring the officers back to the *old discipline* and I anticipate much good . . . in your command."[5]

Eventually the importance of the job and his abiding sense of duty overcame Rodgers's misgivings. There were other capable senior captains who could have restored discipline to the squadron, but no other naval officer was better qualified than Rodgers to deal with the sensitive diplomatic and political situation in the eastern Mediterranean. As the navy's senior officer and an individual imbued with patriotic duty, Rodgers appreciated that he simply could not decline such a critical request from the president and his cabinet. Fully aware of the pain his absence would cause Minerva, Rodgers later wrote as he departed "to beg that you will not suffer your fortitude to forsake you, for be assured that to maintain my own standing in the Navy & promote its interests it had become absolutely necessary, that the sacrifice attending our separation, for a time, should be made."[6]

Although Rodgers preferred the ship of the line *Columbus*, the department designated the *North Carolina* as his flagship. When the cabinet had considered the issue, the secretary of war argued convincingly that since the *Columbus* had already sailed in the Mediterranean, the new seventy-four-gun *North Carolina* should be assigned "to show variety of force" there. In addition to the *North Carolina*, the squadron included the frigate *Constitution* under Captain James Macdonough; the sloop of war *Erie* under Commander David Deacon; and the sloop of war *Ontario* under Commander J. B. Nicholson. Rodgers was to replace Commodore John Orde Creighton, who would return home in the corvette *Cyane* once Rodgers had arrived. Captain Daniel T. Patterson would serve as captain of the fleet; Commander C. W. Morgan as captain of the flagship; and Matthew Calbraith Perry as first lieutenant. One of the midshipmen on the *North Carolina* would be Rodgers's fourteen-year-old son Frederick.

In addition to his sailing orders, Rodgers carried instructions from outgoing Secretary of State and President-elect Adams, who believed it "probable" that in the course of the cruise Rodgers would meet the Turkish fleet commanded "by the Captain Pasha," who had "long entertained favorable sentiments towards the United States." If Rodgers was able to arrange a meeting with the pasha, Rodgers was to ascertain how the United States might obtain "a treaty of commerce, founded upon principles of reciprocity, and by which access to the navigation of the Black Sea should be secured to the commercial shipping of the United States."[7]

Adams assigned George B. English to serve as Rodgers's diplomatic secretary and interpreter. A former marine who had served as an agent of the secretary of state in Constantinople, English had returned to the United States in 1824 to report that European diplomats in the Turkish capital had effectively poisoned American chances of negotiating a commercial treaty. However, English also reported that the pro-American grand admiral had suggested an alternative approach. He offered to meet directly with the American commander of the Mediterranean squadron and then personally convey the terms of a proposed treaty to the Turkish sultan.

On Sunday, 30 January 1825, an entourage of forty dignitaries including

President Monroe, Secretary Southard, congressmen, and senior naval officers toured the *North Carolina* near Ragged Point in the Potomac River. They were entertained by the ship's band, cheered by the crew, and honored by a formal salute. After attending a shipboard religious service, the visitors were led to the ship's 1,100–volume library and then fed a sumptuous lunch. As Rodgers had planned, his guests left with a highly favorable impression of the magnificent new American warship.[8] In February, the *North Carolina* moved to Hampton Roads to make final preparations, which included the issues of discipline and morale in the squadron. In a letter to captain of the ship Morgan and in another to all officers onboard, Rodgers had already served notice of the conduct he expected. In his judgment, a "relaxation of discipline" among junior officers had created "dissentions and bickerings," a "prevalence and frequency of fighting and quarreling," and "indecorous animadversions" in public places." Henceforth, he expected all officers to observe and enforce "due respect and obedience to the laws and regulations" of the navy and would not tolerate the "slightest violation of such laws and regulations." Disputes between officers were to be resolved only through appeal to the captain of the ship. Rodgers later issued additional directives mandating that all officers wear proper uniforms when they went ashore and that midshipmen discontinue the common practice of loaning money and articles of clothing to one another.[9]

The *North Carolina* finally sailed for the Mediterranean on 27 March 1825 and anchored at Algeciras near Gibraltar after a difficult thirty-three-day passage during which "the weather was almost incessantly boisterous and unpleasant." To his "surprise as well as mortification," Rodgers did not find a single squadron vessel there and was initially unable to determine the squadron's whereabouts. He was particularly irritated by the absence of the *Constitution*, which had sailed from the United States the previous October. In fact, the squadron was at Messina and did not join him until June.

Once he had arrived, Rodgers found the fleet to be undisciplined and in disarray. "The insubordination & vices of various kinds that have been prevalent on this station among the officers of a certain class are such as ought never to have been permitted," he privately wrote to Minerva. The absence of the American squadron when Rodgers arrived seemed to Captain Patterson to be a clear case in point. The *North Carolina* had sailed into Gibraltar "with the private signal of the day flying at the Fore, under a full expectation of its being answered by our Squadron" to find "not . . . a single Vessel here to make a reply." Such a "mortifying circumstance" promised to "elicit remarks & give rise to speculations among the foreign Officers, and Citizens of Gibraltar highly disadvantageous to the discipline & organization of our Navy,—the appearance was very bad." Patterson detailed the incident in his journal, concluding that "such occurrences are greatly to be lamented, inasmuch as they may frustrate the views of the Government, evince want of system, or subordination, & great irregularity."[10]

By 1825, officers, sailors, and marines in the squadron had a well-earned reputation for dissipated and rowdy behavior. Brawls between Americans, with sailors of other navies, and with local residents occurred frequently. Dueling persisted as a few oversensitive American officers occasionally defended their personal "honor" against real and imagined insults from fellow Americans and from foreign officers. Before Rodgers reached Spain, a midshipman named Joshua Barney had killed a fellow midshipman. The seconds were also to have fought, but their duel was temporarily delayed and then broken up by Spanish authorities. At Port Mahon, dozens of prostitutes reportedly had been permitted onboard American warships.

Disarray in the squadron had increased under Rodgers's immediate predecessor, Captain John Orde Creighton, even though Creighton was an overbearing commander whom Alfred Thayer Mahan later labeled the "greatest martinet in the navy." Preoccupied with "smartness, order, and spotless cleanliness" in his ship's appearance, Creighton applied "an undue amount of that spirit of the good housekeeper which makes a home unbearable." His fits of anger and verbal abuse of his officers created resentment and personal discomfort among his officers and crew. In 1816, he had survived unscathed a trial for cruelty and oppression in verbally abusing and striking a midshipman on the flagship *Washington* in the Mediterranean. Fifteen years later on the Brazil station, he would survive another court-martial on similar charges brought by several midshipmen and junior lieutenants.[11]

As Rodgers soon learned in 1825, the officers of Creighton's ship, the *Cyane*, seemed to be a particularly unhappy lot enmeshed in constant "bickerings and bad feelings." Rodgers attributed the situation to "an excess of indulgence, such as permitting the younger officers to spend too much of their time on shore in the pursuit not of useful information but of pleasures . . . [sure] to lead them into acts of extravagance calculated not only to produce improvidence in themselves but to reflect no credit on the service." Gambling and borrowing money seemed to be particular culprits. In one case, an irresponsible midshipman without financial resources had managed to borrow $380 from a respectable and well-meaning local merchant by signing an unsecured note. Since the midshipman had "no probable or even possible means of refunding the amount of his note," the transaction was "one of a downright swindling nature." Not only had the local man apparently made other loans, but other local merchants reportedly had lost more than $1,200 in similar transactions. In addition to their negative impact on American officers, these bad loans hurt the confidence of local businessmen in the "honor and integrity of the officers of our Navy."[12]

Rodgers carried a long letter with him detailing the Monroe administration's displeasure with Creighton. In one case, the Navy Department had overturned an attempt by Creighton to appoint a chaplain on the *Cyane* because naval regulations did not authorize a chaplain on a vessel of that size. In another case, the department had reversed a court-martial because Creighton had allowed an unauthorized officer to sit on the court. The department had also reprimanded Creighton for improperly dismissing and sending four midshipmen home. One of the boys, "a mere youth, in American uniform, was left on shore in a foreign country, without friends or protector, and perhaps without money, thus hazarding imminent calamity to himself and disgrace to the station."[13]

Creighton had also created an entirely avoidable incident that embarrassed his country. After local authorities in Naples had temporarily arrested an American officer who was not in uniform, Creighton overreacted and insulted local officials in demanding satisfaction. When the government of Naples complained formally of Creighton's conduct, the Monroe administration "superseded, and recalled him." Secretary Southard instructed Rodgers to deliver the letter personally and to order Creighton to return home.

From the moment that he reached Spain, Rodgers set about to restore the squadron's tarnished reputation, recognizing that his most important assets were his ships and the manner in which they were handled. With the *North Carolina*, he had a magnificent symbol of American naval power. Rated at 74 guns, the battleship actually carried 94 and could mount as many as 102 guns. Although this huge ship of the line would be obsolete within a generation, it nevertheless presented a formidable and awe-inspiring sight in 1825. With a length of 380 feet and a height of 280 feet from the top mainmast to the bottom of the keel, the *North Carolina* carried a crew of 960 officers and men.

Rodgers made sure that his flagship left a memorable impression as it entered Gibraltar Bay on 29 April. Watching from shore, Lieutenant Alexander Slidell Mackenzie described the occasion later: "After much weary expectation . . . I saw her coming down before a gentle levanter, with skysails and studdingsails—a perfect cloud of snow-white canvas. . . . the gallant ship stood boldly into the harbor, with yards a little braced, sails all filled and asleep, and hull careening enough to improve the beauty of the broadside. . . . nothing could exceed the beauty of the spectacle." Rodgers then left the ship with full pomp to pay his respects to local authorities. On deck "double battery, a company of fine-looking soldiers, with burnished and well-brushed attire, were drawn up to salute the departure of the commander." A band attired in Moorish garb was stationed at the stern. On the quarter deck gathered groups of "noble-looking young" officers. When the "Herculean form and martial figure of the veteran commodore" appeared, a "thousand eyes were fixed upon him, a thousand hats were raised; and as he passed over the side, the soldiers presented arms, and the music sent forth a martial melody. I thought I had never seen any array so soul-inspiring, so imposing."[14]

Beyond this theatrical display of his flagship and crew, Rodgers allowed hundreds of local citizens and officials as well as foreign representatives to visit the *North Carolina* in Algeciras, Gibraltar, and Malaga. Rodgers used these visits to create a favorable impression "by display of a ship which may justly be considered one of the finest that has ever been seen in this or any other port of the world." After his stop at Malaga, Rodgers concluded that the visits had left "on the mind of all who visited the ship, impression favorable not only as respects the moral character of the officers of Navy but [also] its strength and discipline."[15]

Within the squadron itself, Rodgers focused on discipline and morale. Rodgers faced a command problem on the *Constitution*, where Captain Thomas Macdonough was seriously ill with consumption. Replacing Macdonough with Captain Patterson, Rodgers sent the hero of the Battle of Lake Champlain home. Macdonough's poor health had been exacerbated by the news of his wife's death, and he, in fact, would die in November before he reached the United States. Rodgers also found himself "beset from all quarters for permission to go home." Most of the requests were for personal reasons; a few related to poor health. He had to delay sending the *Cyane* home because of pending courts-martial for "scandalous behavior," "disobedience," disrespect, and other types of behavior unbecoming to an officer. Rodgers waded through the cases and subsequently imposed his own "Rodgers system of discipline" on the squadron. Officers and crewmen were kept constantly active, drills were increased, shore leaves were reduced, and the observation of rules and regulations was tightened.[16]

Rodgers's methods made an immediate and sharp impression on his men but did not endear him to all. Samuel Francis Du Pont would come to regard Rodgers as a "second father" and go on to a distinguished naval career, but in 1825 he was only a midshipman on the *North Carolina*. "Our commodore says that there has been an unjustifiable relaxation of discipline in the Navy and he is determined to revive it," wrote Du Pont in a letter. "To do [so] he intends punishing every offender to the fullest extent of the laws. The fact [is] that half the officers . . . are half frightened to death. . . . At all events, will see discipline, order & style carried to its highest pitch."[17]

His best intentions notwithstanding, Rodgers confronted grumbling among some men and criticism back home. He informed Minerva that he might well be "lampooned in the newspapers as an arrogant unfeeling tyrant." In assuring her that he would not deviate from his duty, Rodgers stressed that his purpose "for being afloat again was if possible to correct some of the abuses that I knew to exist & if I fail in accomplishing my purpose I shall at least return to you with proud feeling of self approbation—such as . . . nothing on this earth can rob me of." When Rodgers warned Southard that Rodgers's disciplinary actions might produce rumors and attempts to undermine him in Washington, Southard reassured Rodgers that he retained the confidence of the Adams administration. In fact, Southard had "taken some pains to correct them."[18]

As he grappled with discipline and morale, Rodgers also turned to his other naval and diplomatic duties. His first order of business was to protect American commerce. At Gibraltar, Rodgers had observed firsthand both widespread smuggling and privateers menacing peacetime trade. There he observed that "the presence of a respectable force in these seas, is at this time more necessary than ever for the protection of our commerce." In the eastern Mediterranean, the Greek revolutionaries, desperate to win independence from Turkey, created another growing threat to American commerce. As Greek military fortunes deteriorated in 1825, Rodgers predicted that should the Greeks fail to win independence, a "large portion" of the Greek marine "will become pirates, and . . . prey upon every defenseless merchant vessel that falls in their way."[19]

The Greek Revolution also complicated Rodgers's diplomatic mission. While seeking a commercial treaty with Turkey, President John Quincy Adams and his administration remained officially neutral in the Greek struggle but informally very sympathetic to the cause. In fact, in the fall of 1825, the State Department would secretly dispatch an agent to assure Greek officials of American support and to explain that America's policy of nonintervention should not be interpreted by Greek patriots as indifference to their cause. Back home, Americans expressed great public sympathy, raised money, and even provided a few volunteers to fight for Greece. The Turks, of course, were fully aware of American sympathy for Greece and America's corresponding antipathy for Turkey. This presented a delicate test for Rodgers. In the Levant he would need to reassure Greek leaders of American sympathy for their cause while he simultaneously maintained the neutrality of the American flag and tried to convince the Turks of American impartiality.[20]

On 9 July, the *North Carolina*, the *Constitution*, the *Ontario*, and the *Erie* sailed from Gibraltar. After showing the flag briefly at Tunis, the American force reached Smyrna on 20 August. En route, the four ships stopped for five days at Paros to take on water and to allow officers to visit nearby "the relics of antiquity." As an admirer of ancient Greek civilization, Rodgers, like most Americans, sympathized personally with the Greek cause, but the political situation he found at Paros disheartened him. Early in 1825, in support of Turkey, an Egyptian army under Ibrahim Pasha had landed on the peninsula of Morea and proceeded to win a series of military victories. By the time the American squadron had arrived in August, the Egyptians controlled most of the peninsula. Making matters worse in Rodgers's mind were the constant diplomatic machinations of the English, French, and Austrians, all of whom seemed more determined to undermine one another than to help the Greek cause. "I am induced," Rogers reported "to think their cause so desperate, that nothing short of a miracle can sustain them much longer. . . . I have come to the conclusion that without the interposition of some one or more of the European powers, they will be unable to sustain themselves twelve months longer."[21]

However noble and sympathetic the Greek struggle, Rodgers found its military prospects unpromising and its tactics unsavory. He knew that the main threat to American commerce in the area came from Greek pirates and that the revolutionaries were apparently as guilty of outrages against civilians as their Turkish enemies. He was also troubled by an incident that occurred soon after he had anchored at Paros. Two Greeks brought eight captive Turkish women to the ship and offered to sell them to Rodgers for forty dollars each. Rodgers declined the offer but threatened to hold the women's Greek captors as prisoners while he investigated the matter with Greek officials. Under this threat, the Greeks agreed to sell the women for the lump sum of fifty dollars. Rodgers paid the Greeks this sum, kept the women onboard, and subsequently freed them at Smyrna, but he objected to the practice. As a result, a Greek official disavowed the attempt to sell the prisoners and, as proof, sent a copy of a Greek law that outlawed slavery and prohibited the selling of anyone in Greece.[22]

While at Paros, Rodgers also learned that the activities of some American volunteers in Greece were hurting both the cause of Greek independence and the credibility of the United States. Particularly irritating was the presence of William T. Washington, who had attended the U.S. Military Academy and received a commission in the army in 1823. In 1825, he resigned his commission and traveled first to Europe and then to Greece, where he attempted to play a diplomatic role for the cause. Since Washington passed himself off as a nephew of George Washington, both the Greeks and the French "attached some importance to the name of this young man." Washington publicly renounced his American citizenship, placed himself under the protection of French general Roche, and permitted "the French to make a tool of him." To Rodgers, "no excuse can be offered for his inconsistent conduct unless he is insane, & which many a person believes." Washington's foolish conduct angered Rodgers because he was "frequently asked . . . whether Mr. Washington was not really an agent of our Government."[23]

After its brief stay at Paros, the squadron proceeded to Smyrna, where Rodgers conferred with American consul David Offley, met other local officials, and generally received a "flattering reception." In his ongoing effort to etch a sharp impression of American naval power, Rodgers permitted numerous local officials and residents to visit his ships to gain a "most favorable impression concerning the strength and character of our country." Indeed, the squadron's visit pleased local American merchants. "The visit of the squadron will have a beneficial effect," wrote one. The Turks now see that "we are able as well as willing to chastise aggressions. . . . Such a ship [the *North Carolina*] was never before seen in these seas."[24]

At the same time, Rodgers was somewhat surprised to learn that "almost every person of intelligence . . . seems acquainted with all that has been said in our public prints in abuse of their [Turkey's] unrighteous war against the Greeks." And yet, Rodgers noted that the Turks there seemed to realize "our disposition to act so far impartially, as not to compromit [*sic*] our neutrality." Rodgers underscored his country's goodwill when a fire occurred at Smyrna, sending a group of Americans led by Lieutenant Matthew C. Perry to help extinguish the blaze. Near Smyrna, piracy increased during the summer. Offley argued that "our commerce at this time would be unsafe without protection." Accordingly, Rodgers decided that when the squadron returned to the western Mediterranean, he would leave the *Ontario* to protect American trade and to provide convoy protection for four American merchant ships there.[25]

Unfortunately Rodgers was unable to learn the location of the Turkish fleet or its grand admiral. Since his main purpose in coming to Smyrna had been to make contact with the Capudan Pasha, after a brief stay Rodgers left for Napoli de Romania, the capital of the Greek independent government, on the eastern coast of Morea, where Rodgers hoped to gain information about the whereabouts of the Turkish fleet. Here Rodgers paid his respects and was received formally by Greek officials, but he learned nothing about the Turkish fleet. As a result, he decided to return to Gibraltar and postpone his meeting with the Capudan Pasha until the following year.[26]

By October 1825, the squadron was back in Gibraltar. When Rodgers received permission from Spanish authorities to land provisions free of duty at Port Mahon, he decided to make his winter rendezvous there, and, by December, he was settling in. Port Mahon would become the navy's Mediterranean rendezvous for the next two decades. Conveniently placed between Malta and Gibraltar, Port Mahon offered a strategic location and superb harbor. The "harbor is certainly the finest I have ever seen," observed Rodgers, and "certainly one of the finest in the world." A narrow entrance and long channel opened into a deep, sheltered harbor in which even large warships could anchor safely. During a fierce storm in December, Rodgers wrote that "notwithstanding it is at this time blowing about a hurricane the vessels of the squadron are riding with as little motion as if they were in a mill pond." The harbor contained a quarantine island and a hospital island. Onshore was a large lazaretto and a spacious navy yard affording "many conveniences in overhauling the rigging, breaking out the hold, caulking, cleaning and painting the vessels of the squadron."[27]

The town itself had a population of about fifteen thousand. According to Rodgers, it was "well built & very neat & clean, & the inhabitants very civil & well disposed but generally extremely poor." Onshore amusements were plentiful: theater, music, and dancing as well as gambling and drinking. Possibly because of their poverty, the women were known for their easy virtue. In fact, one chaplain ascribed their frequent "aberrations from rectitude . . . less to want of virtue than the yearning instigations of want. Poverty . . . is a prolific source, not only of wretchedness, but of moral turpitude." In any event, naval officers and crewmen liked Port Mahon. For his part, Rodgers was less enthusiastic and pronounced the town without "rational amusement." Although there was "an extraordinary organ" in one of the churches, the theater was laughable. During one performance, the part of Frederick the Great had been played by a local shoemaker who "can neither read nor write."[28]

Port Mahon also offered Rodgers a good location to tighten the discipline of the squadron. He banned gambling by his officers and men because it set a bad example for young officers and would "lead them into acts of improvidence and . . . subject them to ultimate ruin and disgrace." For his midshipmen, Rodgers scheduled classes and set up a dancing school. Without any naval officers and seamen from other nations in the town, no brawls and duels occurred. In addition, local officials were helpful when, during the winter, American sailors on shore leave took to returning to their ships "without the great part of their clothes, sometimes having sold them and sometimes having been robbed of them." In response, the governor of the island issued an order prohibiting residents from taking payment for food or drink by accepting "in pawn any of the clothes" of sailors or selling to them on credit. Still squadron discipline continued to be a major concern of Rodgers. He worried that some younger naval officers were more intent on pursuing their selfish interests and personal feuds than in serving their country honorably.[29]

From home came mixed news from James K. Paulding and Samuel Southard. Paulding reported that the board had fallen into administrative disarray under the leadership of William Bainbridge. "Our friends of the Navy Board, write circulars as if the devil were in them. . . . Morris is sick of it and will no longer return to the Board." Rodgers also learned that one of his senior colleagues, Captain Charles Stewart, had been acquitted in his court-martial trial, but in another trial Captain David Porter had been convicted and suspended. Porter was now engaged in a nasty public feud with Secretary Southard. Rodgers was also chagrined to learn that his old adversary, Captain James Barron, had been permitted to preside at both trials and had subsequently done nothing to punish the officers who had brought the indefensible charges against Stewart. In a letter to Minerva, he lamented the dwindling stature of his beloved navy. "Any black guard now can remain in the navy & transgress its laws with impunity provided he is only the fourth cousin to a member of Congress, or to any other man of political influence." Rodgers worried that rather than "purify" the navy's character and defend it from political reproach, certain officers like Barron were "eagerly seeking" personal and political "popularity" that would be as "short lived as the moon shine of a cloudy night."[30]

At Port Mahon, disciplinary lapses blackened Rodgers's state of mind. At one point, five midshipmen were arrested for violating an order prohibiting gambling at a public gaming house. Although gambling could be considered a rather minor crime, the offense riled Rodgers because he considered it "a horrible and dangerous practice to which some of our young officers have been too much addicted in the Mediterranean for some years past." Since he "had determined to if possible break it up," Rodgers deplored its reappearance.[31]

This setback notwithstanding, Rodgers admitted that "the discipline of the squadron is gradually improving & I begin to believe that the exertions I have made & shall continue to make to restore order & good feeling will not be lost." While they had been "prevalent" before, there had not been "a duel or even a serious quarrel between any two officers of the squadron" since he had arrived in the Mediterranean. Moreover, the midshipman who had borrowed $380 from a merchant with an unsecured note the previous summer had apologized formally to his commander and had allotted one-half of his monthly salary to repay the loan. Rodgers also received reassuring words on his conduct from Southard back in Washington. "We shall see better times—Discipline & order shall be restored," wrote the secretary. "Do not be uneasy about [what] you may hear said about your own course—It is perfectly understood, & the condition of the Squadron [is] an object of approbation."[32]

In the spring of 1826, Rodgers took his squadron to Gibraltar and then sailed for the Levant. His squadron now consisted of the *North Carolina*, the *Constitution*, the schooner *Porpoise*, and the sloops *Erie* and *Ontario*. The *Porpoise* had joined the squadron in February; the *Erie* had previously replaced the *Ontario* in the Greek archipelago. On its eastward cruise, the squadron touched at Algiers, Tunis, Carthage, Milos, Paros, and Delos before reaching Vourla, about twenty miles from Smyrna, on 19 June. Having learned that piracy was not a problem in the area, Rodgers uncharacteristically spent four days each on Milos, Paros, and Delos "rummaging & digging among the broken columns of temples & mouldering tombs . . . of this once enlightened but now unhappy benighted country." Admitting in a letter to Minerva that she would consider him "the least qualified for that of an antiquarian," he had deployed fifty to sixty sailors with "pickaxes & spades" in a search for "rare relicks." Although he doubted he had found anything "intrinsically very valuable," Rodgers nevertheless loaded up the equivalent of ten wagons with relics—various figures, hundreds of medals and coins, as well as "two white marble altars taken from the Temples of Diana & Apollo at Delos." His visit to these sites of antiquity led Rodgers to a pessimistic reflection. "The more one sees of this once enlightened & beautiful but now miserable & degraded Country," observed Rodgers, "the more he has reason to feel ashamed & disgusted with the instability & insignificance of our nature."[33]

For the previous year, rumors about the real purpose of Rodgers's mission had been circulating among European officials in the area. Some speculated that the formidable *North Carolina* had been sent to demand an envoy at Constantinople; others conjectured that the United States wanted to acquire an island in the area for a naval base. Although the precise purpose of the American mission remained unknown, a keen interest in his squadron guaranteed that Rodgers's movements and activities would be closely monitored by European officials.[34]

At Smyrna, Rodgers met with Consul Offley and learned that the Turkish fleet was in the Dardanelles. Joined by Offley, Rodgers sailed the squadron near the entrance to the Dardanelles, bore away, and finally anchored at the island of Tenedos on 2 July. Here the governor of the island informed Rodgers that the Turkish fleet would probably not sail from the Dardanelles for ten or twelve days, but if Rodgers wanted to meet personally with the Capudan Pasha, Rodgers should travel overland about twenty miles to the straits. The governor also offered to arrange passage for Rodgers and to provide guides so that the Americans could visit the nearby plains of Troy, the tombs of Ajax and Achilles, as well as other ancient sites.

On 4 July, a division of the Turkish fleet consisting of twenty-three ships unexpectedly appeared and passed the American squadron as gale force winds blew. When one of the Turkish frigates grounded on a rock and lost her rudder, Rodgers took the opportunity to send Commander Perry in the schooner *Porpoise* to make contact with the ship's captain. Perry returned with information confirming that the Capudan Pasha would be pleased to meet with Rodgers before the main part of the Turkish fleet sailed. Accordingly, Rodgers quickly made arrangements to leave for land, but fate intervened to bring the Turkish admiral to Rodgers, thus saving him "a jaunt by land that I had no desire to undertake if it could be avoided." When the Capudan Pasha learned that one of his frigates had been damaged, he decided to inspect the ship firsthand and to oversee repairs. Arriving on 5 July, he sent word that he would be pleased to meet with Rodgers on shore the next day. Once on board, the Turkish lieutenant and dragoman (or interpreter) who served as messengers asked for and received a thorough tour of Rodgers's ship. To his delight, they explained "that they had seen some of the best ships of England, France and other nations, but that they had seen none that would bear any comparison" to the *North Carolina* and "that the Capudan Pasha on seeing her would think so too."[35]

The next morning at ten a.m., Rodgers, Offley, and interpreter George English met for an hour and a half onshore with the Turkish admiral. During their meeting, Rodgers "was not more struck at the contrast between his brawny, grotesque figure, huge grey beard and the richness of his dress, than I was by his polished manners and polite genteel address." The real name of Capudan Pasha was Khosrew Mehemmet. Lame in one leg, he was the third-ranking government official and held the titles of commander-in-chief of the Turkish fleet, minister of the marine, and inspector of the seas. He was a skilled diplomat but an undistinguished naval commander.[36]

The two naval officers got along well as they exchanged compliments and Rodgers answered the pasha's many questions about the United States. Rodgers expressed the appreciation of his government to the pasha for the protection "he had afforded to our commerce" and assured him that the

United States would avoid taking "any measures which might possibly tend to disturb the friendly relations" between the two nations. Conveying the terms of a formal treaty, Rodgers confirmed to the pasha that the United States would send a diplomatic "agent to Constantinople" as soon as Turkey was willing to negotiate. The pasha responded very favorably, indicating that although an immediate response from the sultan was not possible, Rodgers could expect a "highly satisfactory" result within three or four months. In the course of their conversation, the Turkish admiral described British naval agents at Constantinople "as not being our friends" and as consistently misrepresenting the United States. Now that he "knew us better," the pasha explained that he would know how to "represent us to his sovereign, the Sultan, on his return to Constantinople."[37]

Before the interview, Rodgers had been informed by the Turkish naval officer who came onboard in advance that the Capudan Pasha was "incensed" that one of his frigates had been damaged and quite likely would punish the offending captain by putting him to death unless Rodgers "should intercede for him." Rodgers agreed to make the request as "not only a singular favor conferred on myself, but as one of the highest compliments he [the pasha] could pay my country." When Rodgers did make the request of the pasha during their meeting, the pasha responded that "he would remit punishing him with death . . . provided I would give him a good beating" as punishment. "Seeing that I was at a loss what reply to make . . . he laughed and observed that as I requested it his life should be spared."[38]

Two days later, Rodgers sent Perry in the *Porpoise* to escort the pasha and his "magnificent" barge between Tenedos and the mainland and honor him with a twenty-one-gun salute. During the trip, the pasha "frequently expressed . . . the great delight his meeting us had afforded him." The next day, Rodgers took his ships close to the "entrance to the Dardanelles, so near as to afford a minute view of the batteries on each side of its entrance. . . . [S]ome alarm was occasioned on the display of our colors, that caused the guns of all the batteries to be manned and an express to be sent off to the Capudan Pasha." From here, at five p.m., the squadron "bore away for Mytilene" and an hour later enjoyed a "serene" experience. "The prospect from our decks was peculiarly sublime and interesting," remembered Rodgers, "for just before sunset the following objects of interest, which have been the themes of so much history, poetry and song, presented themselves to view. The entrance of the Dardanelles, the entrance of the River Scamander, the islands of Tenedos, Imbros, Samothrace and Menos, Mount Ida, Mount Athos, Mount Olympus, the tombs of Ajax and Achilles, and Cape Baba were distinctly to be seen from our decks."[39]

At Mytilene on 14 July, the Turkish fleet appeared. It consisted of two ships of the line, seven frigates, seven corvettes, and sixteen smaller vessels. After the Capudan Pasha's flagship had anchored, the remaining Turkish vessels followed in a haphazard manner. The next day the Turkish admiral was received on the *North Carolina* "with the attention due to the rank of the third personage of the Ottoman Empire." During his two-hour tour, the pasha continually expressed "friendship and respect for the American nation" as Rodgers took pains "to render the compliments shown him novel and imposing . . . and accordingly the yards were manned, the men dressed in white, and a salute of twenty-one guns fired, which was immediately returned by the Capudan Pasha's flagship."[40]

The Turkish admiral returned the compliments the following day when Rodgers, his captains, and other officers visited the Turkish flagship. As Rodgers left the ship, the flag of the Turkish admiral "then flying at the Main was struck, and another, bearing the seal of the Sultan, which was never before hoisted except on the occasion of the Sultan's going himself on board the Turkish fleet, was hoisted in its place, and a salute of 21 guns fired." The pasha informed Rodgers that this "extraordinary honor . . . had never been conferred on the flag of any European Nation" and that he should view it as "an indubitable proof of his great respect and friendship for the American Nation."[41]

After Rodgers had returned to his ship, the pasha sent ceremonial gifts to Rodgers and his officers, and let it be known that the pasha "would be glad to receive in return some articles of American Manufacture." Rodgers received a pipe, a shawl, and some articles of Turkish female dress. His officers received lesser but similar gifts. In his report, Rodgers took care to explain to the Navy Department that since these gifts had been "forced upon" him, he would dispose of them as the navy secretary saw fit. "They are mere baubles, of no intrinsic value to those who possess them, further than as mementos of the time, circumstances and interchange of civilities . . . on the first meeting of an American Squadron with the Grand Fleet of the Ottoman Empire."[42]

Rodgers was correct in fearing that "instead of being a gainer I may be a loser by my acceptance of this token of the Pacha's [sic] personal good will." Five months later, Rodgers would purchase and send an estimated $2,000 in gifts, including a diamond ring and a gold snuff-box set with diamonds for the pasha and a fine sword for his dragoman. The pasha had also asked for a stand of one thousand arms for his government plus a musket, bayonet, belt, and cartouche box for himself. Rodgers sent the personal items to the pasha later, but no arms.[43]

On 18 July, the American squadron departed in impressive fashion: "making a tack to windward, each ship bore up in succession and ran down through the Turkish Fleet, and on coming abreast of the Flag of the Capudan Pasha, manned her rigging, the crew dressed in white, and gave him three cheers, the Band at the same time [played] 'Hail Columbia.'" Given the haphazard manner in which the Turkish fleet had anchored at Mytilene, Rodgers thought that his ships had made a "very imposing" exhibition "inasmuch as the several evolutions of getting underway, of making sail, of tacking, of bearing up, of manning the rigging, and of putting the ship under a crowd of sail . . . were performed each with a celerity and precision such as I have never before witnessed, and will, without doubt, leave a lasting impression on the mind not only of the Capudan Pasha, but on that of every other Turk who happened to witness the scene."[44]

Rodgers's diplomatic mission had gone even better than he could have expected. The Turkish government was favorably disposed toward the United States, and the pasha seemed to be a particularly warm friend of the country. Although the pasha made no commitments, his comments were extremely encouraging. In fact, Rodgers had made a strong and enduring impression on the pasha.[45] Rodgers's reports exhibited a strong sense of personal satisfaction. For his part, Rodgers had performed flawlessly, maintaining a personal decorum that was solemn and dignified while treating the pasha with the great respect due his elevated position in the Turkish government. Rodgers also conducted himself and his squadron in a manner carefully designed to impress upon the pasha and his officers the imposing naval strength of the United States. In addition to allowing Rodgers's guests to view in intimate detail the formidable size and armament of the *North Carolina*, he had departed with a flourish.

However, not everyone thought that Rodgers's treatment of the Turkish pasha was laudable. In the squadron, where few officers knew the details of Rodgers's confidential instructions from the Department of State, some privately questioned "the propriety of showing such attention to a Turkish Pasha." Back home, where enthusiasm for the Greek cause ran high, some newspaper editors were appalled by the respect shown the pasha. One newspaper denounced Rodgers for turning American naval officers into "lacqueys [sic] of 'His Highness.'" What a disgrace for Americans to smoke pipes and drink coffee "with the butchers of Scio and Missolonghi [sic]."[46]

Having completed his diplomatic assignment, Rodgers turned to the protection of American commerce in the Greek archipelago. He found the archipelago "much infested by pirates" but reported no attacks on American merchant vessels. The Greek military situation had further deteriorated and seemed even more desperate than it had the year before. After Mesolongi fell to the Turks in April, the "only place of importance in possession of the Greeks" was Napoli di Romania. To Rodgers, the depressing situation in Greece made the struggle seem hopeless. In June, he found so much "anarchy & disunion among them [the Greeks] as to leave no hope that they will under any circumstances be able to hold out much longer" without European assistance. Ever since they had attempted to establish an independent government, Greek misfortunes and failures "have been in proportion to the ignorance, licentiousness, jealousy and restlessness of the people," observed Rodgers, "and the want of energy, talent and honesty in the individuals who have been . . . entrusted with the management of their affairs." Rodgers admired the courage, endurance, and restless disposition of the Greek fighters, but he abhorred the rampant "jealousy and envy" of their political and military leaders. Recently, for example, the Greeks had made two assassination attempts on one of their own naval heroes.[47]

Only European diplomatic intervention could save the Greek cause, according to Rodgers, but that seemed unlikely because the various European agents refused to unite in support of genuine Greek independence. In fact, the "flattery and fair but hollow promises" of the Europeans increased disunity "amongst the miserable, imbecile, shortsighted individuals nominally charged with the administration" of the Greek government. Even in the unlikely event that the Greeks might win independence, Rodgers doubted their ability to maintain sovereignty. Rodgers concurred with "the prevalent opinion among those persons who profess" to know the Greek character best "that the present generation is not capable of self government." In fact, Rodgers had read the situation well. The Greek cause would improve dramatically only with European intervention after Rodgers had left the Mediterranean in 1827.[48]

In August, Rodgers headed back to Port Mahon, ordering the *Erie* to touch at Tripoli and Algiers en route and leaving the *Ontario* behind to protect American commerce. On 10 September, Rodgers reached Port Mahon, where he spent most of the fall waiting for a reply from the sultan of Turkey on the treaty proposal. After Rodgers sent the *Erie* home, the squadron in the western Mediterranean consisted of the *North Carolina*, the *Constitution*, and the *Porpoise*.

By November 1826, Rodgers had learned that Southard wanted Rodgers to fill an upcoming vacancy on the Board of Navy Commissioners, but the department had not yet told Rodgers exactly when he should return home. As he waited during late fall and winter of 1826–27, Rodgers mulled over the offer. He was undecided about accepting because he was "not pleased with what has been done in certain matters since my absence. . . . I feel that I have been neglected by those I least expected it from."[49] As he contemplated his professional future, Rodgers also had time to think about Minerva and his family. Now a man in his early fifties, Rodgers had marked his twentieth wedding anniversary from the Mediterranean. Not surprisingly, his letters lacked the passionate emotion of those he had written two decades earlier. He spoke rarely of how much he missed his wife and family. Instead, he recounted his official activities and described the exotic places he had seen and the people he had met. His letters also reveal that Rodgers felt some guilt about his extended absence. When Minerva assured him that their servants were creating no problems, Rodgers expressed concern over her increased burdens but relief that things seemed to be going well. He reiterated to her the necessity of his mission and regularly described the numerous exotic gifts that he was buying for her at his various stops in the Mediterranean, describing silk, cloth, articles of clothing, earrings, necklaces, and scarves.[50]

In his absence, Minerva had moved the family back to the comfortable surroundings of Sion Hill near Havre de Grace, where she and the children spent most of their time. Rodgers took the precaution of engaging secretary of the board Charles Goldsborough to help look after the Greenleaf Point home in Washington. Her domestic duties kept Minerva busy enough with chores and children to fill the void created by his absence. But she admitted that she often tried to imagine where he might be and what he might be doing at a given moment. As the time for her husband's return approached, Minerva begin to think about "scenes which live only on the page of memory—when the ardent feelings and romantic anticipations of youth lent a charm to every object—'Dim are the long past days. Yet still they please, like sounds half heard, borne on the inconstant breeze.'"[51]

A personal bright spot for Rodgers was observing the continuing development of his son Midshipman Frederick Rodgers. John Rodgers reported to Minerva that Fred "has grown so fat & . . . so tall that you would hardly know him." Having always wanted to be a "sailor," Fred told his father that "he even likes the life better than he ever supposed he should." At a formal dance held onboard, an astonished Rodgers watched his son approaching a young Spanish woman, conversing with her although neither "understood a word of what the other said," and then "in less than a minute . . . capering away with her in a Spanish dance such as I am sure he had never seen or heard of before." As proud as he was of Fred, Rodgers strongly advised his eldest son, Robert, not to enter the navy. In addition to Robert's being "too old" at age seventeen to begin a naval career, a rather jaded Rodgers did "not think it a profession, judging from present appearances, likely to produce much benefit, or probability of reward."[52]

As he neared the end of his cruise, Rodgers could smile at his achievements as commander of the Mediterranean squadron. He had successfully completed the diplomatic mission assigned to him by the State Department. In his diplomatic balancing act in dealing with the warring Greeks and Turks, he had scrupulously preserved the dignity and neutrality of the American flag and effectively protected American commerce in the region. Rodgers had also succeeded in conveying to Greek leaders his sympathy for their cause while convincing the Turks that he and his government were impartial in the conflict. It was an impressive performance. The only minor breach occurred when Commander David Deacon of the *Erie* disobeyed instructions from Rodgers. Consul Offley and Rodgers had agreed to a Turkish request for the *Erie* to transport a Turkish citizen to Alexandria. Instead, Deacon landed the man at Modon, an act that Rodgers believed compromised American neutrality.[53]

Rodgers could also take pride in restoring the Mediterranean squadron to top-class condition. The "discipline, order, & style," of which Midshipman Du Pont had spoken, had, indeed, been "carried to its highest pitch." Duels and brawls virtually disappeared, and incidents of disorderly conduct became rare.[54] On the *North Carolina*, much of the credit for the restoration of discipline went to First Lieutenant Matthew C. Perry, who worked tirelessly to ensure that all rules were followed and the ship remained in impeccable condition. The comments of Midshipman Du Pont are noteworthy in that he worked directly under Perry's supervision and remembered working continuously from daylight to evening "without the least interruption. I can scarcely get my meals, and, indeed, I am never seated at the table more than two minutes, without hearing myself repeatedly called by the first lieutenant with some new order to execute." No one was "more deserving or better qualified," wrote Rodgers when he recommended Perry's promotion in November 1825, "if professional acquirements, moral integrity, & a high sense of honor should be the test."[55]

Rodgers's high regard was reflected in his reliance on Perry to execute a wide array of other tasks. In 1825, on the island of Paros, it had been Perry who negotiated the release from Greek slave traders of the eight Turkish women they held. At Smyrna in 1825, Rodgers ordered Perry to lead the American fire-fighting detachment that helped to extinguish the waterfront fire. In 1826, during negotiations with Pasha Husrev, Rodgers dispatched Perry to convey the pasha ashore and later to greet the Turkish official when he visited the *North Carolina* and to inform him that he was about to be greeted by a twenty-one-gun salute. These and other experiences were important opportunities for Perry. He learned firsthand about the different, and to him sometimes strange, customs and behavior of the Turks. He also benefited from the chance to observe the conduct and actions of Rodgers. While treating the pasha with the utmost respect, Rodgers also understood that the Turks would grant their goodwill only if they respected the formidable power and peaceful intentions of the American naval fleet. Neither man could have known it at the time, but Perry's experiences with Rodgers in the Mediterranean in 1826 would prove to be invaluable preparation for his naval expedition to Japan almost three decades later.

Although most accepted the tough disciplinary regime set by Rodgers and Perry, some crewmen like James Garrison resisted. Garrison, the older brother of abolitionist William Lloyd Garrison, wrote his "confessions" more than a decade after the cruise and included one chapter, "Hell Afloat," that presented a harsh description of life onboard the *North Carolina*. He claimed that discipline was severe, flogging frequent, and conditions harsh. The main object of Garrison's attack was Lieutenant Perry, whom he charged with brutality, uncontrolled anger, abuse of authority, excessive profanity, and even theft from crewmen. Garrison asserted that he was punished on one occasion for whispering while the men stood by their hammocks in silence, on another for singing with his messmates after hammocks were down but before lights were out, and on yet another for refusing an order. In each case, Garrison alleged that Perry was verbally abusive and his punishments excessive. On various occasions, Garrison received thirteen lashes, lost his grog ration for a fortnight or a month, and had his shore leave temporarily suspended.[56]

Although his indictment was potentially telling, Garrison was an unreliable source. A ne'er-do-well and an alcoholic, Garrison was an unhappy sailor and a troubled man who disliked authority in general. A sick man when he wrote his memoirs more than a decade later, he would die in 1842 in his early forties. Even his brother, William Lloyd Garrison, a strong opponent of flogging, chose not to publish his brother's account. Indeed, Garrison's memoir got certain basic facts wrong, and his most dramatic charges are not corroborated by the official record or by any contemporaries. Although Garrison described frequent floggings, the *North Carolina*'s log revealed only thirteen floggings during its twenty-eight-month cruise, a remarkably small number for such a large ship.[57]

In December, Rodgers took the *North Carolina* to Marseilles and Toulon. He also renewed his request for a formal reply from the Turkish government. It was at this time, on behalf of his government, that Rodgers sent the personal gifts—the "diamond ring and a gold snuff box ornamented with brilliants"—that the pasha had suggested when the two met the previous summer. After conveying the American consul to Tunis, the *North Carolina* encountered a severe and protracted northwest wind that finally forced Rodgers to bear up and head for Malta after nearly a month of battling the adverse conditions. He reached Malta on 19 January 1827 with a crew that suffered from various sicknesses, including smallpox, as a result of the exposure and the severe conditions. At one point more than one hundred men had smallpox, and eventually seven died.[58]

After nearly a month of recuperation, Rodgers finally headed for Port Mahon, which he reached on 3 March. Awaiting him were communications from the Navy Department and Turkey. The department ordered him to return to the United States via the West Indies.[59] Unfortunately he would not carry a positive diplomatic response with him. In a letter to Rodgers, the pasha congratulated himself "on account of the gracious complaisance with which he [the sultan] appeared to hearken to my propositions." But the sultan had not provided a "categorical answer" because he was "entirely occupied with the new military system which leaves him little time to think of other things."[60]

As he prepared to leave the Mediterranean, Rodgers continued to brood over his future and the state of the navy. "The principles on which the Navy is at present conducted must sooner or later bring it into contempt," fumed Rodgers, and "altho I am dependent on it for my living, still I am desirous of being as far removed from the scene of its disgrace & [unintangled] with the authors of its misfortunes as possible." Rodgers admitted that because his "zeal & ambition [had] somewhat abated," he was now much less inclined "to make sacrifices of my personal ease & convenience than I was when I was a younger man & had some hope of reward." In spite of his misgivings, Rodgers resigned himself to serving a second term as president the Board of Navy Commissioners. "This I do not like, but as I have objections to going into a navy yard, I suppose my poverty will incline me to accept . . . if I can do nothing better," Rodgers admitted to Minerva. "In the present state of things, I should prefer being unemployed if my circumstances would admit of it."[61] The *North Carolina* finally sailed from Gibraltar on 31 May and reached Hampton Roads on 28 July, after touching briefly at several Caribbean ports. On 3 August, Secretary Southard came aboard to welcome the crew and Rodgers on what would be the last sea command of his career.

Three years before, a large public dinner had honored Rodgers as he prepared for his mission to the Mediterranean. Now with Congress and the president out of town for the summer, the return of the *North Carolina* attracted little attention. In Norfolk, a "large concourse of respectable citizens crowded to the water's edge" to welcome the "splendid ship." But in Norfolk and Washington there were no public dinners nor laudatory newspaper editorials for Rodgers and his officers. And four months later, Secretary Southard praised the "skillful direction" of Rodgers in his yearly report on the navy, but President Adams did not mention Rodgers's cruise in his annual message to Congress. It was in this anticlimactic aftermath of his twenty-eight-month cruise that Rodgers unenthusiastically contemplated his return to shore duty.[62]

10

Last Years, 1827–1838

[The Board of Navy Commissioners] are satisfied that they are incompetent themselves, and have no person under their direction who could furnish them with the necessary information to form a contract for steam engines.

President John Rodgers, speaking for his fellow commissioners
on the subject of steam power in 1835

On 8 October 1827, Commodore John Rodgers resumed his position as president of the Board of Navy Commissioners, a situation he did not relish. For the past year he had mulled over the possibility of assuming command of a navy yard or even of retiring altogether to become a gentleman farmer in Havre de Grace. He was depressed by the turmoil between various naval officers and the general decline in the service's prestige. He also complained that he had not received the personal recognition that he deserved for his service in the Mediterranean. Several factors, however, weighed against retirement. In 1827, Rodgers was still a robust, healthy man in his mid-fifties, one who had never shown any interest in farming and had few hobbies or intellectual interests to occupy his time and energy. And, as he well knew, he also lacked sufficient personal wealth to support Minerva and their family of nine children, seven of whom were less than sixteen years old.

Friends also advised against command of a navy yard or retirement. Rodgers no doubt remembered advice of friend Isaac Chauncey who two years earlier had written to "tell you this secret that the command of a Navy Yard is not a desirable situation." In August 1827, James K. Paulding, who was then the navy agent in New York, congratulated Rodgers on his return: "I hear your cruise has improved your health and made you at least ten years younger, and . . . [that] your firmness and steadiness restored the discipline of the squadron under your command to what it ought to be." On the question of Rodgers's future, Paulding acknowledged the attraction of "shooting canvas backs and playing horse jockey on the shores of the Susquehanna; and if you are sure—I say sure—that you would be happier there, I should say go and shoot and ride and plant corn and tobacco, and turn your sword into a ploughshare and your cocked-hat into a pigeon-house." But Paulding understood that even Rodgers's recent disillusionment with the navy did not prepare him to be a farmer. "I doubt whether a man who has all his life been ploughing the sea will make much figure at ploughing the land. You might make a hand at swapping horses, but upon my soul, my dear commodore, I question whether you would figure greatly in your crops. . . . A Gentleman Farmer is a very pretty kind of gentleman, only he is very apt to get in debt. . . . In the first place you would be cheated, for that is the destiny of a sailor as soon as he puts his foot on the land. The country people moreover make no conscience in cheating a Gentleman Farmer, because as I have often heard them say, 'He don't mind a few dollars.'" Instead, Paulding recommended that Rodgers continue his naval career. "I can't help thinking the Navy Board is the place for you, next to the command of a squadron, and I confess further that I wish to see you there to correct some of the notions and flimflams of certain of your predecessors, or rather successors."[1]

Once he began his second term as president of the board, Rodgers settled comfortably into his personal and professional routine. At Greenleaf Point, six Rodgers children lived at home. The two eldest sons, Robert and Frederick, had already left home, while the third son, John, would join the navy as a midshipman in April 1828. That left Elizabeth (age twelve in 1827), Louisa (ten), Jerusha (eight), William (six), Henry, or Hal (five), and Ann, or Nannie (three), as well as various servants for John and Minerva with whom to contend. In 1829, Augustus, or Gus, the last of the family's eleven children, was born.

The residence at Greenleaf Point furnished an ideal place for a brood of active and often mischievous youngsters. The large lot included various gardens and outbuildings in addition to the two interconnected houses that served as the family's spacious residence. Rodgers delighted in the large garden, which extended from the residence to the river. Bordering the garden were pear, nectarine, fig, and plum trees as well as one large mulberry tree. Along the fences Rodgers planted raspberry bushes. Writing her memoir decades later, Nannie painted a rhapsodic picture of her early childhood there. Although she admitted that the years had dimmed her memory for many facts, the general image of the Greenleaf Point residence and her life there remained vivid. She and her siblings had ample space to romp and roam, numerous animals and pets, and various hiding places. On one porch, coral honeysuckles created a "shady bower" in the summer for the children to "revel" away from their parents' immediate oversight.[2]

The portrait that emerges of John Rodgers from his daughter's memoir is that of a stern, formal, somewhat distant father. Nannie's memoirs and the

Rodgers family legend contain various examples of John's either disciplining his young sons or, in attempting to impose discipline, being outsmarted by them as they avoided detection in some minor act of disobedience. On one occasion in a moment of anger, Rodgers cuffed son John on the head with a new silk hat that Rodgers was shaping at that moment. Much to the private glee of his sons, his hat was permanently misshapen as a result. So, in the privacy of his home, Rodgers seems to have remained the stern, humorless naval commander of his professional life. Lacking are any recollections of Rodgers taking his young children into his arms or onto his lap.[3]

Nannie remembered the atmosphere inside the Rodgers home as being strict. Dinner was a formal affair during which Rodgers presided and was personally served by his servant Butler. The children were "all silent as mice but generally full of repressed merriment that sometimes exploded from the very sense of repression. The offender was immediately dismissed in confusion by a look from our father. . . . We could not speak . . . and never dreamed of asking for anything, but meekly accepted what was put on our plates," remembered Nannie, "the effect of this simple arrangement being, as far as I remember, that we generally received a large portion of something we did not like . . . and a very small share of what we really cared for." "Under such painful restraint," Nannie "did not remember any pleasure relating to the dining room excepting the permission to leave it." Once told they could go, "we escaped and rushed down the hall, speeding to our loved garden haunts, where we might laugh and shout at our will."[4]

In the Rodgers household, the children sought love, comfort, and sympathy from their maternal grandmother, Jerusha, who lived with the family at Greenleaf Point. Nannie remembered her grandmother as a warm person who for the youngest children "was always a peacemaker; she was the ally of my mischievous brothers and told no tales." High praise indeed! The boys went to "Grandma to bind up their wounds and relate their grievances. She seems in my memory to be always administering cakes or salve, or figs or plaster, something to soothe the outer or inner man."

In contrast, Nannie remembered her "own dear mother," now in her mid-forties, as a formal presence, the "autocrat" of the house. Standing between the children and their stern father, Minerva had been raised to play a traditional and formal role as a mother. Nannie described her as a "gentle but spirited creature" with a "natural gift for teaching" who trained the family's servants and taught her children "to love truth and honor. Her sons were brought up to be as chivalric as the knights of old." Minerva "loved fine scenery, good literature, truth and purity and in one way or another she was always teaching some of these things." Using literature to instill important values in her children, Minerva retold stories from her reading and recited both prose and poetry, using "the charm of her musical and well modulated voice" to add grace to the author's words. When Nannie was eight years old, she began to attend school, but years later, even though she could not remember having learned anything at the school or "indeed that they tried to teach me," she never forgot "my mother's lessons and their import" and attributed her own "love of nature and of poetry . . . to my mother's teaching."[5]

Her gentle nature and musical voice notwithstanding, Minerva's voice "had fire in it when she was angry, so had her eyes." She would launch out unexpectedly, sometimes against a recreant child or servant. Particularly offended by her sons' occasional rudeness, she would sarcastically ask: "Can I hope to make a gentleman of *you*? You have the manners of a *boor*. You might as well be a *pig* or a *dog*!!!"[6]

The tranquil life of the Rodgers family was shattered unexpectedly in April 1828, when son Fred drowned. In Norfolk on Saturday, 5 April, Rodgers and three other midshipmen had left the navy yard in a small sailboat for a day of recreation. About three miles from the navy yard, a sudden squall capsized and sunk their boat. One of the young men was trapped under the capsized boat and drowned. Rodgers was an excellent swimmer but weakened himself by attempting unsuccessfully to free his dog, who was trapped in the boat, and then trying again unsuccessfully to save another of his mates, who did not know how to swim. These valiant efforts exhausted Rodgers, who drowned before he could be rescued, leaving only one survivor among the four midshipmen.[7]

When initial efforts to recover the bodies failed, a grief-stricken John Rodgers went to Norfolk and personally supervised recovery efforts. After several days, dragging efforts produced the bodies. Rodgers then returned to Washington with the body of his son, which the father buried in the Congressional Cemetery. The loss of Fred Rodgers and two of his midshipmen friends was enough of a tragedy to attract even the attention of President John Quincy Adams. When informed that Commodore Rodgers's son had drowned, Adams confided to his diary that "I wrote this evening with a heavy heart."[8]

Almost twenty years before, John and Minerva had lost their first child, John Henry, as an infant, but the loss of Fred was more devastating. Fred was "very gay and handsome" with a shining personality. Nannie later remembered him as "Fred the beautiful and the brave . . . always a darling in the family." Less than a month before his death, in time-honored teenage fashion, Fred had written saying that "I am out of cash at present and I think rather too shabby to appear at church on Sundays I wish you would transmit me something by the returning boat." He had also been a favorite of his stern father. As the first Rodgers son to enter the navy, Fred had served as a midshipman on his father's recent Mediterranean cruise, during which John had proudly watched his teenage son mature and emerge as a promising young officer.[9]

Although the youngest children had not known Fred well, the family did not fully recover from the tragedy. "My mother and father," remembered Nannie later, "were never the same again." Most grief-stricken was Fred's older brother, Robert. The two boys had been close friends and constant compatriots in childhood mischief. At the time of Fred's death, Robert was a cadet at the United States Military Academy. He was so "broken down with sorrow" that he left "West Point and return[ed] to the stricken house," never returning to the academy.[10]

In contrast to the tragic turmoil in Rodgers's personal life, the initial years of his second term as board president were uneventful. The main political actors had not changed. President Adams was a strong supporter of the navy, and Rodgers resumed his amicable working relationship with Secretary of the Navy Southard. In the Senate, the navy could count on the support of South Carolinian Robert Y. Hayne, chair of the Committee on Naval Affairs. Given Rodgers's own naval experience and strong persona, he quickly reestablished his authority as president. In fact, turnover on the board further strengthened Rodgers's influence. For almost a year after October 1827, the board had only two members, Rodgers and Lewis Warrington. Then, in the next five years, six different officers (including Rodgers) served on the board.[11]

The work of the board was familiar to Rodgers, but its administrative volume had increased. Meeting six days a week, the board collectively dealt with hundreds of details, appropriations, contracts, and operational requests each year. In addition to its routine bureaucratic duties, the board recommended ways in which the board and the Navy Department could operate more economically and more efficiently. It also pressed for changes in the way in which ships were repaired. By the time Rodgers had rejoined the board, the American navy did not have one operational dry dock. In 1822, Rodgers had invented and patented an inclined plane railroad to serve as a substitute for a dry dock at the Washington navy yard. In 1827, construction was begun on dry docks in Norfolk and Boston, with both being completed in 1833.[12]

As board president, Rodgers also hoped to improve the prestige and discipline of the peacetime navy. Since the board did not control individual personnel matters, there was little it could do to address personal rivalries, disciplinary problems, and tensions between the old and new generations of officers. But Rodgers intended to use the board's control over naval repairs to preserve the navy's public image by saving visible physical examples of its recent past glory. One such symbol was the *Macedonian*, a British frigate that had been defeated and captured by Captain Stephen Decatur in the War of 1812. The recommissioned frigate had served for the next fifteen years as an American warship, but by 1828 the *Macedonian* suffered from such serious decay and rot that she was unseaworthy. The damage to her hull, timbers, and spars was so serious that she would have to be completely rebuilt to be saved. For his part, Rodgers was determined to rebuild the *Macedonian* as a continuing monument to the valor of his friend Decatur and as a visible reminder to American politicians and the public of the navy's past contributions to the nation. A formidable challenge, the project would require all of Rodgers's considerable determination and administrative savvy to overcome the opposition of the Jackson administration and naval officers such as Decatur's old adversary Captain James Barron, who was then the commandant of the Norfolk navy yard, where the *Macedonian* rested. Finally, in 1832, Congress passed legislation to rebuild the famous ship, but it would be another five years before the "rebuilt" *Macedonian*, which in fact was a new ship, was launched in 1837.[13]

Rodgers personally supported changes being proposed at the time to strengthen the navy. From December 1827 to February 1828 in the *Philadelphia National Gazette*, Commander Matthew C. Perry, a Rodgers protégé and his first lieutenant on the *North Carolina*, published a series of articles addressed to Senator Hayne of the Naval Affairs Committee. As a thirty-three-year-old rising star in the navy, Perry agreed with Rodgers about the fundamental reforms needed. Most important, according to Perry, were personnel changes. The officer corps needed to be expanded by immediately promoting one hundred midshipmen to lieutenant and appointing four hundred new midshipmen. Once appointed, the new midshipmen needed to learn by performing numerous duties and by studying "their profession and all the sciences connected with it." To this end, Perry joined others in recommending the establishment of a naval academy, preferably at Annapolis, Maryland.[14]

Perry also recommended a more extensive promotion and personnel classification system. Specifically, new officer ranks needed to be created to achieve parity with the army and to accommodate the growing complexity of the American navy. At the time, the navy had only three officer ranks: lieutenant, master commandant, and captain. A fourth title, commodore, was only an honorary designation that applied to those who commanded a multiship station or squadron. Increasingly, as the number of officers grew and the rate of promotions slowed, officers ended up commanding other officers of the same rank, a situation that created tension and hurt morale. In addition, on overseas stations, Americans captains invariably suffered the embarrassment of being outranked by the admirals of foreign navies with whom they came in contact. To address this problem, Perry endorsed making commodore a formal rank with attendant powers and prerogatives and creating the new ranks of rear admiral and vice admiral. Perry also urged the creation of an apprentice system to supply new American-born recruits for the navy. The current practices of extending bounties and pay advances had serious flaws and produced a navy in which too many foreigners served. Enlisted at age fourteen, the apprentices would be fed, clothed, and trained but not paid a wage. If successful, they could be promoted to the level of master's mate after seven years. According to Perry, such a system would enlist and train hundreds of American boys at a huge cost savings. Focusing on the organization and day-to-day operation of the navy, these recommendations reflected the preoccupations of both Perry and Rodgers. As a commander, Perry had to recruit and train his crews, educate junior officers, and manage the ships he commanded. As board president, Rodgers dealt with the complex but mundane details of peacetime naval administration.[15]

It is clear that in the late 1820s, Rodgers's agenda to strengthen the navy did not include steam technology or address its peacetime commercial and scientific role. Although in the early 1820s, Rodgers had supported the purchase of a small steamer, the Sea Gull, to combat pirates in the shallow waters of the Caribbean, he did not believe that steam power should be employed on large oceangoing battleships such as frigates and ships of the line.[16] Nor did Rodgers embrace the navy's evolving peacetime role. He continued to believe that the navy needed to be comprised primarily of large, sail-powered battleships numerous and powerful enough to defend against a European enemy in wartime while protecting American commerce from pirates, privateers, or Barbary corsairs in peacetime. But the navy would soon begin to play an increasing role in collecting scientific, geographic, and commercial information from around the world. For example, by the 1840s, an arm of the Navy Department would be engaged in helping American whalers chart the likely location of the whale population in the Pacific Ocean. In the late 1820s, the initial project of this kind was a proposed naval exploring and scientific expedition to the South Pacific Ocean (the South Seas). Manned by the navy and assisted by civilian scientists, several warships would approach the South Pole as well as explore, collect scientific information, and chart the waters of Pacific. Aggressively promoted by Jeremiah Reynolds, the proposal captured the interest and support of President Adams.[17]

However, political opposition and numerous problems would delay the expedition for almost a decade before it finally sailed in 1838. One of the initial obstacles was the lack of enthusiasm and, indeed, open opposition of senior naval officers. Reared as they had been in the fighting navy of Thomas Truxtun and Edward Preble, these officers believed it inappropriate to use the ships of an already inadequate American navy to engage in a quixotic attempt to sail to the South Pole and in frivolous efforts to collect the fauna and flora of remote and primitive islands in the Pacific. Although Rodgers did not formally oppose the expedition, he privately discouraged President Adams from proceeding. Still, on 14 July 1828, in a meeting with Secretary Southard and Rodgers, President Adams "earnestly urged that the expedition should at all events be despatched" before the end of the year. In response, Rodgers outlined "the many difficulties to the fitting out of the expedition during the present year, and particularly [noted] that there was no vessel in the navy suited to the service." Several vessels were suggested, including a new sloop, the *Vandalia*, but "all [were] found liable to great objection" from Rodgers and Southard.[18]

The election of Andrew Jackson in 1828 did not augur well for the navy. To his supporters, Old Hickory's triumph signaled that the common people had taken their government back from the special interests and career politicians who allegedly had controlled the Adams administration. Coming to office as a great popular hero with a strong agenda of "reform, retrenchment and economy," Jackson had no naval expertise and little appreciation of maritime issues. Specifically, he intended to remove "corrupt" officeholders from their government jobs, to reduce the size of the federal government, and to limit federal spending in order to eliminate the national debt. Although he was the preeminent military hero of his day, Jackson was a soldier and not a sailor, an Indian fighter from a western, landlocked state. In his very brief inaugural address, Jackson did endorse "the gradual increase of our Navy" but emphasized that "the bulwark of our defense is the national militia."[19]

As his secretary of the navy, Jackson selected an old friend and early political supporter, Senator John Branch from North Carolina. Branch was a wealthy planter and former governor with no background or apparent interest in naval affairs. "By what interest that miserable old woman, Branch, was ever dreamed of no one can tell," observed Jacksonian Louis McLane. Knowing little about the navy, Branch was nevertheless committed to the president's agenda of eliminating corruption and reducing navy spending. Another Jackson appointee also became an active presence in the Navy Department. The modest title of fourth auditor of the treasury gave Jacksonian loyalist Amos Kendall fiscal auditing responsibility for the Navy Department. In his autobiography, Kendall later claimed that in 1829 he found the department riddled with "abuses, frauds, and corruptions, which consumed its means and cankered the morals and honor of our navy." Although he did not charge the navy commissioners with fraud or mismanagement, Rodgers protested vigorously when allegations of board favoritism surfaced. For his part, Kendall later estimated that he had saved the department "more than a half million a year" over the next three years by cracking down on the negligence and abuses of the previous fourth auditor and secretary of the navy in approved but unwarranted, excessive, or fraudulent payments of navy funds. He cited one example in which $2,200 had been paid "for many years" to "mechanics and laborers" at the Philadelphia navy yard without the approval of either the fourth auditor or naval secretary.[20]

Personally, Jackson respected Rodgers and in 1830 sent him a walking stick as a gift made of "Hermitage Hickory," but the new president intended to deemphasize the importance of the navy. In his first annual message to Congress in December 1829, Jackson stated that although the navy constituted "the best standing security of his country" against foreign invasion, the peacetime navy required "no more ships of war than are requisite to the protection of our commerce." Instead of building more large warships, Jackson argued that the navy should accumulate an ample stock of timber and shipbuilding materials so that, in the event of war, American warships could be quickly assembled. The president also recommended that the Board of Navy Commissioners be abolished and replaced by a bureau system.[21]

During Branch's two-year stint as secretary, he responded to Jackson's leadership by proposing efficiencies and administrative reforms, most of which were ignored by Congress. The compensation system for officers needed to be systematized. The number of navy yards should be reduced. Existing personnel regulations needed to be updated. Various irregular fiscal practices must be ended. Most egregious was the unrestricted transfer of funds among the five separate naval appropriation categories. For example, this practice allowed funds appropriated for naval pay to be used to purchase naval provisions or funds appropriated to repair ships to be employed for new construction. In addressing these issues, Branch asked the commissioners how the work of the board might be improved.[22]

In response, Rodgers authored a board report that recommended dividing the administrative work of the department into three general classifications: executive, ministerial, and financial. First, the executive or policy-making functions should remain the duty of the secretary of the navy acting in consultation with the board and under the authority of the president of the United States. Second, the ministerial or general administrative functions should remain the province of the board but should be clearly divided into three areas: the construction, repair, and equipping of the naval vessels; the construction of docks, arsenals, storehouses, and wharves; and the "victualizing" and provisioning of the navy. While acting collectively on questions of principle and administrative policy, each board member would take individual responsibility for one of the three areas and superintend the staff and actual work done therein. In effect, a military bureau system would be created with one commissioner in charge of each of the three bureaus. In time-honored bureaucratic fashion, the board also recommended that a number of new positions be added to allow the commissioners to operate the three bureaus. Third, the financial responsibilities would be divided between the secretary and the board according to their respective administrative duties. While acknowledging that "a single dollar" transferred "intentionally or otherwise, from one appropriation . . . to another . . . is a violation of the law," Rodgers recommended that the president of the United States be empowered to transfer funds between naval appropriation categories in order to meet unexpected contingencies that arose from time to time.[23] In January 1830, Branch recommended these administrative reforms to the house Naval Affairs Committee, but they went nowhere.

In the cabinet reorganization produced by the Peggy Eaton affair, Branch reluctantly resigned and was replaced in May 1831 by New Hampshire senator Levi Woodbury. As a member of the Senate Naval Affairs Committee, Woodbury had an interest in naval matters. Although, as secretary, Woodbury did not press for significant naval expansion, he renewed a number of his predecessor's recommendations, including higher pay for officers and board reorganization. He also used the navy's vessels in a more aggressive manner. For example, in August 1831, he dispatched Commodore John Downes in the frigate *Potomac* to Sumatra to retaliate for an attack against an American ship engaged in the pepper trade. In 1832, Woodbury organized and promoted the diplomatic mission of Edmund Roberts to Japan, Siam, Muscat, and Cochin China. Sailing on the warship *Peacock*, Roberts successfully concluded treaties of commerce and friendship with Muscat and Siam, but he was unsuccessful in Cochin China and decided not to go to Japan. Modest as these diplomatic accomplishments seem in retrospect, they represented an important expansion of the navy's antebellum peacetime diplomatic and commercial role in the Pacific. Although Jacksonian politicians in Washington did not realize the significance of Woodbury's actions, they would inevitably lead to the need for a larger navy and increased naval appropriations.[24]

For Rodgers, 1832 was both a bad year and a turning point in his personal life. In a letter dated 25 May, Rodgers learned that his brother, Commodore George Washington Rodgers of the Brazil squadron, had died suddenly and been buried in Buenos Aires.[25] The two brothers had never been close since John was fourteen years older than his brother and had actually left home by the time George was born in 1787. Still, John had helped George secure his warrant as a midshipman in 1804 and watched approvingly as George distinguished himself in the War of 1812 and later rose to commodore. The unexpected news that his youngest brother was dead came as an unsettling shock to Rodgers.

Then, in September, fifty-nine-year-old Rodgers's own robust health suffered permanently when he contracted Asiatic cholera. That summer a serious cholera epidemic had attacked the United States. From Canada, the disease struck hundreds and then thousands of people as it moved down the eastern seaboard, spread into the Ohio and Mississippi River valleys, and eventually reached New Orleans. Little was known about the disease at the time—only that it struck hard and suddenly. Violent diarrhea, acute spasmodic vomiting, and severe cramps signaled the onset of the disease. Serious dehydration and often cyanosis, which gave the victim's face and skin a dark, bluish tint, followed. Although many cholera victims died within hours of contracting the disease or lingered before succumbing, most victims either recovered fully or survived but indefinitely suffered from the disease's effects.

During the summer of 1832, Washingtonians waited apprehensively as the daily *National Intelligencer* charted the progress of the disease southward. Finally in mid-August, the disease struck the capital. At first, dozens, then hundreds, of cases were alleged. Residents were advised not to eat vegetables or fruits, particularly melons. Those inflicted suffered through the standard medical treatments of the day: bloodletting, the use of laudanum, or the application of cathartic agents such as the chalky mercury compound, calomel. Although huge doses of calomel were given as a popular remedy, some physicians used all three treatments. The *National Intelligencer* published a daily "Cholera Intelligence" section that carried news and statistics on casualties from Washington and other cities, but it readily acknowledged that its statistics were "defective." In addition to recording dozens of deaths, the paper admitted that fatalities were "greater than stated" because there were many cases "not to be found either in the Hospitals (the victims being too ignorant or prejudiced to go there, or to suffer others to take them there) or in private practice." Then, suddenly, the crisis passed. On 1 October, after six weeks of horror, the *Intelligencer* announced that the "cholera has disappeared from the city."[26]

One of the disease's victims was Benjamin Lincoln Lear, son of the late Tobias Lear and one of Rodgers's closest friends. Given the mysterious and frightening nature of the disease, care was not available because "everyone was afraid of him." In this situation, Rodgers personally cared for Lear for days, was with him when he died, and "with his own hands laid Mr. Lear in his grave." The day after the funeral in September, Rodgers himself contracted an acute case of the disease. Violently ill, Rodgers was bedridden for several weeks and survived. But the disease had taken a substantial toll on his constitution. Rodgers never regained his former strength, and both friends and family noticed a gradual and then increased decline in his health and his memory.[27]

Rodgers's last four years as board president from 1833 to 1837 were increasingly difficult ones as his declining health slowly sapped him of his physical strength and mental acuity. Although Rodgers religiously went to work each day, his colleagues, Charles Morris and Isaac Chauncey, assumed more of the workload. In the summer of 1834, Rodgers took the very atypical step of absenting himself from board business for six weeks. In an effort to restore his health, he and Minerva made the tedious overland trek to Warm Springs and then on to White Sulfur Springs in western Virginia, where Rodgers consumed mineral water, took the hot baths, and tried to relax. Rested, he returned to board duties in late September, but his health had not been restored and continued to decline gradually.[28]

In an effort to make his and Minerva's life more convenient, Rodgers built and moved into a large new house on Lafayette Square in 1835. He had never been a religiously devout man, but John and Minerva frequently attended nearby St. John's Episcopal Church, where daughter Louisa sang in the choir and the commodore demonstrated his impatience when sermons ran too long. Although not a wealthy man, Rodgers was financially comfortable. In addition to his salary, Rodgers calculated in 1835 that his assets exceeded $56,000, virtually all of which was in real estate and included his home in Washington, the Greenleaf Point property, and several other holdings in the area. In spite of his intimidating nature, Rodgers could be generous and charitable with friends. In 1824, he had lent $14,150 to David Porter, a loan he had some difficulty collecting. He also tried to protect and assist Mrs. Stephen Decatur with her finances after her husband was killed. Rodgers loaned her money and in 1833 contracted to purchase six of her lots in Norfolk for $7,500. Among his own relatives, Rodgers helped pay for the education of his nephews after his brother George Washington Rodgers died in 1832.[29]

The family move from Greenleaf Point to Lafayette Square was not popular with his youngest children, but it saved John an uncomfortable carriage ride six days a week to and from his office. At the time, Washington was "a straggling, muddy ill kept village," remembered Nannie; "it is really almost impossible to imagine the depth of mud in our principal streets, [and the] bemired appearance of the vehicles that slowly navigated them."[30]

Although there were no major crises during this time, naval discipline languished while tension increased among junior and senior officers. The department also continued to suffer from dilatory leadership. When Woodbury left his position in June 1834 after an undistinguished tenure to become secretary of the treasury, the president replaced him with Senator Mahlon Dickerson from New Jersey. Dickerson was another poor choice to head the Navy Department. Sixty-four years old when appointed, he was in poor health, lacked background in naval affairs, and proved to be a weak administrator.[31]

Clearly adrift, the Navy Department came under continuing criticism, and calls for change and reform persisted. There were complaints of administrative inefficiency, bureaucratic lethargy, and fiscal waste, and also charges of corruption with naval contracts. In April 1833, Amos Kendall and the mayor of Washington came to Rodgers's office to investigate charges of "peculation" against him. Outraged, Rodgers replied that if he was being charged with an "official misdemeanor," he was entitled to a trial by his peers. Refusing to hold himself accountable to his accusers, Rodgers showed them the "door of the office, out of which he recommended them to retire, to save him and them the mortification of his kicking them out, which he should certainly otherwise do." Two days later, the administration newspaper, the *Washington Globe*, denied any intention of trying Rodgers personally, stating that the inquiry related only to "some malversation of his clerks."[32]

Construction and repair projects became another target because they took too long, cost too much, and entailed too much interference by the commissioners. Since 1815, construction of new warships had been done in navy yards under board control. Each yard had a resident constructor who was responsible for design and construction according to the specifications set by the board. This system placed constructors, as the technical experts on naval design, under the control of experienced senior naval officers with no design expertise. Although this should have been an ideal arrangement, it was not because the constructors were not only completely subordinate to the navy commissioners but also insulated from civilian advances in ship design and construction. Moreover, the board could and did change its mind after a design had been approved. As a result, armament could be altered, allowances of stores or crew changed, and the number of boats onboard increased.[33]

In 1826, the construction system was updated with the appointment of Samuel Humphreys as chief naval constructor. All resident constructors reported to Humphreys, who remained subordinate to the board. Although Humphreys was a capable builder and administrator, the board continued to approve design plans and to control the building process. As a result, the quality of naval design and construction suffered. Other than a few vessels, most notably the ship of the line *Ohio*, built after 1815, new American warships did not measure up to the fast and elegant frigates built three decades earlier by private builders. In 1837, an article by an American naval officer lamented American naval architecture had "rather retrograded" in recent years, "during which we have launched some ships that would be a disgrace to the Chinese Navy."[34]

By 1833, civilians and progressive naval officers were renewing their calls to remake the Navy Department by either revamping or eliminating the Board of Navy Commissioners. Other critics urged the abolition of corporal punishment, or flogging, and the elimination of the grog ration in the naval service. A small but active group of junior naval officers pressing for naval reforms included Matthew C. Perry, Alexander Slidell, and Samuel Du Pont. Within a few years they would be joined by other officers, most notably Lieutenant Matthew Fontaine Maury. They initially focused on the education, training, and compensation of officers, but soon these reformers were urging the introduction of modern technologies as well.[35]

In New York, Perry and other officers established a naval lyceum at the Brooklyn navy yard. Founded in 1833 and incorporated two years later, the organization sought "to promote the diffusion of useful knowledge, to foster a spirit of harmony . . . and to cement the links which united us as professional brethren." The membership of the naval lyceum consisted primarily of young commissioned and noncommissioned officers, but the founders were shrewd enough to create an honorary membership category in which they included the president of the United States, the secretary of the navy, and the navy commissioners.[36]

The journal of the lyceum, the *Naval Magazine*, carried "useful information" as well as interesting material for general readers. The periodical did not stress technological change, but it carried abundant information on steam power, explosive ordnance, propellers, and other innovations. In January 1837, the *Naval Magazine* outlined the agenda of the naval reformers. "All of our misfortunes as a nation," claimed the authors, "from the day we became one, have proceeded from the want of a sufficient navy." To remedy this deficiency, the United States needed to build a navy sufficient to protect its far-flung commercial interests, one comparable to the other navies of the world, and one capable of being quickly expanded during an actual war. But an expanded navy and more ships were not enough; internal reforms must be instituted. The present promotion and rank system needed to be revamped so that officers could earn promotion on a systematic and meritorious basis. An apprentice system needed to be formed to create a class of native-born, able seamen. Better discipline and order needed to be established and maintained.[37]

Although reformers such as Lieutenant Matthew Fontaine Maury would later criticize the navy board sharply, Perry and Slidell were careful not to fault the department or the board directly. After all, Perry was a protégé, ally, and friend of Rodgers, and both Perry and Slidell were related to Rodgers by marriage. In fact, Perry continued to praise his mentor. "Our Navy has confer'd such great and lasting honour on our country," wrote Perry, "and to no other perhaps are we more indebted for its efficiency than to Com. Rodgers."[38]

At the same time, the calls for reform subjected the navy and the board to scrutiny and, inevitably, to criticism. The commissioners were especially vulnerable on the issue of steam power, a technology the board opposed. The world's first steam warship had been built by Robert Fulton in 1814 but was not trial tested until after the War of 1812 had ended. The *Demologos*, or *Fulton*, as it was also known, was a primitive but potentially effective weapon designed for harbor defense. Rendered relatively invulnerable by walls almost five feet thick, the *Fulton* displaced 2,475 tons, mounted thirty-two large guns, and could steam at more than 5 knots. Although unappreciated by naval experts for almost two decades, the invention of the steam warship signaled "the most important development" in naval warfare "since the fifteenth century, when the discovery of the art of tacking inaugurated the era of the sailing ship." The commercial arena led the way in developing steam navigation. By the mid-1830s, an estimated seven hundred steam vessels plied the lakes, rivers, and coastal waters of the United States. Virtually all of these ships were small vessels driven by crude steam machinery and limited to short cruises.[39]

In the United States and Europe, naval officials showed little interest in steam power. But by the early 1830s, the British and French had begun to purchase or build steam warships. Within a decade, the British would have forty-nine steam warships in commission and the French thirty-three. While the steam warships were used initially in auxiliary roles, both the British and French quickly realized that the ships represented a vital component of their respective naval forces. In the United States, development of the steam warship was even slower. The *Fulton* had ended up languishing as a receiving ship until an explosion destroyed her in 1829. In 1822, the navy had purchased the small steam galliot the *Sea Gull* to battle pirates in the shallow waters of the Caribbean, but this steamer was permanently out of commission by 1825. Although the naval expansion act of 1816 had authorized the construction of three steam batteries, none was built. During the 1820s and early 1830s, an occasional report or recommendation from the secretary of the navy had suggested that experiments with steam be conducted or that steam batteries be built, but the department took no action.[40]

Resistance to the use of steam power in warships was strong among naval officers everywhere but particularly so in the United States. Professional opposition to steam sprang from several sources. First, the new steam machinery was heavy, bulky, crude, and unreliable. Second, steam technology had inherent drawbacks even when it functioned well. The boilers burned coal rapidly and required a large supply of coal, which occupied valuable space onboard and made the ships less seaworthy. In addition, the large, cumbersome paddle wheels of early steam vessels offered an easy target for enemy guns, as did the high profile of the steam boilers and machinery located on deck above the waterline. Believing that the disadvantages of steam power far outweighed its advantages, many naval officers saw steam-powered ships as cumbersome liabilities, not formidable war machines. The inefficiency of early steam engines also greatly reduced the effective range of steamers. While they might serve well on a coast, in a harbor or a river, or on a lake, steam vessels seemed incapable of making long ocean cruises.

Third, even if and when the technology improved and addressed many of these problems, naval officers, particularly senior officers, still viewed the new technology as offensive, an insult and perversion of naval tradition. Ugly, noisy, and dirty, the steamers offered little challenge of seamanship because, once underway, they could be steered against wind, currents, and tides. In contrast, sailing conventional frigates or ships of the line powered only by the wind required expert seamanship. The commanding officer had to understand and utilize prevailing winds and currents to the ship's advantage. Although a great amount of technical information had to be mastered, sailing a large nineteenth-century warship remained as much an art as a science. A bad tactical decision, a misjudged wind, or a mistake with the complicated sails and rigging could easily spell disaster. Dating back centuries, the traditions and heritage of sailing warships were revered by officers in all navies. Adding to this mystique was the recent advent of huge warships of majestic and formidable dimensions; their tall masts with unfurled sails and intricate rigging created an awe-inspiring sight. Unless they were engaged in an actual battle, these ships were elegant and quiet. They only creaked and groaned, enabling voices onboard to be easily heard. Steamships also threatened to supplant the brave and skilled sailors who had climbed masts and handled rigging and sails with deck-bound coal heavers, mechanics, and firemen. Anyone with a reverence for naval tradition or the romance of the sailing ship could not but resist this technological monster.

The American navy's initial response to steam power was not much different, of course, from the military establishment's initial responses later to the mechanized tank, the airplane, or the submarine. Most senior American officers totally opposed steam power, but even those who embraced its use thought steam useful only for auxiliary purposes, not as a replacement for large, sail-powered battleships. Steam might be used for defense batteries, to tow warships from one point to another, or to power small warships, like the *Sea Gull*, operating for limited distances in shallow coastal waters. But steam-driven warships would never supplant large, oceangoing sailing frigates and ships of the line. Even after steam power had proved itself a superior technology and was widely used in European navies, the U.S. Navy dragged its feet. As late as 1850, the navy listed only seven oceangoing steamers, and four of those were still under construction.[41]

In this context, it is understandable that the navy commissioners resisted the calls for the introduction of steam technology. After all, Rodgers and his two colleagues, Charles Morris and Isaac Chauncey, epitomized the old guard against which ambitious, progressive young officers chafed. In 1833, Rodgers was sixty years old and had been in the navy for thirty-five years. Forty-nine-year-old Morris and sixty-one-yearold Chauncey both had thirty-four years of naval service. With more than one century of collective naval experience among them, the three commissioners had been trained and achieved distinction at sea in the golden days of fighting sail, a period now, in the mid-1830s, almost two decades past. Although they could not know it at the time, the last great naval engagement between sail-powered warships had already occurred in the Mediterranean at Navarino in 1827, when a combined British-French-Russian force had decimated a Turkish and Egyptian squadron.

After years of department and board inaction, Secretary Dickerson finally requested, in June 1835, that the board take immediate steps to begin the construction of a steam warship as authorized by Congress in 1816. Dickerson also asked the board to submit plans for the vessel and its machinery to him for the approval of President Jackson. Thus directed, the board proceeded slowly. Acknowledging that "they [the commissioners] are incompetent themselves, and have no person under their direction" with expertise on steam engines, Rodgers appealed for outside assistance. In February 1836, with a board recommendation, Secretary Dickerson appointed a capable young engineer, Charles Haswell, for two months to "furnish draughts of a high and lower-pressure steam engine and boiler." The department later appointed Haswell as the chief engineer for the new steam warship, the *Fulton*, which was to be commanded by Captain Matthew C. Perry. Progress on the new vessel was slow. Rodgers had actually resigned from the board by the time the new steamship was launched in May 1837, even though its steam boilers had not yet been installed.[42]

As the board fumbled with the steam issue, it also became apparent that the commissioners lacked a strategic vision for a modern navy, an issue raised by a shift in President Jackson's naval policy. In his annual message to Congress in December 1835, the president had acknowledged not only that the existing navy was "inadequate to the protection of our rapidly increasing commerce" but also that the navy, not the militia, furnished "our best security against foreign aggressions." The navy, then, needed a "a speedy increase of the force" as well as an apprentice system to train American boys between thirteen and eighteen years old.[43]

Jackson's about-face was occasioned by two developments. First, the American economy was booming. By 1835, the federal government had eliminated the national debt, and, indeed, the president was able to report a federal surplus of $19 million to Congress. Second, a dispute with France over the payment of outstanding claims had escalated into a diplomatic crisis. Many Americans expected war. France actually appropriated 25 million francs in April to be paid to the United States on the condition that Jackson apologize for previous statements he had made about France in the dispute. When Jackson bluntly refused to apologize in December, the crisis worsened. In January 1836, he recommended reprisals against the French, the completion of a coastal defense, and a large increase in naval expenditures. Although the French crisis was resolved by May, naval appropriations increased dramatically in 1836 and 1837.[44]

In was in this atmosphere that Rodgers, speaking for the board, outlined what was necessary to "place the naval defences of the United States . . . upon the footing of strength and respectability which is due to the security and welfare of the Union." Rodgers began by describing the factors that should determine the nation's naval defenses: the vast geographical separation of the United States from its likely European enemies, the great length of the nation's coastline, the need to secure communications between the entire Mississippi Valley through the Gulf of Mexico with all parts of the East Coast, and the importance of protecting the "widely extended and extremely valuable commerce" of the country.[45]

Having outlined these key factors, Rodgers nevertheless ignored them in estimating how large a naval force was required. Instead, his report estimated that during a war, approximately thirty thousand merchant seamen would be available for naval service. Using the available number of sailors to determine how many ships were required, the board arrived at a force of 135 warships, including 25 ships of the line, 35 frigates, 25 sloops, 25 steamers, and 25 small vessels. Since the navy had a total of only 61 ships currently available, 74 additional ships were required, including 14 ships of the line, 13 frigates, and 25 steamers, as well as 22 smaller warships. Recognizing that a much smaller force was needed in peacetime, Rodgers recommended that 42 ships be placed in active service and divided among six different stations: the Mediterranean, the Indian Ocean, the western Pacific Ocean, the east coast of South America, the West Indies, and along the coastline of the United States.

Although it contained numerical details and fiscal estimates, Rodgers's report contained basic strategic deficiencies. First, the recommendations were based not on factors that defined the defensive job to be done but rather on the number of seamen who might be available. Second, the report did not envision establishing command of the sea, even that portion of the sea proximate to the United States, as a strategic objective. Rather, Rodgers openly acknowledged that American commerce would be seriously disrupted during a war, thus freeing thirty thousand merchant seamen, or about one-third of the nation's total. Third, Rodgers did admit the need for steam vessels, recommending that twenty-five naval steamers be built. But he did not define their role other than to state that the steamers would be used to "protect our great estuaries, [and] to aid the operations of our other naval force."[46] Fourth, Rodgers recommended that naval squadrons be permanently maintained on six different stations, but he defined the role of these squadrons in narrow traditional terms. Ships on these stations were to protect American commerce from disruption and injury, not to help foster or expand it. Rodgers's report remained silent on, and presumably opposed to, the use of naval resources for a commercial and scientific expedition such as the long-delayed U.S. Exploring Expedition, which would finally sail in 1838. As one naval historian has noted, this official report demonstrated that the navy and the board were "still groping for sound principles of naval strategy and organization."[47] Although they requested a total of sixty frigates and ships of the line, they did not indicate any grasp of how to employ such a considerable force. Nor, in their concentration on capital ships, did they show any understanding of the navy's evolving and expanding peacetime commercial and diplomatic role.

On 1 May 1837, Rodgers's declining health forced him to resign from the board. Despite his attempts, he had never fully recovered from his cholera attack in 1832. Although criticism of the board did not cause Rodgers's resignation, the board had clearly outlived its useful life, and its days were numbered. It was an increasingly cumbersome and inefficient administrative mechanism whose members were out of touch. But how does one judge the overall contribution of the board and particularly Rodgers as its president for more than nineteen years of its twenty-seven-year existence?

A number of historians have verbally flogged Rodgers and his fellow commissioners for being inflexible, conservative, or even regressive officers who coveted authority, resisted change, shunned technological innovations, and thereby impeded the development of the U.S. Navy in the quarter-century after 1815.[48] While parts of that critique are on the mark, general condemnation of the board and Rodgers is unfair and inaccurate. First, during its first fourteen years, the board performed well in executing its mandate. The board promptly took control and brought order and system to the construction, repair, arming, and fitting out of naval vessels. In establishing an operational organization in the navy yards, the board tightly controlled the alteration of warships, created procurement procedures, and assigned responsibility for inspection of ships. In other words, the board had successfully replaced the uneven and often amateurish administration of the pre-1815 Navy Department. Essential to these implemented changes were the professional expertise, high standards, personal dedication, and hard work of Rodgers and his board colleagues.[49]

Unfortunately for the board, the late 1820s brought a sea change. Beginning in 1829, a succession of inexperienced and ineffective department secretaries weakened the leadership and the credibility of the navy. It had also become apparent that a three-officer board attempting to deal collectively with the navy's expanding volume of administrative items was an inefficient way to conduct the navy's business. By this time, the board's primary asset, the extensive naval experience of its commissioners, increasingly became a liability. Senior naval officers who had started their careers in the previous century and risen during the age of fighting sail were threatened by new technologies and were not adaptable to the navy's new role. When Commodores Rodgers, Hull, Porter, and Decatur had served on the board in its first five years, each was a relatively young officer in the prime of his professional career. Unfortunately, by 1830, these commissioners had become the old guard, and the board had become a haven for very senior officers past their prime. Because there was no retirement system, they clogged promotion channels. One administrative victim was the board itself, which had no mechanism to infuse its composition with talented young officers and their progressive views. The Board of Navy Commissioners, then, should receive mixed marks. It achieved its initial goals and performed some administrative functions very well. But lacking the means to adapt to various pressures and to embrace changing realities, the board was inevitably marked for the bureaucratic extinction it experienced in 1842.

It is unlikely that Rodgers would have changed his views had he lived and served on the board for another five years, but his naval career was over. In spite of pressures for change, Rodgers believed that senior naval officers were best qualified to control administration of the navy. He recognized and would have supported changes to the board, but he had every reason to fear greater civilian control of the department. After all, since 1801, Rodgers had known and worked with nine naval secretaries. As a second-tier cabinet position, the office was not sought after and did not attract highly talented individuals. While some secretaries such as Robert Smith, William Jones, and Samuel Southard had proven effective and capable, most had been inexperienced and average men at best. Moreover, the recent experience with secretaries Branch, Woodbury, and Dickerson had been a particularly unsettling experience for the naval commissioners.

After resigning from the board in May 1837, Rodgers and his servant Butler traveled to England, where he hoped the bracing climate would restore his health. In England, Rodgers was treated graciously and respectfully received by his civilian and military hosts. But his health did not improve, and he returned to the United States in August. With his condition worsening, Rodgers made a last attempt to restore his health by entering the Philadelphia Naval Asylum. With four teenaged children and an eight-year-old son still at home, Minerva was unable to move the family to Philadelphia, but she did take lodging to be with her husband for extended periods.[50]

At the Naval Asylum, Rodgers placed himself under the care of one of the leading physicians in the navy, surgeon Thomas Harris, who had served during the War of 1812. Stationed in Philadelphia, Harris continued to study medicine, opened a medical school for naval surgeons, served as a professor of surgery at the non-degree-granting Medical Institute of Philadelphia, and became a surgeon at the Pennsylvania Hospital. He had been one of the three naval surgeons who accompanied Rodgers on his mission to the

Key West naval station in 1823 to determine the cause of the epidemic fever there. In 1834, Secretary Woodbury had offered Harris the position of superintendent of medical affairs of the navy, but Harris declined and remained in Philadelphia. In spite of Harris's best efforts, he was not able to reverse the decline of his famous patient. Quietly, on 1 August 1838, Rodgers died in the arms of his trusted servant Butler.[51]

His body was taken to the Philadelphia home of Commodore James Biddle, where it lay until Rodgers was buried in the early evening of 3 August. The procession to the Christ Church cemetery at Fifth and Arch Streets was impressive. Led by the first brigade of the Pennsylvania militia, the cortege marched to the solemn music of the German Washington Guards band and included a detachment of marines, clergymen, naval officers, government officials, and friends. The coffin was draped in the stars and stripes and supported by six pallbearers, including Commodores Biddle and Charles Stewart and Captain William Shubrick. The solemn occasion attracted "many thousands" of observers to the cemetery, where Reverend Stephen Tying read the Episcopal burial rites, the coffin was lowered into the grave, and the marines fired a final three-volley salute.[52] Philadelphia was not to be Rodgers's final resting place. In 1839, his body was moved to the family burial site in the Congressional Cemetery in Washington. There he joined his son, Frederick, and there he would be united thirty-eight years later with his beloved Minerva.

By 1838, the navy's public image had lost much of the glitter it had enjoyed twenty-four years earlier, when the United States was last at war and Rodgers was at the apex of his career. Americans were now preoccupied with an economic depression and fixed on westward territorial expansion. Not surprisingly, an old naval hero was praised for a time but soon receded as a dim memory. Still, John Rodgers had left a considerable, if not fully appreciated, historical legacy. The preeminent naval officer of his era, Rodgers had dominated American naval affairs for more than a quarter of a century and as no other officer would in the nineteenth century. As a young officer, he had risen quickly and made his mark in war and peace. Within a decade, he had won public acclaim, earned the regard of civilian leaders, and emerged as the most influential officer in the navy. By 1821, only twenty-three years after joining the navy, Rodgers had become its senior officer, a distinction he would enjoy for almost two decades. Although he usually disagreed with his superiors on how large the navy should be, Rodgers won the respect of the five U.S. presidents as well as the most capable of the nine naval secretaries under whom he had served. Presidents Madison and Monroe had offered to appoint him secretary of the navy, a position he declined each time.

During his long career, he served with genuine distinction and made enviable contributions during three wars and a long period of peace. Rodgers first won acclaim in 1799 as first lieutenant under Captain Thomas Truxtun on the *Constellation* in the dramatic capture of *L'Insurgente* during the Quasi-War with France. Promoted to captain before he was thirty years old, Rodgers served ably as ship and squadron commander in the Mediterranean from 1803 to 1807 during the Barbary Wars. Later, on four cruises during the War of 1812, he managed to elude and frustrate his British adversary in the Atlantic for months, but, alas, he captured few ships and failed to strike a combat blow against the enemy. In the successful defense of Baltimore in 1814, Rodgers played a critical role in bolstering American morale and defenses in the immediate aftermath of the British capture of Washington.

While fellow officers such as Hull, Decatur, Perry, Porter, and Bainbridge basked in the glory of their naval exploits, a chagrined Rodgers had to content himself with the satisfaction of having escaped, distracted, and frustrated the British. He may not have won a great combat victory as a commander, but at least he had suffered no defeats or significant embarrassments. In an age when the American navy won great victories, it also endured the capture of the frigate *Philadelphia* in 1803, the shelling of the *Chesapeake* in 1807, and the loss of various warships during the War of 1812. Rodgers was associated with none of these embarrassments. As a commander, Rodgers was unlucky in never being at the right place at the precise moment when he might have gained the immortality he sought. He was also a man of imperfect judgment, at times too impetuous, at others too careful. Although the *Little Belt* affair did not harm his reputation, he was embarrassed to have mistaken the British sloop to be a much larger vessel than, in fact, she was. Then, in the War of 1812, he was impatient in his chase of the *Belvidera* but later overly cautious as he overestimated the size of enemy warships on several occasions, thus losing the chance to engage and defeat them. He also suffered from uneven luck. He might well have taken the *Belividera* in 1812 had his own guns not exploded at the outset of the engagement.

After the War of 1812, Rodgers emerged as a dominant force in the peacetime navy in his two terms as president of the Board of Navy Commissioners, which brought order, system, and efficiency to the administration of the navy. He and the board revised naval regulations, improved financial practices, introduced contract purchasing, took control of naval construction and repair, and created checks against fraud. The board also proposed progressive personnel reforms in the recruitment of sailors, the education of young officers, and the rank and promotion structure. Although they were not approved during Rodgers's terms, these recommendations were well conceived. And even though the board eventually became the target of increasing criticism by the mid-1830s as an outmoded body and would be replaced in 1842, it had made a significant contribution to the peacetime navy during its first two decades.

Rodgers's tenure as board president was broken by an important twenty-eight-month cruise of the Mediterranean squadron, which he commanded. From 1825 to 1827, he restored the frayed discipline of the squadron, maintained American neutrality during the Greek Revolution between the rebels and their Turkish rulers, and laid the groundwork for an unprecedented diplomatic and commercial treaty with Turkey.

Critical elements in Rodgers's influence and public stature were his character and professional conduct. A family man of absolute probity, Rodgers did not gamble, carouse, or drink hard liquor. As a young officer, he embraced the model of excellence created by his first commander, Captain Thomas Truxtun. He was never involved in the periodic scandals and nasty feuds that marred the navy's public image. Although sensitive and protective of his personal honor, Rodgers never allowed arguments with fellow officers to degenerate into duels or prolonged public quarrels. Setting high standards for himself, Rodgers also demanded that those who served under him aspire to the same level of professional excellence. He established operating routines and practices, known as the "Rodgers system of discipline," which became the preferred disciplinary norm for decades. Like other officers who adhered to the same high ideal, Rodgers set demanding standards of which the nation could be rightfully proud, to which future American naval officers would aspire, and which won him a host of friends and admirers among his naval peers. His longtime naval friends included some of the most distinguished officers of their time—Thomas Tingley, Stephen Decatur, Charles Morris, Isaac Hull, and Isaac Chauncey, as well as rising young officers such as Matthew C. Perry, Alexander Slidell, and Samuel F. Du Pont, all of whom served under and had great respect for Rodgers.

Rodgers was a man of few, but passionate, devotions. He was a fervent patriot who loved the navy. The navy always came first. Everything in his personal life for forty years revolved around and was secondary to his devotion to the navy, even though he adored and was intensely devoted to his wife and to their children. Like many other leading public figures of his era, Rodgers was motivated by high-minded principles. As a man of courage, honor, and ambition, he hoped that a career of naval service would bring him fame, glory, and fortune. In the prevailing ethos of his day, the pursuit of immortal fame through sacrifice and service to country was regarded as a worthy and admirable motive. Essentially a practical man of action who was deadly serious in all that he did, Rodgers was not a man of hobbies or amusements. He apparently liked to read books such as Cooper's tales of the sea, but he did not have broad intellectual interests. In the eastern Mediterranean, he visited famous ancient sites and gathered relics, but he undertook these activities in a perfunctory way. He clearly did not share the historical fascination with antiquity of fellow officers such as Daniel T. Patterson and Matthew C. Perry.

Stout, muscular, and physically intimidating, Rodgers exhibited a forceful manner, an indomitable will, and great physical energy. He also evinced a quick temper and a dark visage when angry. Some found Rodgers's demeanor overbearing or even insufferable. Certainly, that was the initial impression of Minerva Denison and her mother when they first met Rodgers in 1802. His relationship with his brother George Washington was stiff and distant. Over the years Rodgers also attracted his share of enemies and detractors. During the War of 1812, the British despised what they considered Rodgers's vainglorious arrogance.

His strong feelings, passionate nature, and quick temper won him animosity and scorn among some of his peers. Thomas Truxtun, his first commander, was initially an admirer and strong supporter of Rodgers but later became and remained a sharp critic. By 1811, Truxtun, himself an embittered former naval officer who was possibly jealous of Rodgers's stature, confided to a friend that "I have long since lost all opinion of Rodgers, and he knows it—he is a trifler and a sycophant—such men I despise and I despise Rodgers." Rodgers and Edward Preble were natural rivals who instinctively disliked each other. Rodgers and James Barron had a long-standing animosity that almost led to a duel in 1807 and produced several unseemly incidents later. Ironically, for two days before he was buried, Rodgers's coffin lay at the Philadelphia home of Commodore James Biddle, who fifteen years earlier had sharply criticized Rodgers. After Rodgers had sided with Isaac Hull against Biddle during a navy trial, Biddle privately condemned Rodgers's "base gratification of personal malignancy—. . . . I despise Comr Rodgers as much as I detest his character."[53]

Most assuredly not warm and comforting, Rodgers's personality and demeanor never made him a popular officer or beloved commander or won him the adulation of other officers or the general public. In an era when sailors often bestowed descriptive, and usually good-natured, nicknames on their commanders, Rodgers had none. While he struck an impressive presence in his uniform, he clearly lacked the charisma of militia heroes like Andrew Jackson or the flamboyance of naval heroes like Stephen Decatur and Oliver Hazard Perry. Nevertheless, in spite of his lack of flair, Rodgers came to epitomize the ideal American naval officer. His distinguished record, his command presence, his exceptional ability, and his high ideals combined to overcome the fact that he was not a combat hero. One of the great senators of his era remembered Rodgers as an idyllic symbol. Serving in the Senate from 1820 to 1850, Missourian Thomas Hart Benton was an outspoken and loyal Jacksonian Democrat from a landlocked western state. In his autobiography published in the 1850s, Benton vividly recollected Rodgers. "He was to me the complete impersonation of my idea of the perfect commander— person, mind, and manners; with the qualities of command grafted on the groundwork of a good citizen and good father . . . and all lodged in a frame to bespeak the seaman and officer."[54] Coming from an observer who could be harsh in his judgments of others, this was high praise. Certainly no other naval officer of his generation had earned such rock- solid stature.

Notes

Abbreviations

ASP	American State Papers
HSP	Historical Society of Pennsylvania
JRP	John Rodgers Papers
LC	Library of Congress
NA	National Archives, Navy Department, Record Group 45.
NASP	New American State Papers
NHF	Naval Historical Foundation, Library of Congress
NYHS	New York Historical Society
R	Microfilm reel or roll number
RFP	Rodgers Family Papers
WLCL	William L. Clements Library, University of Michigan.

Preface

1. Paullin, *Rodgers*; K. Jack Bauer, "John Rodgers: The Stalwart Conservative," in Bradford, *Command under Sail*, 220; McKee, *Preble*, vii.

2. Benton, *Thirty Years' View*, 2: 144.

Chapter 1. Maryland Merchant Captain and Navy Lieutenant, 1773–99

1. Shelley, "Ebenezer Hazard's Travels," 53.

2. "Biographical Notice of Com. John Rodgers," typescript, RFP, LC.

3. Autobiography of John Rodgers, typescript, RFP, LC.

4. Shelley, "Ebenezer Hazard's Travels," 47; Preston, *History of Harford County*, 249; C. Wright, *Our Harford Heritage*, 312.

5. Risjord, *Chesapeake Politics*, 9–10; U.S. Bureau of the Census, *A Century of Population Growth*, 199; see also Scharf, *History of Maryland*, 2: 60–61.

6. "Biographical Notice of Com. John Rodgers," typescript, RFP, LC; statement on Rodgers's early life, n.d., JRP, WLCL.

7. There are a number of excellent summaries of Baltimore in the 1780s and 1790s, including Olson, *Baltimore: The Building of an American City*, 26–40, and Browne, *Baltimore in the New Nation*, 19–50.

8. Paullin, *Rodgers*, 74; "Biographical Notice of Com. John Rodgers," typescript, RFP, LC; statement on Rodgers's early life, JRP, WLCL.

9. "Biographical Notice of Com. John Rodgers," typescript, RFP, LC.

10. "Autobiography of John Rodgers," typescript, RFP, LC.

11. Ibid.

12. "Abstract of Cases of Capture of American Vessels by French," in Knox, *Naval Documents Related to the Quasi-War between the United States and France* (hereafter cited as *Quasi-War*), 1: 28.

13. Paullin, *Rodgers*, 32–33; McKee, *A Gentlemanly and Honorable Profession*, xi-xii,

14. Chapelle, *History of the American Sailing Navy*, 129, 130, 536.

15. John J. Carrigg, "Benjamin Stoddert," in Coletta, *American Secretaries of the Navy*, 1: 62, 71–72.

16. Ferguson, *Truxtun*, v-vii, 127, 138–41; McKee, *A Gentlemanly and Honorable Profession*, 165–67.

17. Truxtun to ——— [a junior officer], 9 February 1799, Truxtun Papers, Library Company of Philadelphia.

18. [Porter], *Constantinople and Its Environs*, 2: 10–11.

19. Ferguson, *Truxtun*, 140–41.

20. Truxtun to Simon Goss, 30 August 1797, in *Quasi-War*, 1: 15.

21. J. Adams to commanders of armed vessels, 28 May 1798, in *Quasi-War*, 1: 88.

22. Statement of Truxtun, 2 July 1798, in *Quasi-War*, 1: 156–58.

23. Ibid.; orders of Truxtun, 29 June, 22 July, and 10 August 1798, Truxtun Papers, HSP; also in *Quasi-War*, 1: 233, 291.

24. McKee, *A Gentlemanly and Honorable Profession*, 255–57; muster roll of the *Constellation*, 17 November 1798, in *Quasi-War*, 1: 312.

25. Stoddert to Truxtun, 2 July 1798, in *Quasi-War*, 1: 158; extract from journal of Truxtun, 31 August 1798, ibid., 1: 365. The journal of the *Constellation* for 1798–99 is in Truxtun Papers, HSP.

26. Truxtun to Cowper, 15 August 1798; see also Truxtun to Triplett, 10 August 1798, both in *Quasi-War*, 1: 298–99, 290–91.

27. Stoddert to Truxtun, 18 December 1798; see also Stoddert to Truxtun, 16 January 1799, both in *Quasi-War*, 2: 95–96, 242–43.

28. Stoddert to Truxtun, 8 December 1798, in *Quasi-War*, 2: 73–74.

29. Truxtun to Stoddert, 3 February 1799, in *Quasi-War*, 2: 303–4.

30. Truxtun to Stoddert, 10 February 1799, in *Quasi-War*, 2: 326–27; journal of the *Constellation*, ibid., 2: 328–29 and 2: 336–37; letter from Andrew Sterrett to his brother Charles, 14 February 1799, ibid., 2: 334–35.

31. Rodgers to Truxtun, 15 February 1799; Truxtun to Stoddert, 14 February 1799, both in *Quasi-War*, 2: 336–37, 330.

32. Goldsborough, *United States Naval Chronicle*, 132–33. Truxtun did not mention the incident in his official report. Truxtun to Stoddert, 10, 14 February 1799, in *Quasi-War*, 2: 326–31. In addition to his written account, Goldsborough told the story publicly at a dinner in honor of Rodgers on 22 July 1824; see the *Daily National Intelligencer*, 24 July 1824.

33. Among those who accept the likely validity of the story are Paullin, *Rodgers*,

46–47; Pratt, *Preble's Boys*, 203–4; Long, *Nothing Too Daring*, 9; Porter, *Memoir*, 22–23.

34. Stoddert to J. Adams, 25 May 1799; Stoddert to Truxtun, 31 May 1799, both in *Quasi-War*, 3: 252–253, 285–86.

35. Ferguson, *Truxtun*, 170–72; Paullin, *Rodgers*, 50.

36. Ferguson, *Truxtun*, 175–76.

Chapter 2. Captain in the Caribbean, 1799–1802

1. Stoddert to Rodgers, 13 June 1799; Stoddert to Truxtun, 31 May, 10 June 1799; Stoddert to Adams, 25 May 1799, all in *Quasi-War*, 3: 335, 285, 322, 252–53.

2. J. Buchanan to secretary of state, 5 September 1799, in *Quasi-War*, 3: 159; Rodgers to Stoddert, 14 September, RFP, HSP.

3. Quarter bill of the *Maryland*, JRP, WLCL; for an excerpt from Rodgers's regulations, see Paullin, *Rodgers*, 56–60; J. Buchanan to secretary of state, 5 September 1799, in *Quasi-War*, 3: 159.

4. Stoddert to Rodgers, 5 September 1799, in *Quasi-War*, 4: 159; Stoddert to Rodgers, 29 December 1799, RFP, LC.

5. Rodgers to Stoddert, 20 September 1800, in *Quasi-War*, 6: 365.

6. Letter from officer of *Maryland*, 21 November 1799, in *Quasi-War*, 4: 437–38.

7. T. Tufts to Stoddert, 3 February 1800, in *Quasi-War*, 5: 181.

8. Stoddert to Decatur, 5 April 1800; Rodgers to Stoddert, 20 September 1800 (two letters), all in *Quasi-War*, 5: 386, 6: 364, 367.

9. Rodgers to General Megan, military commander, Suriname, 7 December 1799, RFP, HSP.

10. Rodgers to Stoddert, 20 September 1800, in *Quasi-War*, 6: 367–68.

11. Tufts to secretary of state, 31 January 1800, in *Quasi-War*, 5: 154–57.

12. Rodgers to Stoddert, 20 September 1800; Rodgers to Stoddert, 20 September 1800, both in *Quasi-War*, 6: 182–83, 312.

13. Rodgers to Stoddert, 20 September 1800, in *Quasi-War*, 6: 364–65. For a critical assessment of Rodgers, see Palmer, *Stoddert's War*, 194–95.

14. Stoddert to Rodgers, 18 March 1801; see also Stoddert to Rodgers, 7 March 1801 (two letters), all in *Quasi-War*, 7: 148, 141.

15. Symonds, *Navalists and Antinavalists*, 86; Sprout and Sprout, *Rise of American Naval Power*, 52.

16. U.S. Bureau of the Census, *Historical Statistics*, Part 2: 1104; 335–38, 466–71. The definition of the federal fiscal year was changed in 1843 to run from 1 July to 30 June.

17. Malone, *Jefferson and His Time*, 4: 12; Symonds, *Navalists and Antinavalists*, 87–88.

18. [The] *Maryland*, in *Quasi-War*, 7: 368; Smith to Rodgers, 22 October 1801, ibid., 7: 292.

19. Malone, *Jefferson*, 4: 251, 252.

20. Ott, *Haitian Revolution*, 145–54.

21. Brighton, *Checkered Career of Tobias Lear*, 191.

22. "Autobiography of John Rodgers," 2; "Biographical Notice of Comm. John Rodgers," 25, both typescripts in RFP, LC; Brighton, *Lear*, 190–92.

23. Logan, *Diplomatic Relations*; Ott, *Haitian Revolution*, 155–59; Brighton, *Lear*, 192–93.

24. [Rodgers], "Narrative of Facts Relative to My Imprisonment in Cape Francois," typescript, RFP, NHF, LC.

25. "Biographical Notice of Comm. John Rodgers," typescript, RFP, LC.

26. Rodgers to Pinkney, 20 November 1802, RFP, HSP.

27. G. Denison to W. Crozier, 26 April 1792, RFP, HSP.

28. [Minerva Denison], "Memoir," typescript, RFP, LC; for a summary of her descendants, see W. V. Cox to M. Meigs, 2 February 1892, JRP, WLCL. Minerva's older sister died as an infant.

29. Ibid.

30. Ibid.

31. Ibid.

Chapter 3. Commodore in the Mediterranean, 1802–6

1. Smith to Rodgers, 25 August, 18 September 1802, JRP, WLCL. Built in Charleston, South Carolina, the *John Adams* had actually been constructed by two different contractors. As a result, the frigate had a delicacy of beam on one side that meant that she sailed faster on one tack than on the other. Paullin, *Rodgers*, 100–101.

2. Irwin, *Diplomatic Relations*, 1–19; Field, *America and the Mediterranean World*, 27–49. The ruler of Algiers was usually referred to as the dey; the ruler of Morocco, which was independent, as the emperor; the ruler of Tripoli as the pasha; and the ruler of Tunis as the bey.

3. Frank L. Owsley, "Robert Smith," in Coletta, *American Secretaries of the Navy*, 1: 77–90.

4. G. Allen, *Our Navy and the Barbary Corsairs*, 1–2.

5. The Tunisian agent claimed that Eaton had promised that the $22,000 loan would be repaid by Morris, an assertion that Eaton vigorously denied. Morris blamed the "insult" on the "duplicity of Eaton." Morris claimed that, had he been forewarned, he would not have gone ashore and placed "myself in the power of the Bey of Tunis." Morris to Smith, 30 March 1803, in Knox, *Naval Documents Related to the United States Wars with the Barbary Powers* (hereafter cited as *Barbary Powers*), 2: 383–84.

6. Long, *Nothing Too Daring*, 21.

7. Rodgers to Morris, 30 June 1803; see also Rodgers to Smith, 4 December 1803, both in *Barbary Powers*, 2: 465–66, 459–60.

8. Rodgers to Smith, as quoted in McKee, *Preble*, 147. For an excellent article on the use of broad pendants, or pennants, see Langley, "Squadron Flags," 234–42.

9. McKee, *Preble*, 146–47, 309.

10. Preble to Rodgers, 15 September 1803, in *Barbary Powers*, 3: 46–47.

11. Rodgers to Preble, 15 September 1803, in *Barbary Powers*, 3: 47.

12. T. Lear to secretary of state, 26 September, 18 October 1803; E. Preble to secretary of navy, 15, 17 October 1803, in *Barbary Powers*, 3: 80–89, 146–53, 138–43; "Report [of Lear] on Commodore Preble's Negotiations . . . with Morocco . . . 13–26 September 1803," Tobias Lear Papers, WLCL; see also McKee, *Preble*, 148–72.

13. Message to Congress, 5 December 1803, in Richardson, *Messages of the Presidents*, 1: 365. Congress compensated the captors of the *Meshuda* and the *Mirboka*.

14. "Memoir of Minerva Denison," typescript, RFP, LC.

15. Minerva Denison to Ann Pinkney, 5 November 1802, RFP, LC.

16. Pinkney to Rodgers, 29 May 1803, RFP, LC.

17. Rodgers to Pinkney, [December] 1803, RFP, LC; Pinkney to Rodgers, 9 December 1803, RFP, NHF, LC.

18. Smith to Rodgers, 21 December 1803, in *Barbary Powers*, 3: 282–83.

19. Minerva Denison to Rodgers, 3 April, 13 March 1804, RFP, LC.

20. Rodgers to Minerva Denison, 13, 29 January, 8 February 1804, RFP, LC.

21. "Memoir of Minerva Denison," typescript, RFP, LC; Rodgers to Minerva Denison, 18 March 1804; Minerva Denison to Rodgers, 5 March 1804, both in RFP, LC; Rodgers to Mrs. J. Denison, 18 March 1804, JRP, WLCL. See also H. Campbell to Rodgers, 10 March 1804, JRP, WLCL.

22. Rodgers to Minerva Denison, 7, 29 March 1804; Minerva Denison to Rodgers, 5 March 1804, all in RFP, LC.

23. An excellent account is Spencer Tucker, *Stephen Decatur: A Life Most Bold and Daring*, 45–56, and xi for Nelson's comment.

24. Rodgers to Smith, 17 August 1804; Rodgers to S. Barron, 17 August 1804; see also Rodgers to J. Simpson, 27 August 1804, all in *Barbary Powers*, 4: 422–24, 469–70.

25. Rodgers to Smith, 30 August 1804, in *Barbary Powers*, 4: 486–88.

26. Rodgers to S. Barron, 27 October 1804, in *Barbary Powers*, 5: 102–3.

27. S. Barron to Rodgers, 26 October 1804; Rodgers to S. Barron, 27 October 1804; Rodgers to Smith, 6 November 1804; all in *Barbary Powers*, 5: 100, 103, 124.

28. S. Barron to Rodgers, 3, 27 November 1804, in *Barbary Powers*, 5: 117–18, 163–64.

29. Rodgers to Smith, 30 December 1804; Lear to Rodgers, 16 October 1804, both in *Barbary Powers*, 5: 226–27, 88.

30. Rodgers to W. Jarvis, 1, 4, 5, 16, 20, 21 January 1805; Rodgers to Smith, 1, 26, 27 January 1805; Jarvis to Rodgers, 1, 2, 3, 7, 19, 22, 23 January 1805; Jarvis to secretary of state, 5 January 1805, all in *Barbary Powers*, 5: 245–315 passim.

31. Rodgers to Smith, 4, 16 February 1805, in *Barbary Powers*, 5: 328, 356–57.

32. S. Barron to Rodgers, 28 February 1805; Rodgers to S. Barron, 19 March 1805 (two letters), all in *Barbary Powers*, 5: 377–78, 425–26.

33. Rodgers to Lear, 17 April 1805, *Barbary Powers*, 5: 518.

34. Lear to Rodgers, 1 May 1805; S. Barron to Rodgers, 1 May 1805, both in *Barbary Powers*, 6: 1, 2.

35. Edwards, *Barbary General*, 5.

36. Lear to Eaton, 6 June 1805, in *Barbary Powers*, 6: 92.

37. S. Barron to Smith, 22 May 1805; S. Barron to Rodgers, 22 May 1805, both in *Barbary Powers*, 6: 33–34, 31–32.

38. "Third Article of the Preliminary Articles of a Treaty of Peace. . . .," *ASP*, Foreign Relations, 2; 713–19.

39. Lear to secretary of state, 5 July 1805, *ASP*, Foreign Relations, 2: 718. In previous private discussions with Lear, Rodgers had claimed that if the pasha would release the American prisoners without making peace, Rodgers would ransom the Americans for $200,000 by personally raising the amount in excess of the $60,000 from the American naval officers in the squadron. Ibid., 2: 718.

40. Rodgers to S. Barron, 3 June 1805, in *Barbary Powers*, 6: 78.

41. Folayan, *Tripoli*, 40–42; see also Irwin, *Diplomatic Relations*, 155–58; G. Allen, *Barbary Corsairs*; 251–57; Long, *Gold Braid and Foreign Relations*, 31–32, Field, *America and the Mediterranean World*, 54; Paullin, *Diplomatic Negotiations*, 88–89.

42. Rodgers to Smith, 8 June 1805, *ASP*, Foreign Affairs, 2: 715.

43. "The Relative Force of the Four Squadrons Sent to the Mediterranean," [22 May 1805], in *Barbary Powers*, 6: 31.

44. Rodgers to Davis, 11 June 1805; Rodgers to bey of Tunis, 1 July 1805, in *Barbary Powers*, 6: 109, 146–47.

45. As quoted in Goldsborough, *United States Naval Chronicle*, 280–81.

46. Davis to Rodgers, 3 August 1805, in *Barbary Powers*, 6: 204.

47. Bey of Tunis to Rodgers, 5 August 1805; bey of Tunis to Lear, 9, 10 August 1805, all in *Barbary Powers*, 6: 208–9, 221–22.

48. As quoted in Goldsborough, *United States Naval Chronicle*, 284.

49. Rodgers to Hamuda, 16 August 1805, in *Barbary Powers*, 6: 233.

50. Rodgers to Smith, 21 August 1805; see also Rodgers to W. Higgins, 21 August 1805, both in *Barbary Powers*, 6: 240, 241–42.

51. Rodgers to Smith, 1 September 1805, in *Barbary Powers*, 6: 261, 263.

52. Bey of Tunis to President Thomas Jefferson, 31 August 1805, in *Barbary Powers*, 6: 256.

53. Rodgers to Smith, 21 August 1805, in *Barbary Powers*, 6: 240.

54. Letters of W. Allen, 30 April 1804, 31 August 1805, in Tatum and Tinling, "Letters of William Henry Allen," 1: 118, 128.

55. Rodgers to Porter, 24 December 1805; Rodgers to seamen and marines of the U.S. squadron in the Mediterranean, 23 December 1805; Rodgers to Smith, 3 January 1806, all in *Barbary Powers*, 6: 325, 324, 332.

56. Rodgers to Smith, 22 May 1806, in *Barbary Powers*, 6: 429.

Chapter 4. Peacetime Interlude, 1806–8

1. Rodgers to Lear, 27 May 1806, in *Barbary Powers*, 6: 436; Bainbridge to Porter, 10 July 1805, Naval History Society Collection, NYHS.

2. Paullin, *Rodgers*, 176.

3. Rodgers to J. Barron, 24 July 1806, in Paullin, *Rodgers*, 178; Barron to Rodgers, 29 July 1806, JRP, WLCL; see also Stevens, *Affair of Honor*, 56–57.

4. Jefferson to Rodgers, 8 August 1806, RFP, LC.

5. Rodgers to Minerva Denison, 28 July 1806, RFP, LC.

6. Rodgers to Minerva Denison, 21, 29 August 1806, RFP, LC.

7. Smith to Rodgers, 3 October 1806, NA, M149, R7; Tingley to Rodgers, 5 October 1806; Gale to Rodgers, 20 October 1806, both in RFP, LC.

8. Tingley to Rodgers, 6 February 1807, JRP, WLCL; see also Tingley to Rodgers, 25, 30 January 1807, JRP, WLCL; Tingley to Rodgers, 31 January 1807, RFP, NHF, LC; Gale to Rodgers, 21 January 1807, RFP, LC.

9. "Biographical Notice of Com. John Rodgers"; "Memoir of Minerva Denison," both in RFP, LC. The story was also reprinted in Rodgers's obituary notice, 11 August 1838, *Niles National Register*, 54: 373.

10. Minerva Rodgers to Rodgers, 4 March 1807, RFP, LC.

11. Minerva Rodgers to Rodgers, 4 March 1807; Rodgers to Minerva Rodgers, 7, 9 April 1807; see also Minerva Rodgers to Rodgers, 12 April 1807, all in RFP, LC.

12. Tucker and Reuter, *Injured Honor*, 1–17; an excellent brief account is Hagan, *This People's Navy*, 65–67.

13. For the American response, see Tucker and Reuter, *Injured Honor*, 71–72, 84–85; Gene Smith, *"For Purposes of Defense,"* 49–56.

14. Smith to Rodgers, 9, 13 July 1807, NA, M149, R7.

15. For the letters and Jefferson's report to Congress, "Efficiency of Gunboats in Protecting Ports and Harbors," 10 February 1807, *ASP*, Naval Affairs, 1: 163–64. For Jefferson's policy, see Symonds, *Navalists and Antinavalists*, 115–19; Gene Smith, *"For Purposes of Defense,"* 48–49; S. Tucker, *Jeffersonian Gunboat Navy*, 10–30. An excellent article on Jeffersonian naval policy is Macleod, "Jefferson and the Navy: A Defense."

16. Richardson, *Messages of the Presidents*, 1: 419–21.

17. Hagan, *This People's Navy*, 64.

18. Symonds, *Navalists and Antinavalists*, 86–89, 117–18.

19. Hagan, *This People's Navy*, 70; Love, *History of the U.S. Navy*, 1:91; Symonds, *Navalists and Antinavalists*, 122–30.

20. Rodgers to Smith, 25 July 1807, RFP, LC.

21. Smith to Rodgers, 21, 23, 24, 28 July; 1, 4, 5, 15 August 1807, NA, M149, R7; Tucker and Reuter, *Injured Honor*, 108.

22. Rodgers to Smith, 5 September 1807, NA, M125, R8; Tucker and Reuter, *Injured Honor*, 111.

23. Rodgers to Minerva Rodgers, 8, 21, 20 July 1807, RFP, LC.

24. Minerva Rodgers to Rodgers, 23, 26 July 1807, RFP, LC.

25. Rodgers to Minerva Rodgers, 1 August 1807, RFP, LC.

26. J. Denison to Rodgers, 15 August 1807; Minerva Rodgers to Rodgers, 17 August

1807, both in RFP, LC. The letter from Minerva's mother included a brief note from Minerva.

27. Rodgers to J. Denison, 18, 20 August 1807, RFP, LC. The letter of 18 August included a brief note to Minerva.

28. Minerva Rodgers to Rodgers, 15 September 1807; see also 5 October 1807, Rodgers to Minerva Rodgers, 20 October 1807, both in RFP, LC.

29. Smith to Rodgers, 13 November 1807, NA, M149, R7.

30. *Norfolk Gazette and Publick Ledger*, 3 July 1807, as quoted in Tucker and Reuter, *Injured Honor*, 104.

31. William Allen to "Dearest sir," 24 June 1807, in "Letters of William Henry Allen," ed. Tatum and Tinling, 1: 216.

32. As quoted in Tucker and Reuter, *Injured Honor*, 141.

33. Ibid., 162.

34. Smith to Rodgers, 9 December 1807, JRP, WLCL; Stevens, *Affair of Honor*, 80.

35. Smith to Rodgers, 7 December 1807, NDA, M149, R7.

36. A balanced account of the trial is Tucker and Reuter, *Injured Honor*, 164–88.

37. *Proceedings of the General Court Martial Convened for the Trail of Commodore James Barron. . . 1809*, 93, 105–7, 180, 204.

38. An excellent assessment of the verdict is Tucker and Reuter, *Injured Honor*, 188.

39. Minerva Rodgers to Rodgers, 21 December 1807, RFP, LC.

40. Minerva Rodgers to Rodgers, 17 January 1808; see also Minerva Rodgers to Rodgers, 30 January 1808, both in RFP, LC.

41. Rodgers to Minerva Denison, 25 January, 29 January 1808; see also Rodgers to Minerva Rodgers, 4 February 1808, all in RFP, LC.

42. Rodgers to Minerva Rodgers, 20 February 1808; see also Rodgers to Minerva Rodgers, 16 February 1808, both in RFP, LC.

Chapter 5. To the Brink of War, 1808–11

1. Bauer, "Naval Shipbuilding Programs," 32. Eventually only 176 of the 256 authorized vessels were built.

2. Richardson, *Messages of the Presidents*, 1: 433.

3. Rodgers to Smith, 28 July 1808, NA, M125, R12.

4. An excellent assessment of the dueling problem in the navy is McKee, *A Gentlemanly and Honorable Profession*, 403–6; see also Valle, *Rocks and Shoals*, 88–90. Charles O. Paullin's "Dueling in the Old Navy" includes an annotated list of eighty-two duels involving American naval officers from 1799 to 1850.

5. Rodgers to Goldsborough, 31 March 1808, NA, M125, R10; Rodgers to Smith, 9 November, 8 July 1808, NA, M125, R13.

6. Rodgers to Smith, 31 July 1808, NA, R45, R12.

7. Smuggling and evasion of the law were, in fact, serious problems for the ad-

ministration. Spivak, *Jefferson's English Crisis*, 156–77; see also S. Tucker, *Jeffersonian Gunboat Navy*, 32. For a different view, see Sears, *Jefferson and the Embargo*, 91–96.

8. Rodgers to J. Jones, 26 April 1808; Rodgers to commanders of gunboats, April 1808, both in NA, M125, R11. "Board Reports" of the New York Flotilla, 1808–9, JRP, WLCL; see also "Record Book, 1808–1809 of Commercial Vessels Boarded by the New York Flotilla, RFP, HSP.

9. Rodgers to Smith, 5 July 1808, NA, M125, R12.

10. Smith to Rodgers, 25 July 1808, NA, M149, R8; Rodgers to Smith, 12 August, 14 September 1808, NA, M125, R12; Gallatin to Jefferson, 6 August 1808, as quoted in Spivak, *Jefferson's English Crisis*, 165.

11. Rodgers to Mrs. J. Denison, 16, 25 August 1808; Rodgers to H. Denison, 22 September 1808; Minerva Rodgers to "My Dear Mother," 26 August–October 1808, all in RFP, LC.

12. Rodgers to Minerva Rodgers, 22 December 1808, RFP, LC.

13. Symonds, *Navalists and Antinavalists*, 137–43.

14. Frank L. Owsley, "Paul Hamilton," in Coletta, *American Secretaries of the Navy*, 1: 93–98.

15. Hamilton to Senator J. Anderson, 6 June 1809, *ASP*, Naval Affairs, 1: 195, 194.

16. Smith to Rodgers, 2 February 1809, NA, M149, R8; Rodgers to Smith, 22 February, 3, 13 March 1809, NA, M125, R14; Rodgers to Hamilton, 1 December 1809, NA, M125, R17.

17. Rodgers to Hamilton, 19 July 1809, NA, M125, R16.

18. Hamilton to Rodgers, 6 August 1809, NA, M149, R8; Rodgers to Hamilton, 11, 21 August 1809, NA, M125, R16; Rodgers to Hamilton, 26 October, 3 November 1809, NA, M125, R17.

19. Rodgers to Minerva Rodgers, 2 January 1810, RFP, LC.

20. Rodgers to Minerva Rodgers, [April], 26 April 1810 (two letters), RFP, LC.

21. Truxtun to R. Dale, May 1801, Truxtun Papers, HSP.

22. Hamilton to Rodgers, 2, 5, 20 June 1810, NA, M149, R9.

23. Hamilton to Rodgers, 9 June 1810, NA, M149, R9.

24. Rodgers to Hamilton, 16 June 1810, NA, M125, R19; Rodgers to Hull, 4 August 1810, NA, M125, R19.

25. Rodgers to Hamilton, 15, 22 July 1810, NA, M125, R19. See also Rodgers to Hamilton, 23, 25, 27 August, 17 September, 4, 9, 12, 28 October 1810, NA, M125 R19 & 20.

26. Hutcheon, *Fulton*, 93–106; Hamilton to Rodgers, 29 March 1810, JRP, WLCL.

27. *Torpedo War and Submarine Explosions* is printed as "Use of the Torpedo in the Defense of Ports & Harbors," 26 February 1810, *ASP*, Naval Affairs, 1: 211–27.

28. Ibid., 220, 221.

29. Ibid., 225.

30. Ibid.

31. Rodgers to Hamilton, 16 February 1810 (two letters), NA, M125, R18.

32. Rodgers to Minerva Rodgers, 13 March 1810, RFP, LC; Rodgers to Goldsborough, 13 March 1810, NA, M125, R18.

33. Rodgers to Hamilton, 2 April, 4 September 1810, NA, M125, R18 & 20.

34. "Statement of Facts and Observations in Relation to Experiments Exhibited by Mr. Robert Fulton, Explanatory of His System or Torpedo War . . . 1810," *ASP*, Naval Affairs, 1: 236; extract from Rodgers's journal, 24 September 1810, ibid., 1: 240. Correspondence and documents pertaining to the experiments are printed ibid. 1: 234–45.

35. "Statement of Facts. . . .," *ASP*, Naval Affairs, 1: 236.

36. Letter of citizens to Hamilton, 22 January 1811, *ASP*, Naval Affairs, 1: 235; Rodgers to Hamilton, 21 November 1810, NA, M125, R20; extract from Rodgers's journal, *ASP*, Naval Affairs, 1: 242–43; Fulton to Hamilton, 1 February 1811, ibid., 1: 245.

37. Extract from Rodgers's journal, 1 November 1810, *ASP*, Naval Affairs, 1: 242; Hutcheon, *Fulton*, 114.

38. Rodgers to Hamilton, 10 November 1810, 8 March 1811, NA, M125, R21 & 21; Chauncey to Rodgers, 13 January 1811, RFP, LC.

39. Rodgers to Hamilton, 9, 16 April, 2, 8 May 1811, NA, M125, R21.

40. For Rodgers's account, see Rodgers to Hamilton, 28 May 1811, NA, M125, R21. It is also printed in *ASP*, Foreign Affairs, 3: 497–98.

41. *ASP*, Foreign Affairs, 3: 498.

42. Ibid.

43. For correspondence and documents on the *Little Belt* affair, see *ASP*, Foreign Affairs, 3: 491–99. One American naval officer who was not sympathetic was James Biddle, who later snidely commented that Rodgers "mistook a sloop for a frigate and fired into her in time of peace." Biddle to T. Cadwalader, 5 February 1823, as quoted in Long, *Sailor-Diplomat*, 107.

44. Hamilton to Rodgers, 28 May 1811, NA, M149, R9; Goldsborough to Rodgers, 27 May 1811, RFP, WLCL.

45. Hamilton to Rodgers, 28, 29 May 1811, NA, M149, R9; Rodgers to Hamilton, 31 May, 3, 4 June 1811, NA, M125, R21 & 22.

46. Hamilton to Rodgers, 29 June 1811, NA, M149, R9; Rodgers to Hamilton, 9 June, 11 July 1811, NA, M125, R22.

47. Rodgers to Hamilton, 16 July 1811 (two letters), NA, M125, R22; Hamilton to Rodgers, 24 July 1811, NA, M149, R9; "Sworn Statement of William Burket," RFP, WLCL.

48. Statement by officers of the *Little Belt*, 29 May 1811, *ASP*, Foreign Relations, 3: 473–74. The proceedings of the court and pertinent documents are printed ibid., 3: 473–96.

49. Rodgers to Court of Inquiry, [September 1811], *ASP*, Foreign Relations, 3: 496.

50. Ibid., 3: 496–97; Hamilton to Rodgers, 29 August 1811; Hamilton to Decatur, 28 September 1811, both in JRP, WLCL.

51. For a partisan British viewpoint, see James, *Naval History*, 6: 17–20. James

contends that, as the commander of a neutral warship, Rodgers should have returned Bingham's hail even though he thought his was first; that Rodgers fired the first shot "unintentionally"; that both commanders were too "precipitate"; and that Rodgers intended to inflict excessive human damage by firing low not only with "round and grape shot, but with every scrap of iron that could possibly be collected."

Chapter 6. Commodore at Sea in the War of 1812

1. Hagan, *This People's Navy*, 75.
2. Love, *History of the U.S. Navy*, 1: 98.
3. Richardson, *Messages of the Presidents*, 1: 492, 494.
4. Symonds, *Navalists and Antinavalists*, 148–69; Mahan, *Sea Power*, 1: 259–63.
5. Rodgers to Hamilton, 23 January, 28 February 1812; NA, M125, R23; see also Hamilton to Rodgers, 14 January, NA, M149, R9.
6. Mahan, *Sea Power*, 1: 263–64; H. Adams, *History of the United States*, 2: 433–34.
7. Hamilton to Rodgers, 9, 13 April 1802, NA, M149, R10; Rodgers to Hamilton, 29 April, 27 May 1812, NA, M125, R25.
8. Minerva Rodgers to Rodgers, 25 April, 17, 19 May 1812, RFP, LC.
9. Minerva Rodgers to Rodgers, 19 May 1812, RFP, LC.
10. Minerva Rodgers to Rodgers, 26 May, 1 June 1812, RFP, LC; see also Minerva Rodgers to Rodgers, 5, 11, 19 June 1812, RFP, LC.
11. Rodgers to Minerva Rodgers, [June], 12 June 1812, RFP, LC.
12. Rodgers to Minerva Rodgers, 19 June 1812, RFP, LC.
13. Hamilton to Rodgers, 21 May 1812, NA, M149, R10.
14. Rodgers to Hamilton, 3 June 1812, NA, M125, R23.
15. Ibid.
16. Decatur to Hamilton, 8 June 1812, NA, M125, R23. The letters between Decatur, Rodgers, and Hamilton are reprinted in Dudley, *Naval War of l812*, 1: 118–24.
17. Rodgers to Hamilton, 2 June 1812, NA, M125, R24. While A. T. Mahan supports the soundness of Rodgers's proposed strategy, others, such as Linda Maloney, have been critical. See Mahan, *Sea Power*, 1: 315–16, and Maloney, "The War of 1812: What Role for Sea Power?" in Hagan, *In Peace and War*, 47–53.
18. Hamilton to Rodgers, 18 June 1812, NA, M149, R10.
19. Hamilton to Rodgers, 22 June 1812, NA, M149, R10.
20. Hamilton to L. Cheves, chairman of House Naval Committee, 3 December 1811; Dudley, *Naval War of 1812*, 1: 53–60; "Annual Abstract of the Ships and Vessels Belonging to the British Navy . . . 1812," in James, *Naval History of Great Britain*, 6: Appendix; Knox, *History of the United States Navy*, 82.
21. Mahan, *Sea Power*, 1: 283–84.
22. Rodgers to Hamilton, 21 June 1812, NA, M125, R24.
23. Rodgers to Hamilton, 21 (two letters), 16, 19 June 1812, NA, M124, R24.
24. Extracts from Rodgers's journal, 23 June 1812, and Byron to Vice Admiral Sawyer, 27 June 1812, in Dudley, *Naval War of 1812*, 1: 154–60; see also the enclosure

included in Rodgers to Hamilton, 1 September 1812, NA, M125, R25. A handwritten copy of Byron's account is in JRP, WLCL.

25. Byron to Sawyer, 27 June 1812, in Dudley, *Naval War of 1812*, 1:157–59; Hagan, *This People's Navy*, 79; Mahan, *Sea Power*, 1: 323; Hull to Hamilton, 28 August 1812, NA, M125, R24.

26. Rodgers to Hamilton, 31 August, 1 September 1812, NA, M125, R24 & 25.

27. Rodgers to Hamilton, 31 August 1812, NA, M125, R24.

28. Rodgers to Hamilton, 14, 4 September 1812, NA, M125, R25.

29. Rodgers to Hamilton, 14 September 1812, NA, M125, R25; see also C. W. Goldsborough to Rodgers, 8 September 1812, RFP, LC.

30. Hamilton to Rodgers, 9, 26 September 1812, NA, M149, R10.

31. Rodgers to J. Smith, 12 October 1812, JRP, WLCL.

32. Rodgers to Hamilton, 3 October 1812, NA, M125, R25.

33. Rodgers to Hamilton, 17 October 1812, NA, M125, R25. James contends that Rodgers passed up an excellent opportunity to pursue and engage the *Galatea*, a thirty-six-gun frigate, which was ninety-three men short of her crew complement and "scarcely could have resisted an attack." James, *Naval History of Great Britain*, 6: 181.

34. Rodgers to Hamilton, 1 November 1812, NA, M125, R25; Mahan, *Sea Power*, 1: 408–9.

35. Rodgers to Hamilton, 2 January 1813, NA, M125, R26.

36. Edward K. Eckart, "William Jones: Mr. Madison's Secretary of the Navy, 96: 167–82; see also Frank L. Owsley, "William Jones, 1813–1814," in Coletta, *American Secretaries of the Navy* 1: 101–10.

37. Jones to Rodgers, Bainbridge, Decatur, Stewart, and Morris, 22 February 1813, NA, M149, R10; Rodgers to Jones, 8 March 1813, NA, M125, R27.

38. Lear to Rodgers, 9 April 1813, JRP, WLCL; Rodgers to Jones, 22 April l813, NA, M125, R28; Jones to Rodgers, 29 April 1813, JRP, WLCL.

39. Petrie, "Ransoming of the *Eliza Swan*"; Rodgers to Jones, 27 September 1813, NA, M125, R31.

40. James contends that Rodgers missed an opportunity to engage the British on favorable terms when he seriously misjudged the thirty-two-gun frigate *Alexandria* to be a ship of the line and the sixteen-gun schooner the *Scourge* to be a frigate. "Will any one pretend, that the flight of Commodore Rodgers was all the effect of a delusion?" James, *Naval History of Great Britain*, 6: 309–12.

41. Lossing, *Pictorial Field-Book*, 735–37. Hutchinson vehemently denied that he took any personal possessions from Rodgers's house in Havre de Grace. Hutchinson to Rodgers, 11 October 1813, JRP, WLCL.

42. Rodgers to Jones, 27 September 1813, in Dudley, *Naval War of 1812*, 2: 252–53.

43. Jones to Rodgers, 4 October 1813, NA, M149, R11; G. Blakely to Rodgers, 1 October 1813, RFP, LC. See also E. Jones to Rodgers, 4 October 1813; L. W. Tazewell to Rodgers, 5 October 1813, both in RFP, LC.

44. Rodgers to Jones, 19 February 1814, NA, M125, R34. Paullin, *Rodgers*, 273. James agrees that Rodgers missed another opportunity to engage a smaller enemy ship by misjudging the thirty-eight-gun frigate *Loire* to be the seventy-four-gun ship of the line *Plantagenet*. At the time, the *Loire* had a crew of not more than 220 men out of a full complement of 352 men. James, *Naval History of Great Britain*, 6: 410–13.

45. Rodgers to Jones, 5 March 1814, NA, M125, R35.

46. In 19 March, 9 April 1814, *Niles Weekly Register*, 6: 44, 101.

47. Emmons, *Navy of the United States*, 60–61.

48. Positive assessments of Rodgers include Mahan, *Sea Power*; Mahan, *From Sail to Steam*, 5–6; Pratt, *Preble's Boys*, 56–57; Paullin, *Rodgers*, 275–77. A critical view is Maloney, "The War of 1812: What Role for Sea Power?" in Hagan, *In Peace and War*, 46–53.

49. Valle, "Navy's Battle Doctrine."

Chapter 7. The Defense of the Chesapeake, 1814

1. *Polyanthus*, as quoted in Lossing, *Pictorial Field-Book*, 737; Rodgers to Jones, 20 February, 16 March 1814, NA, M125, R34 & 35.

2. Rodgers to Jones, 26 February, 5 March 1814, NA, M125, R35; Jones to Rodgers, 16 April 1814, NA, M149, R11.

3. Contemporary accounts include [Sparks], "Conflagration of Havre de Grace," 157–65; B. H. Latrobe to R. Fulton, 4 May 1813, as quoted in Earle, *Chesapeake Bay Country*, 245–46.

4. Letter of [William Pinkney], 14 May 1813, RFP, NHF, LC; Latrobe to Fulton, 4 May 1813, in Earle, *Chesapeake Bay Country*, 245–46; Paullin, *Rodgers*, 279–80.

5. H. Adams, *History of the United States*, 1: 807–9.

6. Ibid., 1: 811–12, "Outrages at Hampton, in Virginia," *ASP*, Military Affairs, 1: 375–82.

7. Rodgers to C. W. Morgan, 13 May 1814; see also Rodgers to Jones, 28 May 1814, both in NA, M125, R36.

8. Rodgers to Jones, 25 June 1814, NA, M125, R37.

9. Rodgers to Jones, 14 July 1814, NA, M125, R37.

10. H. Adams, *History of the United States*, 1: 1000.

11. Jones to Rodgers, 19 August 1814, NA, M149, R11; Rodgers to Minerva Rodgers, 23 August 1814, JRP, WLCL; Jones to Rodgers, 23 August 1814, NA, M149, R11; see also Rodgers to Minerva Rodgers, 24 August 1814, RFP, LC.

12. Horsman, *War of 1812*, 201–3; Hickey, *War of 1812*, 197–201.

13. Minerva Rodgers to Rodgers, 25 August 1814; Rodgers to Minerva Rodgers, 28 August 1814, both in RFP, LC.

14. Porter to Jones, 27 August 1814, in RFP, NHF, LC; Rodgers to Jones, 27, 29 August 1814, NA, M125, R38.

15. Rodgers to Jones, 29 August 1814, NA, M125, R38; Rodgers to Minerva Rodgers, [31 August 1814], JRP, WLCL.

16. Rodgers to Jones, 4, 9 September 1814, NA, M125, R39.

17. Spence to Rodgers, 31 August 1814, in Dudley, *Naval War of 1812*, vol. 3, 261, ed. Michael J. Crawford; Smith to Rodgers, 2 September 1814, in Friend, "Defense of Baltimore Correspondence," 443–44.

18. An excellent characterization of Smith is found in Cassell, *Merchant Congressman*, 181.

19. Ibid., 181–97.

20. Rodgers to A. Murray, 9 September 1814, in Dudley, *Naval War of 1812*, vol. 3, 263, ed. Michael J. Crawford. See also Lord, *Dawn's Early Light*, 248, and Paullin, *Rodgers*, 292–93.

21. Various British accounts of the battle are included in Dudley, *Naval War of 1812*, vol. 3, 272–91, ed. Michael J. Crawford. American accounts are in ibid., 292–304.

22. Rodgers to Jones, 14 [September] 1814, in ibid., 3: 293. Excellent secondary accounts are Horsman, *War of 1812*, 206–8; Hickey, *War of 1812*, 203–4.

23. Cassell, *Merchant Congressman*, 209.

24. S. Smith to J. Monroe, 19 September 1814, in Crawford, *Naval War of 1812*, 3: 298; Spence to Rodgers, 29 September 1814, in Friend, "Defense of Baltimore Correspondence, 446–47.

25. Rodgers to Jones, 18, 23 September 1814, RFP, NHF, LC.

26. Rodgers to Jones, 23 November 1814, NA, M125, R41; Rodgers to C. W. Morgan, 1 October, 12 December 1814, RFP, HSP.

27. Homans to Rodgers, 14, 24 December 1814, NA, M149, R11; Rodgers to Homans, 31 December 1814, NA, M125, R41.

28. Rodgers to Madison, 29 November 1814; RFP, NHF, LC; Madison to Rodgers, 4 December 1814, RFP, LC.

29. Minerva Rodgers to Rodgers, 14 December 1814; Rodgers to Minerva Rodgers, 24 December 1814; Minerva Rodgers to Rodgers, 27 December 1814, all in RFP, LC.

Chapter 8. President of the Board of Navy Commissioners, 1815–24

1. Schroeder, *Shaping a Maritime Empire*, 3–10.

2. White, *The Jeffersonians*, 269.

3. Jones to House of Representatives, 2, 3, 4 February 1813, *ASP*, Naval Affairs, 1: 285–86.

4. "Report on Reorganization of the Navy Department," 9 January 1815, *ASP*, Naval Affairs, 1: 354–59.

5. Rodgers to Madison, 29 November 1814, RFP, LC.

6. "Report on Reorganization of the Navy Department," *ASP*, Naval Affairs, 1: 354; *U.S. Statutes at Large*, 3: 202–3, 231, as cited in Paullin, *Paullin's History of Naval Administration*, 168.

7. Rodgers to Crowninshield, 11 February 1815, as quoted in Paullin, *Naval Administration*, 168–69. (Original source is the *Proceedings of the Massachusetts Historical Society*, 2nd ser., 4: 207–8.) See also Maloney, *Captain from Connecticut*, 263–64.

8. Rodgers to Minerva Rodgers, 14 February 1815, RFP, LC.

9. Minerva Rodgers to Rodgers, 18 February 1815, RFP, LC.

10. Rodgers to Minerva Rodgers, 27 February 1815, RFP, LC.

11. Hull to Rodgers, 8 March 1815, RFP, LC; S. Smith to Rodgers, 25 May 1815; Rodgers to S. Smith, 28 May 1815, both in JRP, WLCL.

12. Paulding to Rodgers, [1816]; Paulding to H. Brevort, 1 December, 25 September 1815; all in Aderman, *Letters of James Kirke Paulding*, 48, 43, 42.

13. Rodgers memo, 21 January 1823; draft manumission document, both in RFP, LC. The prize-money figure is from McKee, *A Gentlemanly and Honorable Profession*, table 33, p. 494. Rodgers's partners in the lumber business were Howes and Charles Goldsborough; their venture did not prove financially successful. The correspondence from Charles Goldsborough on the business is in JRP, WLCL.

14. The first offices of the board were in a rented house some distance from the office of the secretary of the navy. In 1820, the board moved its offices to the old navy building, about 200 yards west of the White House. Paullin, *Naval Administration*, 174.

15. Entries of 2, 3 December 1818, J. Q. Adams, *Memoirs of John Quincy Adams*, 4: 185; see also 21 October 1818, ibid., and Long, *Nothing Too Daring*, 177.

16. Journal of the Board of Navy Commissioners, 25 April 1815, vol. 1, NA.

17. Edwin M. Hall, "Benjamin W. Crowninshield," in Coletta, *American Secretaries of the Navy*, 1: 113–20.

18. Board of Navy Commissioners to Crowninshield, 19 May 1815, letters sent by the Board of Navy Commissioners, vol. 1, NA.

19. Board of Navy Commissioners to Madison, 25 May 1815, letters sent by the Board of Navy Commissioners, vol. 1, NA; Madison to Crowninshield, 12 June 1815, in *Letters and Other Writings of James Madison*, 2: 603–6.

20. Madison to Crowninshield, 12 June 1815, in *Letters and Other Writings of James Madison*, 2, 605–6; a copy is in the journal of the Board of Navy Commissioners, vol. 1, NA.

21. Porter, *Nothing Too Daring*, 183–84.

22. During Rodgers's first term on the board, Isaac Chauncey and Charles Morris also served on the board. Porter, *Nothing Too Daring*, 183–84.

23. Paullin, *Naval Administration*, 201.

24. S. Tucker, *Arming the Fleet*, 136–37; Paullin, *Rodgers*, 319.

25. "Rules, Regulations, and Instructions, for the Naval Service," 20 April 1818, *ASP*, Naval Affairs, 1: 510–34; quote is from 512.

26. Ibid., 1: 512.

27. Ibid., 1: 517–18.

28. Bauer, "Naval Shipbuilding Programs," 34.

29. Hall, "Crowninshield," 1: 116; Hall, "Smith Thompson," in Coletta, *American Secretaries of the Navy*, 1: 123–24, 126–27.

30. Symonds, *Navalists and Antinavalists*, 223–24.

31. As quoted in ibid., 226.

32. Rodgers to Thompson, 31 January 1820, *ASP*, Naval Affairs, 1: 649–52.

33. Ibid., 651; Symonds, *Navalists and Antinavalists*, 228–29.

34. Stevens, *Barron*, 159; *Proceedings of a Court of Enquiry*, 92–99.

35. For background on the duel, see Seitz, *Famous American Duels*, 176–223; Cochran, *Noted American Duels*, 51–69; Forester, "Bloodshed at Dawn," 41–45, 73–74.

36. Long, *Nothing Too Daring*, 185–86.

37. On the frequency of dueling among American naval officers, see McKee, *A Gentlemanly and Honorable Profession*, 403–6.

38. Accounts of the duel include Seitz, *Famous American Duels*, 223–26; Cochran, *Noted American Duels*, 69–79; Forester, "Bloodshed at Dawn," 41–45, 74–76.

39. Seitz, *Famous American Duels*, 224.

40. John H. Schroeder, "Stephen Decatur," in Bradford, *Command under Sail*, 213; Stevens, *Barron*, 146–47.

41. An excellent account of the affair is Maloney, *Captain from Connecticut*, 349–57.

42. Long, *Nothing Too Daring*, 215–16.

43. Southard to Monroe, 21 September 1823; Southard to Rodgers, 29 September 1823, both in *ASP*, Naval Affairs, 1: 1116–7.

44. Randolph to Rodgers, 15 October 1823, RFP, LC; Rodgers to Perry, 26 November 1823, RFP, HSP. Rodgers's letterbook containing correspondence on the mission to Key West is in RFP, HSP.

45. Rodgers to Southard, 16, 1 November, 25 October 1823, NA M125, R84 & 85.

46. T. Harris, B. Washington, and R. K. Hoffman to Rodgers, 29 October 1823, NA, M125, R85.

47. Rodgers to Southard, 16, 24 November 1823, NA, M125, R85. See also Rodgers's pocket journal, November 1823, RFP, HSP.

48. *Daily National Intelligencer*, 24 July 1824.

Chapter 9. Commodore of the Mediterranean Squadron, 1825–27

1. Southard to Rodgers, 15 December 1824, RFP, LC.

2. Entry for 26 May, 1824, J. Q. Adams, *Memoirs of John Quincy Adams*, 6: 238.

3. Maloney, *Captain from Connecticut*, 292.

4. As quoted in Birkner, *Samuel L. Southard*, 90.

5. Chauncey to Rodgers, 5 February 1825, JRP, WLCL.

6. Rodgers to Minerva Rodgers, 31 January 1825, RFP, LC.

7. J. Q. Adams to Rodgers, 7 February 1825; see also H. Clay to Rodgers, 6 September 1825, both in Diplomatic Instructions, Special Missions, 1: 27–31, Department of State, NA.

8. *Daily National Intelligencer*, 2 February 1825.

9. Rodgers to Morgan, 12 January 1825; Rodgers to officers, 30 April 1815, both in RFP, LC; Rodgers to Southard, 30 April 1825, NA, M125, R92; Rodgers to Patterson, 11, 13 May 1825, JRP, WLCL. See also Rodgers to Minerva Rodgers, 1 May 1825, RFP, LC; "Journal of Commodore Daniel Patterson," 1825, typescript, LC, 1–3.

10. Rodgers to Minerva Rodgers, 31 July 1825, RFP, LC; "Journal of Commodore Daniel Patterson," 1825, typescript, LC, 4–5.

11. Mahan, *Admiral Farragut*, 54–55; Valle, *Rocks and Shoals*, 259–61. A contemporary account is McNally, *Evils and Abuses*, 23–24.

12. Rodgers to Southard, 2 July 1825, NA, M125, R93.

13. Southard to Rodgers, 15 January 1825, NA, M149, R15.

14. Mackenzie, *Year in Spain*, 263–65.

15. Rodgers to Southard, 17 June 1825, NA, M125, R93.

16. Rodgers to Southard, 26 June 1825, NA, M125, R93; see also Rodgers to Southard, 9 May 1825, NA, M125, R92.

17. E. I. Du Pont to Rodgers, 2 February 1827, RFP, LC; Merrill, *Du Pont: The Making of an Admiral*, 39; see also Merrill, "Midshipman Du Pont and the Cruise of the North Carolina."

18. Rodgers to Minerva Rodgers, 31 July 1825, RFP, LC; Southard to Rodgers, 6 July, 12 September 1825, RFP, NHF, LC.

19. Rodgers to Southard, 26 May, 7 July 1825, NA, M125, R92 & 93.

20. Larrabee, *Hellas Observed*, 65–75; Field, *America and the Mediterranean World*, 121–33.

21. Rodgers to Southard, 30 August 1825, NA, M125, R95.

22. Secretary of state of Greece to Rodgers, 15 August 1825, RFP, LC.

23. Rodgers to Southard, 30 August 1825; NA, M125, R95; see also Rodgers to Southard, 12 October 1825, NA, M125, R101.

24. Larrabee, *Hellas Observed*, 79; see also Rodgers to Southard, 20 December 1825, NA, M125, R98.

25. Rodgers to Southard, 30 August 1825, NA, M125, R95.

26. Before leaving the eastern Mediterranean, Rodgers addressed a letter of goodwill to the captain pasha and sent it confidentially to Consul Offley with instructions to deliver it to the Turkish admiral in the event that Offley came in contact with him. Rodgers to captain pasha, 20 September 1825, *NASP*, Naval Affairs, 2: 312–13,

27. Rodgers to Southard, 18 October 1825, NA, M125, R96; Rodgers to Southard, 20 December 1825, NA, M125, R98; Rodgers to Minerva Rodgers, 20 December 1825, RFP, LC. Another description of the harbor is [G. Jones], *Sketches of Naval Life*, 1: 68–69.

28. Rodgers to Minerva Rodgers, 20 December 1825, 6, 22 January 1826, RFP, LC; [G. Jones], *Sketches of Naval Life*, 1: 71–72.

29. General Order, 3 December 1825; Rodgers to Minerva Rodgers, 30 December 1825, RFP, LC; Order of Don Joseph Taverner, 4 February 1826, Daniel T. Patterson Papers, LC.

30. Southard to Rodgers, 28 December 1825, RFP, LC; Paulding to Rodgers, 8 August 1825, as quoted in Long, *Ready to Hazard*, 296; Rodgers to Minerva Rodgers, 31 July 1825, RFP, LC.

31. Rodgers to Minerva Rodgers, 24 February 1825, RFP, LC. For a later relapse, see Nicholson to Rodgers, 4 August 1826, RFP, LC.

32. Rodgers to Southard, 24 February 1826, RG45, M125, R101; Southard to Rodgers, 29 December 1825, RFP, LC.

33. D. Deacon to Rodgers, 14 April 1826; RFP, LC; Rodgers to Minerva Rodgers, 27 June 1826, RFP, LC.

34. Larrabee, *Hellas Observed*, 75; Paullin, *Rodgers*, 340.

35. Rodgers to Southard, 18 July 1826, NA, M125, R105. This fourteen-page letter is Rodgers's formal report to the Navy Department.

36. Ibid.; see also Rodgers to Minerva Rodgers, 12 September 1826, RFP, LC. Another description of the meeting is in [G. Jones], *Sketches of Naval Life*, 1: 159. For various spellings of Khosrew's name, see Field, *America and the Mediterranean*, 118.

37. Rodgers to Clay, 19 July 1826, RFP, LC.

38. Rodgers to Southard, 18 July 1826, NA, M125, R105.

39. Ibid.

40. Ibid.

41. Ibid.

42. Ibid.

43. Ibid.; see also Rodgers to Capudan Pasha, 19 December 1826, RFP, LC.

44. Rodgers to Southard, 18 July 1826, NA, M125, R105.

45. Finnie, *Pioneers East*, 56–57, 73, 258.

46. Larrabee, *Hellas Observed*, 85, 307 n. 44.

47. Rodgers to Southard, 25 June 1826, NA, M125, R104; Rodgers to Southard, 16 September 1826, NA, M125, R107.

48. Rodgers to Southard, 16 September 1826, NA, M125, R107.

49. Rodgers to Minerva Rodgers, 6 November 1826; Southard to Rodgers, 3 August 1827, both in RFP, LC.

50. For Rodgers's reports on the gifts, see Rodgers to Minerva, 31 July, 16 October 1825, 16 May, 27 June, 12 September, 8 December 1826; see also Rodgers's notebook, 1826–27, in which he recorded his personal purchases, including ninety-six cases of wine; all in RFP, LC.

51. Minerva Rodgers to Rodgers, 22 March 1827, RFP, LC. Minerva was quoting "Sonnet #6" by Robert Southey.

52. Rodgers to Minerva Rodgers, 11, 12 May, 17 June, 29 August 1825, 6 November 1826, all in RFP, LC.

53. Rodgers to Southard, 11 September 1826, NA, M125, R107. Rodgers's letter includes attached correspondence about the incident.

54. For allegations that Rodgers lost his temper on a number of occasions, see Bauer, "John Rodgers," in Bradford, *Command under Sail*, 235–36.

55. Merrill, *Du Pont*, 28; Rodgers to Southard, 26 November 1825, NA, M125, R97; see also Rodgers to Minerva Rodgers, 31 July 1825, RFP, LC.

56. Garrison, *Behold Me Once More*, 82–85 passim.

57. Schroeder, *Matthew Calbraith Perry*, 50–51; Valle, *Rocks and Shoals*, 45; Mayer, *All on Fire*, 270. In the Black (or Discipline) Book of the *North Carolina* for 1825–27,

Garrison is listed only twice. In April 1826, the offense was intoxication, which was forgiven. In July 1826, he received twelve lashes for leaving the ship without permission. Black Book, *North Carolina*, 1825–27, RFP, HSP.

58. Rodgers to Capitan Pasha, 19 December 1826; see also Rodgers to Minerva, 12 September 1826, both in RFP, LC; Report of Board of Health, Malta. . . ., 7 February 1827, RFP, LC.

59. Southard to Rodgers, 7, 17, 20 February and 20 March 1827, RFP, LC.

60. Khosrew Mehemmet Pasha to Rodgers, 7 February 1827, RFP, LC.

61. Rodgers to Minerva Rodgers, 26 April 1827, RFP, LC; journal of the *North Carolina*, 3 August 1827, RFP, HSP.

62. *Daily National Intelligencer*, 15 August, 28 September 1827; "Report from the Department of the Navy. . . ," ibid., 15 December 1827.

Chapter 10. Last Years, 1827–38

1. Chauncey to Rodgers, 5 February 1825; Paulding to Rodgers, 2 August 1827; see also Chauncey to Rodgers, 31 August, 18 October 1827, all in JRP, WLCL.

2. Mrs. J. N. Macomb, "Memoir of My Girlhood Days in Washington," typescript, RFP, LC.

3. Ibid.

4. Ibid.

5. Ibid., 61, 66–67.

6. Ibid., 77.

7. P. J. Rodriguez to Rodgers, 6 April 1828; C. Harris to Rodgers, 6 April 1828, both in JRP, WLCL; Rodriguez to Rodgers, 13 April 1828, RFP, LC. Rodgers to G. W. Rodgers, 19 April 1828, RFP, LC; Macomb, "Memoir of My Girlhood Days," typescript, RFP, LC, 98–99.

8. Entry for 8 April 1818, in J. Q. Adams, *Memoirs of John Quincy Adams*, 7: 501.

9. F. Rodgers to Rodgers, 9 March 1828, JRP, WLCL; Macomb, "Memoir of My Girlhood Days," typescript, RFP, LC, 98–99. For a long, unfinished poem on the death of her brother, see Commonplace Book of Louisa Rodgers, 1829–1836, RFP, HSP.

10. Macomb, "Memoir of My Girlhood Days," typescript, RFP, LC, 98, 100; Minerva Rodgers to Mrs. I. Hull, 16 June 1828, JRP, WLCL; Robert did not return to West Point but instead became a civil engineer.

11. Langley, "Robert Y. Hayne," 311–30. Daniel T. Patterson served from 1828 to 1832, Charles Stewart from 1830 to 1833, Charles Morris from 1832 to 1841, and Isaac Chauncey from 1833 to 1840.

12. Draft remarks on advantages of the Board of Navy Commissioners, [undated, but late 1820s], RFP, LC; "Rodgers' Marine Railway, or Inclined Plane," 27 January 1823, *ASP*, Naval Affairs, 1: 872–76; "Patent to John Rodgers, 24 June 1822, RFP, NHF, LC.

13. de Kay, *Chronicles of the Frigate* Macedonian, 191–206

14. *Philadelphia National Gazette*, 15, 24 December 1827. The articles appeared

in the newspaper on 15, 24 December 1827, 7, 15, 26 January, and 5, 12 February 1828. On Perry's authorship, see Langley, *Social Reform* 100–101, n. 10.

15. *Philadelphia National Gazette*, 7, 15 January, 12 February 1828.

16. The board recommended the rejection of a proposal by John Stevens to purchase the machinery for steam batteries for coastal defense. "Defense of the Seacoast," 17 January 1821, *ASP*, Naval Affairs, 1: 685.

17. Stanton, *Great United States Exploring Expedition*, 1–25; Philbrick, *Sea of Glory*, 18–41.

18. Entry for 14 July 1828, in J. Q. Adams, *Memoirs of John Quincy Adams*, 8: 57.

19. Remini, *Andrew Jackson*, 199–200; Richardson, *Messages of the Presidents*, 2: 437–38.

20. As quoted in Remini, *Andrew Jackson*, 163–64; Kendall, *Autobiography of Amos Kendall*, 299–300, 316; Rodgers to J. W. Webb, 29 June, 3 August 1829; Webb to Rodgers, 2 July, 9 September 1829, all in RFP, HSP. See also Cole, *A Jackson Man*, 126–27, 130–31.

21. [President's Overseer] to Rodgers, 31 March 1830, RFP, LC; W. Patrick Strauss, "John Branch," in Coletta, *American Secretaries of the Navy*, 1: 143–49; John H. Schroeder, "Jacksonian Naval Policy, 1829–1837," in [Harrod], *New Aspects of Naval History*, 121–27.

22. For the partially successful efforts to improve naval pay, see Chisholm, *Waiting for Dead Men's Shoes*, 140–56.

23. Rodgers to Branch, 23 November 1829, *ASP*, Naval Affairs, 3: 396–402.

24. W. Patrick Strauss, "Levi Woodbury," in Coletta, *American Secretaries of the Navy*, 1: 151–53.

25. B. Cooper to Rodgers, 25 May 1832; J. Redue to Rodgers, 30 May 1832, both in RFP, LC. For a letter that reveals the formal nature of their relationship, see G. W. Rodgers to Rodgers, 4 January 1822, RFP, LC.

26. In 10 September, 1 October 1832, *National Intelligencer*. See also Rosenburg, *Cholera Years*, 3–4, 65–68; Margaret Bayard Smith to Mrs. Kirkpatrick, 3, 7, 8, [9] September 1832, in M. Smith, *First Forty Years*, 334–40.

27. Macomb, "Memoir of My Girlhood Days," typescript, RFP, LC, 83–84.

28. An excellent firsthand description of the trip is in Minerva Rodgers to [Mrs. Richard Bland Lee], 7 August 1834, RFP, LC.

29. Promissory notes and legal documents regarding loan by Rodgers to Porter, December 1823–April 1824, David Porter Papers, WLCL; Indenture between Rodgers and Mrs. S. Decatur, 2 February 1833; Mrs. George Rodgers to Rodgers, 4 March 1835, both in JRP, WLCL.

30. Rodgers memo, 12 November 1835; Macomb, "Memoir of My Girlhood Days," typescript, 77, both in RFP, LC. Rodgers actually first contracted to have the home built in 1830. Rodgers agreement with Jacob Swinley, 10 February 1830, RFP, LC.

31. Langley, "Hayne," 328; W. Patrick Strauss, "Mahlon Dickerson," in Coletta, *American Secretaries of the Navy*, 1: 155–63.

32. Entry for 12 April 1833, in J. Q. Adams, *Memoirs of John Quincy Adams*, 8: 540; see also Rodgers to I. Bergen, 12 October 1833, RFP, LC.

33. Chapelle, *History of the American Sailing*, 349.

34. Ibid., 313, 349, 353–54, 417–19; "Thoughts on the Navy," *Naval Magazine* 1 (1837): 33. Slidell and Perry were the anonymous coauthors of this article.

35. For Rodgers's fifty-nine-page response to a proposal to revamp the board, see Rodgers to [Southard], 11 April 1834, RFP, HSP; [Alexander Slidell Mackenzie], "Report of the Secretary of the Navy." Slidell changed his name to Alexander Slidell Mackenzie in about 1838. Samuel Eliot Morison, *"Old Bruin,"* 54.

36. "The Naval Lyceum" and "Constitution and By Laws," 1836, *Naval Magazine* 1: 5–18, 31–42.

37. "Thoughts on the Navy," ibid., 1: 9–10.

38. Perry to Rodgers, 25 February 1835, RFP, LC. Rodgers's youngest brother, George Washington Rodgers, had been married to Perry's sister Anna Marie Perry in 1815. Alexander Slidell was the younger brother of Perry's wife, Jane Slidell Perry. On the regressive nature of the board, see Chapelle, *American Sailing Navy*, 415.

39. Bennett, *Steam Navy of the United States*, 9–11; Brodie, *Sea Power*, 20–21, 18.

40. Brodie, *Sea Power*, 30–31, 21 n. 14; the *Sea Gull* was laid up in 1825 and not used again. Bennett, *American Steam Navy*, 16.

41. Sprout and Sprout, *Rise of American Naval Power*, 125–26; Bauer, "Naval Shipbuilding Programs," 37–38; Brodie, *Sea Power*, 36.

42. Rodgers to Dickerson, 30 December 1835; Dickerson to Haswell, 19 February 1836, both as quoted in Bennett, *American Steam Navy*, 18, 19.

43. Richardson, *Messages of the Presidents*, 3: 173.

44. Ibid., 3: 161; Schroeder, "Jacksonian Naval Policy," in [Harrod], *New Aspects of Naval History*, 125. For Jackson and France, see Belohlavek, *"Let the Eagle Soar,"* 90–126.

45. John Rodgers, report from the Navy Department, 31 March 1836, *ASP*, Military Affairs, 6: 399–403. For similar ideas, see John Rodgers, "Statement on the Maximum Amount That Can Be Beneficially Expended . . . for the Navy," 27 April 1836, *ASP*, Naval Affairs, 4: 953–56.

46. Rodgers, report from the Navy Department, 1836, *ASP*, Military Affairs, 6: 400.

47. Sprout and Sprout, *Rise of American Naval Power*, 109.

48. Harsh critics include Long, "The Navy under the Board of Navy Commissioners, 1815–1842," in Hagan, *In Peace and War*, 63–78, and Sprout and Sprout, *Rise of American Naval Power*, 106–9. More evenhanded are Paullin, *Paullin's History of Naval Administration*, 175, 201–3; White, *The Jeffersonians*, 279–80; White, *The Jacksonians*, 216–18; Chapelle, *American Sailing Navy*, 414–25.

49. Chapelle, *American Sailing Navy*, 307.

50. For a firsthand account, see Butler [servant of Rodgers] to Minerva Rodgers, 2 July 1837, RRP, LC.

51. Roddis, "Thomas Harris, M.D."; see also Langley, *History of Medicine*, 253, 276, 298, 343.

52. In 11 August 1838, *Niles Weekly Register*, 54: 372–73.

53. Truxtun to J. Biddle, June 1811, as quoted in Palmer, *Stoddert's War*, 195; Biddle to T. Cadwalader, 5 February 1823, as quoted in Long, *Biddle*, 107; see also N. Morris to Preble, as quoted in McKee, *Preble*, 309–10.

54. Benton, *Thirty Years' View*, 2: 144.

Bibliography

Primary Sources

UNPUBLISHED OFFICIAL RECORDS AND MANUSCRIPTS

John S. Barnes Collection of the Naval Historical Society. New York Historical Society, New York City.

Barron, James. Papers. Manuscript Division, Library of Congress.

Cockburn, George. Papers (microfilm). Manuscript Division, Library of Congress.

Journal of the *President*, 1812. Rodgers Family Papers, Historical Society of Pennsylvania, Philadelphia.

Lear, Tobias. Papers. Manuscript Division, Library of Congress.

Lear, Tobias. Papers. William L. Clements Library, University of Michigan.

Letterbook of Isaac Chauncey, 1809–12 (microfilm). New York Historical Society, New York City.

Logbook of the *Constellation*, 1798–99. Historical Society of Pennsylvania, Philadelphia.

Naval Historical Society Collection. New York Historical Society, New York City.

Patterson, Daniel T. Papers. Manuscript Division, Library of Congress.

Porter, David and David D. Papers. William L. Clements Library, University of Michigan.

Preble, Edward. Papers. Library of Congress.

Rodgers, John. Papers. William L. Clements Library, University of Michigan.

"Rodgers Family Papers." Historical Society of Pennsylvania, Philadelphia.

"Rodgers Family Papers." Manuscript Division, Library of Congress.

"Rodgers Family Papers." Naval Historical Foundation, Manuscript Division, Library of Congress.

"Rodgers Papers." New York Historical Society, New York City.

Shaw, John. Papers. Naval Historical Foundation, Library of Congress.

Truxtun, Thomas. Papers. Historical Society of Pennsylvania, Philadelphia.

U.S. Department of the Navy Records, National Archives. Journal of the Board of Navy Commissioners, 1815–42. 19 vols. RG45. The volumes of the journal are not numbered consecutively.

———. Letters received by the Board of Navy Commissioners from the secretary of the navy, 1815–42. 11 vols. RG45.

———. Letters received by the secretary of the navy from captains ("Captains' Letters"), 1807–61. 370 vols. RG45, M125.

————. Letters sent by the Board of Navy Commissioners to the secretary of the navy, 1815–42. 7 vols. RG45.

————. Letters sent by the secretary of the navy to officers ("Letters to Officers of Ships"), 1798–1868. 86 vols. RG45, M149.

————. Miscellaneous letters sent by the Board of Navy Commissioners, 1815–42. 8 vols. RG45.

————. Register of the Board of Navy Commissioners, 1825–1842. 6 vols. RG45.

BOOKS, ARTICLES AND PERIODICALS

Adams, John Quincy. *Memoirs of John Quincy Adams, Comprising Portions of the Diary from 1795 to 1848.* Edited by Charles Francis Adams. 12 vols. Philadelphia: J. B. Lippincott, 1875.

Aderman, Ralph M., ed. *The Letters of James Kirke Paulding.* Madison: University of Wisconsin Press, 1962.

Bassett, John Spencer, ed. *Correspondence of Andrew Jackson.* 7 vols. Washington, D.C.: Carnegie Institution, 1929.

Bauer, K. Jack, ed. *The New American State Papers, 1798–1966.* Naval Affairs. 10 vols. Wilmington, Del.: Scholarly Resources, 1981.

Benton, Thomas Hart. *Thirty Years' View; OR A History of the Working of the American Government for Thirty Years, From 1820 to 1850.* 2 Vols. New York: D. Appleton, 1854.

Bigelow, Andrew. *Travels in Malta and Sicily . . . .* 2 vols. New York: E. Bliss, 1831.

Dudley, William S., and Michael J. Crawford, eds. *The Naval War of 1812: A Documentary History.* Vols. 1, 2, edited by Dudley. Vol. 3, edited by Crawford with foreword by Dudley. Washington, D.C.: Naval Historical Center, 1985–2002.

Emmons, George F. *The Navy of the United States from the Commencement, 1775 to 1853.* Washington, D.C.: Gideon, 1853.

Friend, Melind K. "Defense of Baltimore Correspondence, 1814." *Maryland Historical Magazine* 86 (1991): 443–49.

Garrison, James Holley. *Behold Me Once More: The Confessions of James Holley Garrison.* Edited by Walter McIntosh Merrill. Cambridge, Mass.: Houghton, Mifflin, 1954.

Hopkins, James F., ed. *The Papers of Henry Clay.* 9 vols. Lexington: University Press of Kentucky, 1959–88.

Hoxse, John. *The Yankee Tar: An Authentic Narrative of the Voyages and Hardships of John Hoxse and the Cruises of the U.S. Frigate Constellation . . . .* Northampton, Mass.: John Metcalf, 1840.

[Jones, George]. *Sketches of Naval Life with Notices of Men, Manners and Scenery, on the Shores of the Mediterranean . . . .* 2 vols. New Haven: Hezekiah Howe, 1829.

Kendall Amos. *Autobiography of Amos Kendall.* Edited by William Stickney. 1872. Reprint, New York: Peter Smith, 1949.

Knox, Dudley W., ed. *Naval Documents Related to the Quasi-War between the*

United States and France. 7 vols. Washington, D.C.: Government Printing Office, 1935–38.

———. *Naval Documents Related to the United States Wars with the Barbary Powers.* 6 vols. Washington, D.C.: Office of Naval Records and Library, 1939–44.

Mackenzie, Alexander Slidell. *A Year in Spain.* 2 vols. 5th ed. 1831. New York: Harper and Brothers, 1847.

Madison, James. *Letters and Other Writings of James Madison.* 4 vols. Philadelphia: J. B. Lippincott, 1867.

McNally William. *Evils and Abuses in the Naval and Merchant Service Exposed; with Proposals for the Remedy and Redress.* Boston: Cassady and March, 1839.

Morris, Charles, *The Autobiography of Commodore Charles Morris.* Boston: A. Williams, 1880.

Niles Weekly Register (Baltimore), 1811–38.

Norfleet, Fillmore, ed. "Baltimore As Seen by Moreau De Saint-Mery in 1794." *Maryland Historical Magazine* 35 (1940): 221–40.

[Porter, David]. *Constantinople and Its Environs, in a Series of Letters . . . by an American.* 2 vols. New York: Harper and Brothers, 1835.

Porter, David D. *Memoir of Commodore David Porter of the United States Navy.* Albany: J. Munsell, 1875.

Proceedings of a Court of Enquiry, Held at the Navy Yard, Brooklyn, N.Y., upon Captain James Barron, of the United States Navy, in May 1821. Washington, D.C.: Jacob Gideon Jr., 1821.

Proceedings of the General Court Martial Convened for the Trial of Commodore James Barron, Captain Charles Gordon, Mr. William Hook, and Captain John Hall, of the United States Ship Chesapeake, in the Month of January 1808. Washington, D.C.: Jacob Gideon Jr., 1822.

Richardson, James D., ed. *A Compilation of the Messages and Papers of the Presidents, 1789–1902.* 10 vols. Washington, D.C.: Bureau of National Literature and Art, 1903.

Semmes, Raphael, ed. *Baltimore As Seen By Visitors, 1783–1860.* Baltimore: Maryland Historical Society, 1953.

Shaler, William. *Sketches of Algiers, Political, Historical, and Civil.* Boston: Cummings, Hilliard, 1826.

Shelley, Fred., ed. "Ebenezer Hazard's Travels through Maryland in 1777." *Maryland Historical Magazine* 46 (1951): 44–54.

Smith, Margaret Bayard. *The First Forty Years of Washington Society.* Edited by Gaillard Hunt. New York: Charles Scribner's Sons, 1906.

Sowerby, E. Millicent, ed. *Catalogue of the Library of Thomas Jefferson.* 5 vols. Washington, D.C.: Library of Congress, 1952–59.

[Sparks, Jared]. "Conflagration of Havre de Grace." *North American Review* 5 (1817): 157–65.

Tatum, Edward H., Jr., and Marion Tinling, eds. "Letters of William Henry Allen, 1800–1813." *Huntington Library Quarterly* 1 (1937–38): 101–32, 203–43.

Tracy, Nicholas, ed. *The Naval Chronicle. The Contemporary Record of the Royal Navy at War.* 5 vols. Consolidated edition. London: Chatham, 1999.

U.S. Bureau of the Census. *A Century of Population Growth from the First Census of the United States to the Twelfth, 1790–1900.* Washington, D.C.: Government Printing Office, 1929.

———. *Historical Statistics of the United States: Colonial Times to 1970.* 2 Parts. Washington, D.C.: Government Printing Office, 1975.

U.S. Congress. *American State Papers.* Class 1: Foreign Relations. 6 vols. Washington, D.C.: Gales and Seaton, 1832–59.

———. American State Papers. Class 5: Military Affairs. 7 vols. Washington, D.C.: Gales and Seaton, 1832–61.

———. *American State Papers.* Class 6: Naval Affairs. 4 vols. Washington, D.C.: Gales and Seaton, 1834–61.

Washington Daily National Intelligencer. 1813–38.

Secondary Sources

Adair, Douglass. "Fame and the Founding Fathers." In *Fame and the Founding Fathers: Essays by Douglass Adair,* edited by Trevor Colbourn, 3–26. New York: W. W. Norton, 1974.

Adams, Henry. *History of the United States of America . . . .* 1889–90. 9 vols. Reprint, New York: Antiquarian Press, 1962.

Aderman, Ralph M., and Wayne R. Kime. *Advocate for America: The Life of James Kirke Paulding.* Selinsgrove: Susquehanna University Press, 2003.

Albion, Robert Greenhalgh. *Makers of Naval Policy, 1798–1947.* Annapolis: Naval Institute Press, 1980.

Allen, Gardner. *Our Naval War with France.* Boston: Houghton Mifflin, 1909.

———. *Our Navy and the Barbary Corsairs.* Boston: Houghton Mifflin, 1905.

Allen, Max P. "William Pinkney's First Public Service." *Maryland Historical Magazine* 39 (1944): 277–92.

Allgor, Catherine. *Parlor Politics; In Which the Ladies of Washington Help Build a City and a Government.* Charlottesville: University Press of Virginia, 2000.

Allison, Robert. *The Crescent Obscured: The United States and the Muslim World.* New York: Oxford University Press, 1995.

Bauer, K. Jack. "Naval Shipbuilding Programs, 1794–1860." *Military Affairs* 29 (1965): 29–40.

Belohlavek, John M. *"Let the Eagle Soar!": The Foreign Policy of Andrew Jackson.* Lincoln: University of Nebraska Press, 1985.

Bennett, Frank M. *The Steam Navy of the United States. A History of the Growth of the Steam Vessel of War in the U.S. Navy, and of the Naval Engineer Corps.* 2 vols. Pittsburgh: Warren, 1897.

Birkner, Michael. *Samuel L. Southard: Jeffersonian Whig.* Rutherford, N.J.: Fairleigh Dickinson University Press, 1984.

Bradford, James, ed. *Command under Sail: Makers of the American Naval Tradition, 1775– 1850.* Annapolis: Naval Institute Press, 1985.

Brant, Irving. *James Madison.* 6 vols. Indianapolis: Bobbs-Merrill, 1941-61.

Brewer, David. *The Greek War for Independence.* New York: Overlook Press, 2001.

Brighton, Ray, *The Checkered Career of Tobias Lear.* Portsmouth, N.H.: Portsmouth Marine Society, 1985.

Brodie, Bernard. *Sea Power in the Machine Age.* Princeton: Princeton University Press, 1941.

Browne, Gary Lawson. *Baltimore in the New Nation, 1789–1961.* Chapel Hill: University of North Carolina Press, 1980.

Bruchey, Stuart. *Robert Oliver, Merchant of Baltimore, 1783–1819.* Baltimore: Johns Hopkins University Press, 1956.

Brugger, Robert. *Maryland: A Middle Temperament, 1634–1980.* Baltimore: Johns Hopkins University Press, 1988.

Byron, Gilbert. *The War of 1812 on the Chesapeake.* Baltimore: Maryland Historical Society, 1964.

Caffey, Kate. *The Twilight's Last Gleaming: Britain vs. America, 1812–1815.* New York: Stein and Day, 1977.

Carson, David A. "Jefferson, Congress and Leadership in the Tripolitan War." *Virginia Magazine of History and Biography* 94 (1986): 410–24.

Cassell, Frank A. *Merchant Congressman in the Young Republic: Samuel Smith of Maryland, 1752–1839.* Madison: University of Wisconsin Press, 1971.

Chapelle, Howard. *The History of the American Sailing Navy: The Ships and Their Development.* Reprint, New York: Bonanza, 1988.

Chisholm, Donald. *Waiting For Dead Men's Shoes: Origins and Development of the U.S. Navy's Officer Personnel System, 1793–1941.* Stanford, Calif.: Stanford University Press, 2001.

Cochran, Hamilton, *Noted American Duels and Hostile Encounters.* Philadelphia: Chilton, 1963.

Cole, Donald B., *A Jackson Man: Amos Kendall and the Rise of American Democracy.* Baton Rouge: Louisiana State University Press, 2004.

Coletta, Paolo E., ed. *American Secretaries of the Navy.* 2 vols. Annapolis: Naval Institute Press, 1980.

Cooper, James Fenimore. *The History of the Navy of the United States of America.* 1846. Reprint, Annapolis: Naval Institute Press, 2001.

———. *Lives of Distinguished American Naval Officers.* 2 vols. Philadelphia: Carey and Hart, 1846.

Crenson, Matthew. *The Federal Machine: Beginnings of Bureaucracy in Jacksonian America.* Baltimore: Johns Hopkins University Press, 1975.

Dakin, Douglas. *The Greek Struggle for Independence, 1821–1833.* Berkeley and Los Angeles: University of California Press, 1973.

Davies, G. E. "Robert Smith and the Navy." *Maryland Historical Magazine* 14 (1919): 305–22.

de Kay, James Tertius. *Chronicles of the Frigate* Macedonian, *1809–1922*. New York: W. W. Norton, 1995.

———. *A Rage for Glory: The Life of Commodore Stephen Decatur, USN*. New York: Free Press, 2004.

Duffy, Stephen W. H. *Captain Blakeley and the* Wasp*: The Cruise of 1814*. Annapolis: Naval Institute Press, 1999.

Dye, Ira, *The Fatal Cruise of the* Argus*: Two Captains in the War of 1812*. Annapolis: Naval Institute Press, 1994.

Earle, Swepson. *The Chesapeake Bay Country*. Baltimore: Thomsen-Ellis, 1924.

Eckert, Edward K. *The Navy Department in the War of 1812*. Gainesville: University of Florida Press, 1973.

———. "William Jones: Mr. Madison's Secretary of the Navy." *Pennsylvania Magazine of History and Biography* 96 (1912): 167–82.

Edwards, Samuel. *Barbary General: The Life of William H. Eaton*. Englewood Cliffs, N.J.: Prentice-Hall, 1968.

Ellet, Elizabeth F. *The Court Circles of the Republic, or the Beauties and Celebrities of the Nation*. Hartford, Conn.: Hartford Publishing Co., 1869.

Ferguson, Eugene. *Truxtun of the* Constellation*: The Life of Commodore Thomas Truxtun, U.S. Navy, 1755–1822*. Baltimore: Johns Hopkins University Press, 1956.

Field, James A., Jr. *America and the Mediterranean World, 1776–1882*. Princeton: Princeton University Press, 1969.

Finnie, David H. *Pioneers East: The Early American Experience in the Middle East*. Cambridge: Harvard University Press, 1967.

Folayan, Kola. *Tripoli during the Reign of Yusuf Pasha Qaramanli*. Ile-Ife, Nigeria: University of Ife Press, 1979.

Forester, C. S. "Bloodshed at Dawn." *American Heritage* 15 (1964): 41–45, 73–76.

Fowler, William. *Jack Tars and Commodores: The American Navy, 1789–1815*. Boston: Houghton Mifflin, 1984.

Goldsborough, Charles W. *The United States Naval Chronicle*. Washington, D.C.: James Wilson, 1824.

Green, Constance M. *Washington: Village and Capital, 1800–1950*. 2 vols. Princeton, N.J.: Princeton University Press, 1962–63.

Guernsey, R. S. *New York City and Vicinity during the War of 1812–15*. 2 vols. New York: Charles L. Woodward, 1889.

Guttridge, Leonard, and Jay D. Smith. *The Commodores*. New York: Harper and Row, 1969.

Hagan, Kenneth J., ed. *In Peace and War: Interpretations of American Naval History, 1775–1984*. 2nd ed. Westport, Conn.: Greenwood Press, 1984.

———. *This People's Navy: The Making of American Sea Power*. New York: Free Press, 1991.

[Harrod, Frederick S.], ed. *New Aspects of Naval History: Selected Papers from the Fifth Naval History Symposium*. Baltimore: Nautical and Aviation Publishing Company of America, 1985.

Hickey, Donald. *The War of 1812: A Forgotten Conflict*. Urbana: University of Illinois Press, 1989.

Horsman, Reginald. *The Causes of the War of 1812*. Philadelphia: University of Pennsylvania Press, 1962.

———. *The War of 1812*. New York: Alfred A. Knopf, 1969.

Humphreys, Margaret. "No Safe Place: Disease and Pain in American History." *American Literary History* 14 (2002): 845–57.

Hutcheon, Wallace, Jr. *Robert Fulton: Pioneer of Undersea Warfare*. Annapolis: Naval Institute Press, 1981.

Irwin, Ray W. *The Diplomatic Relations of the United States with the Barbary Powers, 1776–1816*. Chapel Hill: University of North Carolina Press, 1931.

James, William. *A Full and Correct Account of the Naval Occurrences of the Late War between Great Britain and the United States of America. . . .* London: Joyce Gold, Printer, 1817.

———. *The Naval History of Great Britain: From the Declaration of War by France, in February, 1793 to the Accession of George IV—, in January, 1820*. 1826. 6 vols. Reprint, London: Richard Bentley and Son, 1886.

Jones, Robert F., "The Naval Thought and Policy of Benjamin Stoddert, First Secretary of the Navy, 1798–1801." *American Neptune* 24 (1964): 61–69.

Jay, Peter, ed. *Havre de Grace: An Informal History*. Havre de Grace, Md.: Susquehanna Press, 1986.

Johnson, Robert E. *Rear Admiral John Rodgers, 1812–1888*. Annapolis: Naval Institute Press, 1967.

Langley, Harold D. *A History of Medicine in the Early U.S. Navy*. Baltimore: Johns Hopkins University Press, 1995.

———. "Robert Y. Hayne and the Navy." *South Carolina Historical Magazine* 82 (1981): 311–30.

———. *Social Reform in the United States Navy, 1798–1862*. Urbana: University of Illinois Press, 1967.

———. "Squadron Flags of the United States." *Military Collector and Historian* 55 (Winter 2003–4): 234–42.

Larrabee, Stephen A. *Hellas Observed: The American Experience of Greece, 1775–1865*. New York: New York University Press, 1957.

Lewis, Charles Lee. *The Romantic Decatur*. Philadelphia: University of Pennsylvania Press, 1937.

Liss, Peggy, K. *Atlantic Empires: The Network of Trade and Revolution, 1713–1826*. Baltimore: Johns Hopkins University Press, 1983.

Logan, Rayford W. *The Diplomatic Relations of the United States with Haiti, 1776–1891*. Chapel Hill: University of North Carolina Press, 1941.

Long, David F. *Gold Braid and Foreign Relations: Diplomatic Activities of U.S. Naval Officers, 1798–1883*. Annapolis: Naval Institute Press, 1988.

———. *Nothing Too Daring: A Biography of David Porter, 1780–1843*. Annapolis: Naval Institute Press, 1970.

——. *Ready to Hazard: A Biography of Commodore William Bainbridge*. Boston: University Press of New England, 1981.

——. *Sailor-Diplomat: A Biography of Commodore James Biddle, 1783–1848*. Boston: Northeastern University Press, 1983.

Lord, Walter. *The Dawn's Early Light*. New York: W. W. Norton, 1972,

Lossing, Benson J. *The Pictorial Field-Book of the War of 1812*. New York: Harper Brothers, 1868.

Love, Robert W., Jr. *History of the U.S. Navy, 1775–1941*. Vol. 1. Harrisburg: Stackpole Books, 1992.

Mackenzie, Alexander Slidell. *A Year in Spain*. 2 vols. 5th ed. New York: Harper and Brothers, 1847.

[Mackenzie, Alexander Slidell]. "Report of the Secretary of the Navy to the President of the United States, December 1, 1829." *North American Review* 30 (year TK): 361–89.

Maclay, Edgar S. *A History of American Privateers*. New York: D. Appleton, 1899.

MacLeod, Julia H. "Jefferson and the Navy: A Defense." *Huntington Library Quarterly* 8 (1945): 153–84.

Mahan, A. T. *Admiral Farragut*. New York: D. Appleton, 1892.

——. *From Sail to Steam; Recollections of Naval Life*. 1907. Reprint, New York: De Capo, 1968.

——. *Sea Power in Its Relations to the War of 1812*. 1905. 2 vols. Reprint, New York: Greenwood, 1968.

Mahon, John. *The War of 1812*. Gainesville: University of Florida Press, 1972.

Malone, Dumas. *Jefferson and His Time*. 6 vols. Boston: Little, Brown, 1948–81.

Maloney, Linda M. *The Captain From Connecticut: The Life and Naval Times of Isaac Hull*. Boston: Northeastern University Press, 1986.

Mannix, Richard. "Gallatin, Jefferson, and the Embargo of 1808." *Diplomatic History* 3 (1979): 151–72.

Marine, William M. *The British Invasion of Maryland, 1812–1815*. Baltimore: John H. Saumenig, 1913.

Mayer, Henry. *All on Fire: William Lloyd Garrison and the Abolition of Slavery*. New York: St. Martin's, 1998.

McDonald, Forrest. *The Presidency of Thomas Jefferson*. Lawrence: University Press of Kansas, 1976.

McKee, Christopher. *Edward Preble: A Naval Biography, 1761–1807*. Annapolis: Naval Institute Press, 1972.

——. *A Gentlemanly and Honorable Profession: The Creation of the U.S. Naval Officer Corps, 1794–1815*. Annapolis: Naval Institute Press, 1991.

McNamara, Peter. *The Noblest Minds: Fame, Honor and the American Founding*. New York: Rowman and Littlefield, 1999.

Merrill, James M. *Du Pont: The Making of an Admiral. A Biography of Samuel Francis Du Pont*. New York: Dodd, Mead, 1986.

Merrill, James M. "Midshipman Du Pont and the Cruise of the *North Carolina*, 1825–1827." *American Neptune* 40 (1980): 211–25.

Morison, Samuel Eliot. *"Old Bruin": Commodore Matthew Calbraith Perry, 1794–1858*. Boston: Little, Brown, 1967.

Nash, Howard P., Jr. *The Forgotten Wars: The Role of the U.S. Navy in the Quasi War with France and the Barbary Wars, 1798–1815*. New York: A. S. Barnes, 1968.

Neeser, Robert W. *Statistical and Chronological History of the United States Navy*. 2 vols. New York: Macmillan, 1909.

Olson, Sherry H. *Baltimore: The Building of an American City*. Rev. ed. Baltimore: Johns Hopkins University Press, 1997.

Ott, Thomas O. *The Haitian Revolution, 1789–1804*. Knoxville: University of Tennessee Press, 1973.

Pack, James. *The Man Who Burned the White Hourse: Admiral Sir George Cockburn*. Annapolis: Naval Institute Press, 1987.

Palmer, Michael A. *Stoddert's War: Naval Operations during the Quasi-War with France, 1798–1801*. Columbia: University of South Carolina Press, 1987.

Paullin, Charles O. *Commodore John Rodgers; Captain, Commodore, and Senior Officer of the American Navy, 1773–1838*. 1910. Reprint, Annapolis: Naval Institute Press, 1967.

———. *Diplomatic Negotiations of American Naval Officers, 1778–1883*. Baltimore: Johns Hopkins University Press, 1912.

———. "Dueling in the Old Navy." *United States Naval Institute Proceedings* 35 (1909): 1155–97.

———. *Paullin's History of Naval Administration, 1775–1911*. Annapolis: Naval Institute Press, 1968.

Peden, Henry. *Revolutionary Patriots of Harford County, Maryland, 1775–1783*. Bel Air, Md.: Bel Air Copy Center, 1985.

Perkins, Bradford. *Prologue to War: England and the United States*. Berkeley and Los Angeles: University of California Press, 1961.

Petrie, Donald A. "The Ransoming of the *Eliza Swan*." *American Neptune* 53 (1993): 98–108.

Philbrick, Nathaniel. *Sea of Glory: America's Voyage of Discovery: The U.S. Exploring Expedition, 1838–1842*. New York: Viking, 2003.

Philip, Cynthia Owen. *Robert Fulton: A Biography*. New York: Franklin Watts, 1985.

Pinkney, William. *The Life of William Pinkney*. 1853. Reprint, New York: De Capo, 1969.

Pratt, Fletcher. *Preble's Boys: Commodore Preble and the Birth of American Sea Power*. New York: William Sloane, 1950.

Preston, Walter W. *History of Harford County, Maryland*. Baltimore: Press of Sun Book Office, 1901.

Remini, Robert V. *Andrew Jackson and the Course of American Liberty, 1822–1832*. New York: Harper and Row, 1981.

Renzulli, L. Marx. *Maryland: The Federalist Years*. Rutherford, N.J.: Fairleigh Dickinson University Press, 1972.

Risjord, Norman. *Chesapeake Politics, 1781–1800*. New York: Columbia University Press, 1978.

Roddis, Louis H. "Thomas Harris, M.D., Naval Surgeon and Founder of the First School of Naval Medicine in the New World." *Journal of the History of Medicine and Allied Sciences* 5 (1950): 236–50.

Roland, Alex. *Underwater Warfare in the Age of Sail*. Bloomington: Indiana University Press, 1978.

Roosevelt, Theodore. *The Naval War of 1812, or the History of the United States during the Last War with Great Britain*. 1882. 2 vols. Reprint, New York: G. P. Putnam's Sons, 1900.

Rosenburg, Charles. *Cholera Years; The United States in 1832, 1849 and 1866*. Chicago: University of Chicago Press, 1962.

Sale, Kirkpatrick. *The Fire of Genius: Robert Fulton and the American Dream*. New York: Free Press, 2001.

Scharf, J. Thomas. *Chronicles of Baltimore: Being a Complete History of "Baltimore Town" and Baltimore City from the Earliest Period to the Present Time*. Baltimore: Turnbull Brothers, 1874.

———. *History of Maryland from the Earliest Period to the Present Day*. 1879. 3 vols. Reprint, Hatboro, Pa.: Tradition Press, 1967.

Schroeder, John H. *Matthew Calbraith Perry: Antebellum Sailor and Diplomat*. Annapolis: Naval Institute Press, 2001.

———. *Shaping a Maritime Empire: The Commercial and Diplomatic Role of the American Navy, 1829–1861*. Westport, Conn.: Greenwood Press, 1985.

Sears, Louis Martin. *Jefferson and the Embargo*. Durham, N.C.: Duke University Press, 1927.

Seitz, Donald C. *Famous American Duels*. New York: Thomas Y. Crowell, 1929.

Shippen, Edward. "Some Account of the Origin of the Naval Asylum at Philadelphia." *Pennsylvania Magazine of History and Biography* 7 (1883): 117–42.

Shryock, Richard H. *The Development of Modern Medicine: An Interpretation of the Social and Scientific Factors Involved*. New York: Alfred A. Knopf, 1947.

Smith, Gene A. *"For Purposes of Defense": The Politics of the Jeffersonian Gunboat Program*. Newark: University of Delaware Press, 1995.

Smith, Geoffrey. "The Navy before Darwin: Science, Exploration, and Diplomacy in Antebellum America." *American Quarterly* 18 (1976): 41–55.

Spivak, Burton. *Jefferson's English Crisis: Commerce, Embargo, and the Republican Revolution*. Charlottesville: University Press of Virginia, 1979.

Sprout, Harold, and Margaret Sprout. *The Rise of American Naval Power, 1776–1918*. Princeton, N.J.: Princeton University Press, 1939.

Stagg, J.C.A. *Mr. Madison's War: Politics, Diplomacy and Warfare in the Early Republic, 1783–1830*. Princeton, N.J.: Princeton University Press, 1983.

Stanton, William. *The Great United States Exploring Expedition of 1838–1842*. Berkeley and Los Angeles: University of California Press, 1975.

Stevens, William Oliver. *An Affair of Honor: The Biography of Commodore James Barron, U.S.N.* Williamsburg, Va.: Norfolk County Historical Society in Cooperation with the College of William and Mary, 1969.

Symonds, Craig. *Navalists and Antinavalists: The Naval Policy Debate in the United States, 1785–1827*. Newark: University of Delaware Press, 1980.

Tracey, Nicholas, *Attack on Maritime Trade*. Toronto: University of Toronto Press, 1991.

Tucker, Glen. *Dawn Like Thunder: The Barbary Wars and the Birth of the U.S. Navy*. Indianapolis: Bobbs-Merrill, 1963.

Tucker, Spencer. *Arming the Fleet: U.S. Navy Ordnance in the Muzzle-Loading Era*. Annapolis: Naval Institute Press, 1989.

———. *The Jeffersonian Gunboat Navy*. Columbia: University of South Carolina Press, 1993.

———. *Stephen Decatur: A Life Most Bold and Daring*. Annapolis: Naval Institute Press, 2005.

Tucker, Spencer, and Frank T. Reuter. *Injured Honor: The Chesapeake-Leopard Affair, June 22, 1807*. Annapolis: Naval Institute Press, 1996.

Valle, James E. "The Navy's Battle Doctrine in the War of 1812." *American Neptune* 44 (1984): 171–78.

———. *Rocks and Shoals: Order and Discipline in the Old Navy, 1800–1861*. Annapolis: Naval Institute Press, 1980.

Watson, Paul B. *Commodore James Barron: The Tragic Career of Commodore James Barron*. New York: Coward-McCann, 1942.

Watts, Steven. *The Republic Reborn: War and the Making of Liberal America, 1790–1820*. Baltimore: Johns Hopkins University Press, 1987.

Wharton, Anne Hollingsworth. *Social Life in the Early Republic*. 1902. Reprint, Williamstown, Mass.: Corner House, 1970.

Whipple, A.B.C. *To the Shores of Tripoli: The Birth of the U.S. Navy and Marines*. New York: William Morrow, 1991.

White, Leonard, *The Jacksonians: A Study in Administrative History*. New York: Macmillan, 1954.

———. *The Jeffersonians: A Study in Administrative History*. New York: Macmillan, 1951.

Whitman, T. Stephen. *The Price of Freedom: Slavery and Manumission in Baltimore and Early National Maryland*. Lexington: University Press of Kentucky, 1997.

Williams, Frances Leigh, *Matthew Fontaine Maury: Scientist of the Sea*. New Brunswick, N.J.: Rutgers University Press, 1963.

Wright, Louis B., and Julia B. MacLeod. *The First Americans in North Africa: William Eaton's Struggle for a Vigorous Policy against the Barbary Pirates, 1799–1805*. Princeton, N.J.: Princeton University Press, 1945.

Wright, C. Milton. *Our Harford Heritage: A History of Harford County, Maryland.*
    Baltimore: French-Bray, 1967.

Young, James Sterling. *The Washington Community, 1800–1828.* New York: Colum-
    bia University Press, 1966.

Index

John H. Schroeder is professor of history at the University of Wisconsin, Milwaukee. He is the author of *Matthew Calbraith Perry: Antebellum Sailor and Diplomat* (2001).